Joyce Molyneux grew up during the  war-time evacuation to a farm n desire to begin culinary training. F farm's self-sufficiency proved a valuable lesson for Joyce which is still evident today in her philosophy of cooking at The Carved Angel – making full use of absolutely fresh ingredients and the best produce in season.

She started her career in Stratford-upon-Avon, before joining the Hole in the Wall restaurant in Bath, owned by George Perry-Smith, the 'patriarch of post-war British chefs', whose unorthodox but successful approach to running a restaurant had a great influence on her during her thirteen years there. In 1974, Joyce and Tom Jaine, together with George Perry-Smith and Heather Crosbie, opened The Carved Angel in Dartmouth.

Praised and admired by many of today's top chefs, Joyce Molyneux's recipes have been chosen to appear in collections celebrating the best of British cooking, and she has made appearances on TV, including the immensely popular *Floyd on Fish.*

Sophie Grigson is the cookery columnist of the *London Evening Standard* and the *Sunday Express* magazine.

The Carved Angel Cookery Book

JOYCE MOLYNEUX
With Sophie Grigson

Grafton
An Imprint of HarperCollins*Publishers*

Grafton
An Imprint of HarperCollins*Publishers*
77–85 Fulham Palace Road,
Hammersmith, London W6 8JB

Published by Grafton 1992
1 3 5 7 9 8 6 4 2

First published in Great Britain by
William Collins Sons & Co. Ltd 1990

ISBN 0 586 21344 9

Set in Meridien

Printed in Great Britain by
HarperCollinsManufacturing Glasgow

FOR MY PARENTS

Irene Mary Molyneux and Maurice William Molyneux

Contents

Foreword

One of the pleasures of writing this book has been the making of new friends, and I would like to thank all those who have helped me along the way. Primarily, Sophie Grigson who co-operated in the writing and so skilfully interpreted and set out the recipes; her assistance was marvellous. Also, Martin Brigdale and his team for the beautiful photographs; and Hugh Marshall for his delightful illustrations. At Collins, I would like to thank Louise Haines and Robin Wood who foresaw the possibilities for the book.

And for their support, all at The Carved Angel, especially Nick Coiley, Sallie Turvey, for her invaluable secretarial skills, and Meriel, who has always been an intelligent and sensitive partner.

Finally, my thanks to Steven, the rock, who gave me a Catalan home and introduced me many years ago to the varied delights of other cuisines.

Joyce Molyneux
Dartmouth, 1990

Introduction

By the time I was sixteen I knew without doubt that I wanted to cook. But my decision to leave school after taking O levels to go to the local domestic science college did not meet with the approval of my headmistress. At the bottom of the card announcing my exam results, she wrote: 'I still think it is a great pity that you are not coming back to us in the autumn . . .' A training in catering was only an option for those who weren't bright enough to study Latin or something more academic.

I emerged from the two-year course, limited still by post-War austerity and rationing, adept at baking a wide selection of scones, but ignorant of most of the basics of a restaurant kitchen. I didn't even know how to section an orange, let alone anything more technical.

My serious culinary training began when I went to work at a small restaurant in Stratford-upon-Avon, the Mulberry Tree. At last I was working with a good chef, with a real feeling for food. From Mr Sutherland, I gained a thorough grounding in classic cooking. I stayed for almost ten years.

The Hole in the Wall

Although in the late 1950s there wasn't the same kind of media interest in restaurants as there is now, George Perry-Smith's

Hole in the Wall in Bath had already earned a wide reputation. I still remember clearly the first time I ever went there. As I walked in, my gaze was instantly caught by the huge bowl on the entrance table, with a pure blue lining, piled high with the most beautiful pink and white mushrooms.

The famous cold table was laid out before us, every plate filled with enticing foods, nothing fussy, no unnecessary frills and garnishes, no wilting lettuce leaves or tired salads. It looked marvellous precisely because there was no disguise or artifice, and it needed none. Everything about the dining room inspired a feeling of abundance and relaxed elegance. We ate a simple, delicious meal. The occasion made a huge impact on me, and I knew immediately that I wanted to work there.

A few months after I'd left the Mulberry Tree, I answered an advertisement in the *Lady* magazine for a general assistant at the Hole in the Wall and, to my delight, was taken on. When I first started, I did everything – waiting at tables and cooking. Gradually, I spent more and more time in the kitchen. George was a terrific influence. He expected his staff to think for themselves, and to have opinions about the food they were cooking and serving.

He was very good at training people to work under pressure, willingly and to a common cause. Everyone knew what they were working for, and they all agreed that it was worth it. We felt involved in the running of the restaurant. Unlike many chefs, George treated his staff with great respect. He addressed everyone by name, and made each of us feel that our contribution was essential to the success of the restaurant.

As I became more confident, I began to help with the menu planning. The organization of the long menu, in which everything was integrated, was something that George excelled at. There was never any waste at all. The main menu remained unchanged from day to day, but was supplemented by a changing daily menu that relied on the market and unused food and trimmings from the previous day. Then, of course, there was the cold table which took leftover salmon, or vegetables, say.

But it never became a dustbin for jaded scraps – many dishes on the main menu were chosen because they could be served hot one day, and would taste just as good, if not better, cold the next day.

I learnt to plan a menu economically, without ever compromising on quality. Naturally, this influences the way you buy your ingredients. George never bought in vast quantity, even though we might be feeding over one hundred people on a Saturday night, because he needed to be sure of having the freshest ingredients. We never went to wholesale greengrocers, preferring to take our custom to small retailers, often bringing in supplies twice a day.

George's approach was way ahead of his time, and seemed extraordinarily unorthodox to established restaurateurs. The catering business was really very conservative. At the end of the War it had blithely picked up the threads again as if nothing had changed. George came in from the outside, with no professional training and a fresh eye. He broke all the old-school rules about 'portion control' and proved that his method could be profitable.

When he decided to include a new dish in the menu, his starting point was always the taste. If it passed that hurdle he then set about weaving it into the menu, never mind whether it was 'suitable' for a restaurant. The cost and pricing became incidental, and was never allowed to interfere with the way a dish was presented or cooked.

This approach was epitomized by the way we served Tarragon Chicken: roast chicken scented with lots of tarragon, and finished with a butter and cream sauce, in the Elizabeth David style. There was no question of carefully measured, equal portions. The whole chicken, in its full glory, was taken out into the restaurant and carved at the table, and diners could choose how much, and which parts they wanted.

This complete abandoning of portion control might have appeared a sure recipe for financial disaster, but in fact was quite the opposite. An elderly lady here wanted just a thin slice of breast, and over there a man asked for a whole leg and a piece of breast. Each of them got just what they wanted, everyone was delighted, and in the end it all balanced out. The carcass was returned to the kitchen where it was assiduously picked clean of all meat, to become part of a cold dish, and the bones went straight into the stock pot.

In a similar way, soft summer fruits were displayed in big bowls. Instead of measuring out a precise quantity when anyone asked for strawberries, the entire bowl was set in the centre of the table, so that people could help themselves. The sheer pleasure given by such displays of generosity paid its way.

George sold the Hole in the Wall in 1972. I stayed on for a year with the new owners, but for me it lost much of its magic. I left to join George and his partner Heather Crosbie in their new venture.

Setting up The Carved Angel

They had been scouring the West Country to find the right premises for two new restaurants. They settled on the Riverside at Helford, and the waterfront bistro at Dartmouth that was to become The Carved Angel. Tom Jaine, George's stepson, and I were brought in to make the partnership up to four. We were to run the Angel, while George and Heather ran the Riverside.

Tom and George set about reorganizing and designing the Dartmouth bistro, turning it into the light, airy restaurant it is now, with its view across the River Dart to the Kingswear on the opposite bank. The kitchen was quite deliberately left open on to the dining room, marked off only by a waist-high counter. This is one of the most successful things about the Angel, from everyone's point of view.

The customers can see the food being prepared and it gives them a sense of involvement. The muted backdrop of kitchen noises puts people instantly at ease without intruding on conversation. The first diners to arrive never have to endure that awful intimidating hush of an empty room. It gives a human scale to the business, and makes for an easy manner between customers and staff.

It is lovely, too, for those of us working in the kitchen because we're not cut off from what is happening in the front of house. We can see how people react to their meal and knowing that we are cooking for individuals, not some faceless crowd, gives us all an extra feeling of responsibility. Newcomers to the staff are often a bit nervous about being so exposed to the scrutiny of the customers. But they soon settle down, and discover that being able to see the pleasure created by something they have just cooked is immensely rewarding.

We finally opened the doors of The Carved Angel in July 1974. It takes its name from the wooden angel who gazes calmly over the dining room. Initially, the idea was that both the Angel and the Riverside could share the same wine list, with centralized buying and so on. This was fine in theory, but in practice, with a hundred miles between the two places, it was not so convenient. We started, too, with identical menus, but soon began to diverge.

Being in charge of a kitchen, even with George's advice and help, was a daunting prospect. For both Tom, who was quite new to the restaurant business, and me those first months were nerve-racking. He adapted quickly and managed the front of house with great efficiency and a warm welcome. He took charge, too, of building up an excellent wine list.

Tom also had a very stimulating effect on the food and kitchen, bringing a fresh questioning mind to bear. So we gradually acquired charcoal grills, bamboo steamers and widened our repertoire to include dishes from many regions beyond the Mediterranean. At the same time, he was writing a monthly food and wine magazine. I am always grateful for and appreciative of his contribution to the success of the restaurant.

Despite all our efforts, that first summer was awful. Desperately quiet and very depressing after the hustle and bustle of the Hole in the Wall. We watched an endless stream of holiday-makers and locals strolling up and down the waterfront, but few of them ever came through our door.

I suppose that our prices did seem very high for the area and the kind of food we were offering was not what local people or most visitors were used to. Our style was beginning to change and evolve too, as we started to discover the wealth of small suppliers in the area, and adapted the menu to fit the best ingredients that there were to hand.

The turning point finally came that autumn. There was an article in *The Times* about George and chefs he had trained at the Hole in the Wall, who were now setting up their own restaurants – Colin and Gwen White at the Jews House in Lincoln, Michael Waterfield at Canterbury, and Tom and I at The Carved Angel, among others. Not that it immediately opened up the floodgates to hundreds of people beating a path to our door, but it gave us the courage to persevere, reassuring us that we weren't entirely on the wrong track.

The Carved Angel today

Tom left the business in 1984 and, a few months later, Meriel Boyden, George's niece, stepped into his shoes. It has been a successful and enduring partnership. Meriel is supportive, and entirely in tune with the way the restaurant is run and the kind of food we offer. We have basically the same ideas and attitudes.

The general philosophy of the restaurant has not changed over the years. I want to make customers feel comfortable, relaxed and welcome, and that is every bit as important as the quality of the food and wine. Neither the staff nor I are here to show off or score points. To that end we try to make service as unobtrusive as possible, anticipating people's wants, without constantly fluttering around them.

The wording of the menu is kept as simple and straightforward as possible. There are explanations where necessary, with no glossy frills, so that diners have a clear idea of what they are ordering. I can't bear the current vogue for coy, irrelevant adjectives like 'dew-gathered', or 'morning-fresh'.

Much the same principle applies to the way the food is presented. It should be simple and attractive, with no garnishing for garnishing's sake. Everything on the plate is there for a reason, and to be eaten. Food should look like what it is. Good ingredients, thoughtfully prepared and combined, have an inherent beauty.

And we are blessed with excellent raw ingredients in this part of Devon. When we first opened we had to do all our own footwork, following up every possible lead. Gradually word has worked its way around the community that we will take all kinds of fresh produce, often in small quantities, as long as the quality is high. The phone is always ringing with new offers. 'Would you be interested in a basketful of this or that?' and more often than not, I am.

Marvellous fresh fish and shellfish, from both sea and river, are landed every day, virtually on our doorstep. Independent fishermen, even holiday-makers, may bring in smaller catches. Commercial market gardeners have become more adventurous, changing with the times as they discover that there is a market for a much wider range of fruit and vegetables. Many of the herbs and vegetables that I once had to grow myself on my allotment, on the hillside above Dartmouth, are now easy to buy.

Fresh supplies are often the catalyst for experiments and the development of new recipes to add to the repertoire. I think it is important to involve every member of staff in the process of working out new dishes; their opinions are immensely valuable, and wide ranging.

When I began cooking at The Carved Angel, I was very much an Elizabeth David cook, like George Perry-Smith, and I still am. But, little by little, I started to explore other areas as well, developing along my own route. Cookery writers like Madhur Jaffrey and Claudia Roden have been great influences. I read cookery books avidly, drawing ideas from this side and that. I now mix Eastern, Mediterranean and European flavours with classic French.

I don't want to turn the Angel into an ethnic restaurant, but I do try to bring in the overtones and subtleties of foreign styles, weaving them into our regular dishes. One of the best examples, and one that I love making, is a first course of aubergine salads. Aubergines are cooked all over the world in hundreds of different ways, so they offer enormous scope. On one plate, I can arrange, say, an Italian aubergine caponata, aubergine with sesame sauce, and aubergine cooked with Szechwan pepper. With subtle spicing, they can all be drawn together, each keeping its individuality without clashing or dominating.

We go on regular staff outings, and I encourage individual staff members to eat out as often as possible to experience other restaurants from the customers' point of view. I do think it's important to keep abreast with how other chefs are working, and it's often reassuring to find that they are heading in the same directions as us. And, of course, I may also come across new ideas.

I suppose I have a natural magpie instinct, picking up a method here, a combination there, and blending them into the way I cook. I'm always pleased when members of staff feel confident enough to add their suggestions. Georges Blanc's recipe for Basil Ice Cream (page 286) was a discovery of Nick Coiley, who has been with me for several years now. The unusually light and delicious Nut Loaf on page 269 was the contribution of a girl who worked with us for a while, and is now something we make regularly for vegetarians. All these new dishes sit happily side by side with old Perry-Smith stalwarts, like his popular Pheasant with Celery (page 200).

The British have become much less conservative about what they will eat. Holidays abroad and the ever increasing number of ethnic restaurants have brought a more open attitude to food. Many of the people who come to eat at The Carved Angel are positively keen to try things they haven't dared to eat before, or that they might not get at home. When one woman was so enthused by a dish of stewed eels that she rushed off to buy some to cook herself, I took it as a great compliment. Although I always make sure that there are a few very straightforward things on offer, this widening interest in food has given me much greater freedom.

Recipes from The Carved Angel

The joy of cooking, and what makes it an endlessly absorbing occupation, is the pleasure it gives to other people, and the satisfaction of having created something. I still remember the excitement of my first attempt at making puff pastry. I went through all that rolling and folding again and again. And at long last, the moment came when I opened the door of the oven to see the trays of beautifully risen, golden brown *mille feuilles*. Sheer magic – it had worked. Even now I get that thrill out of cooking, deriving a great personal pride, whether it is something I've made a hundred and one times before or something that is quite new.

Cooking is a continuous voyage of discovery, much more than the mere acquisition of a few practical skills. It exercises the mind, the imagination, pulling different bits of knowledge, shreds of information together, to create a whole on the plate that is the perfect balance of its components. In short, it is what each individual cares to make it.

When Meriel and I sat down to choose the recipes for this book, we kept this in mind. As we riffled through the well-thumbed kitchen files, we tried to resist the temptation to include the eternally popular but better known dishes, like *coq au vin*. It resurfaces time and again on our menu, a classic that survives time and fashion. But there are recipes by the handful for *coq au vin* in countless cookery books, and it would take several volumes to cover our entire collection.

We ended up with what is really an eclectic selection, bringing together tastes from all over the world. Many of the recipes are favourites from other authors and chefs whom I admire tremendously, some in their original form, some adapted and changed here and there to fit my style of cooking. I hope that I have given them full credit where due. Some of my best-loved recipes, tried and tested and tweaked into shape over many years, have become such a fundamental part of The Carved Angel's repertoire, that it is hard to recall their origins. Was this my idea? Have I altered it so much that with time it has become my idea? Or do I owe some forgotten author a debt of gratitude? If, inadvertently, I have failed to acknowledge this debt, I offer my apologies.

I have tried to avoid the overly 'chef-like' and complicated. All of the recipes have been written up for me by Sophie Grigson so that they are suitable for cooking at home. Most of them are fairly easy to tackle. There is usually room to manoeuvre and adapt, and no one should feel that they must follow my recipes slavishly. One or two may seem tricky, and indeed, may require a little patience and time, but taken step by step even they are not outside the range of any competent cook. Try them out when you have an afternoon to indulge in the sheer pleasure of creating something special.

I hope that readers will use this book in the way that I use cookery books, as a springboard for ideas, trying out recipes and tempering them to their own way of eating. If it gives them the confidence to use an unfamiliar ingredient or a familiar one in a new way, then it will have been worth while.

A Note on Ingredients

Bouquet garni: The classic bouquet garni is made up of a sprig of thyme, a bay leaf, and half-a-dozen or so parsley stalks, tied with a piece of string, or wrapped in a single fold of leek, so that it can be fished out before serving. To this you can add a small twig of rosemary, or a leaf of sage, or indeed, any other herb that will enhance the flavour.

Edible leaves and flowers: We keep a trough of scented-leaved geraniums (pelargoniums) in the back yard of the restaurant, about six varieties ranging from *quercifolium* – very long leaved, to *filicifolium* – which has a very finely divided leaf and is everybody's choice for decorating puddings. The one we use for infusing in custards and ice creams is 'Lady Plymouth'.

In late May, early June we look forward to elderflowers, which we try to collect away from main roads, picking those free of black fly; the leaves are used unwashed. Also, the leaves of all the very fragrant hybrid roses such as 'Ena Harkness' and 'Etoile de Hollande', or ragosa roses, can be used to give a delicate flavour to ice creams, sorbets and creams. We gather these as close to time of use as possible.

Nasturtiums and pot marigolds are easy annuals to cultivate and are both very decorative in salads or with charcuterie, especially the leaves of the variegated 'Alaska' nasturtium. Marigold petals are strewn particularly over potato salads. Both nasturtium and marigold flowers are used whole. The pure blue of borage flowers looks lovely on a sorbet or ice cream; we gently lift off the flower, rejecting the hairy stem behind.

Peach leaves, picked any time from May to September, can be used in custards and ices, while blackcurrant leaves for sorbet are best gathered in June and July. Many people now have a vine in their garden and shouldn't forget to use the vine leaves in midsummer before they get tough. They are ideal for wrapping small birds such as quail, or for making little parcels of rice and meat Greek style.

Eggs: Throughout the recipes in this book I have used large eggs.

Flour: I always use unbleached flour, for preference stone-ground. This traditional method of milling preserves more flavour, since the grains and resultant flour are kept cool throughout the process. I used to buy in bulk for the restaurant, but soon realized that this was a false economy. Breads and brioches made from the flour at the bottom of the bag did not have the same light texture. For the same reason, only buy flour from a shop with a quick turnover.

In recipes where I have not specified the type of flour, use plain flour.

Herbs: When The Carved Angel first opened in the mid-1970s, fresh herbs, apart from the occasional bunch of parsley, were a hard-to-come-by commodity. What supplies there were, were erratic and limited. In those days we grew most of our herbs ourselves on the allotment at the top of the hill. Now, however, the only herbs growing there are the rarer ones – great lusty swathes of lovage; fern-leaved, aniseedy sweet cicely; tart sorrel, and borage with its pretty blue flowers.

Fresh thyme, marjoram, rosemary, chives, basil, coriander, mint, sage, chervil – they are all easy to come by these days. We buy from a greengrocer near the restaurant, or more usually from Capton Fruit Farm near Dittisham, from whom we get excellent fresh produce. Even in mid-winter there's a good choice of herbs flown in from hotter climates to supplement the evergreen rosemary, thyme and bay in our garden.

Most herbs can be frozen – chopped finely and packed tightly into ice-cube trays. Basil is best puréed with a little olive oil before freezing, and the last of the summer's fresh tarragon keeps most of its impact when blended with butter and frozen in neat rolls. Slice a disc or two off to serve with grilled fish or chicken, or to whisk into sauces.

Dried herbs come a poor second. A few dry comparatively well, retaining enough original character to warrant occasional use – thyme, rosemary, mint – but even they impart a dusty, musty undertaste along with aromatic interest. On the whole, it's better to improvise than resort to a faded echo. If the recipe suggests basil, use marjoram, or even fresh coriander, instead. Experimenting with herbs is a joy . . . you may find that you like a new combination, born out of necessity, as much as or even better than the original.

Lettuces and salad leaves: In the wake of the enthusiasm for fresh herbs, commercial growers have realized that there is a market for interesting lettuces, too. Alongside the classic Webb and Cos lettuces, sit the newcomers: frisée with its bitter edge; escarole; bronzed and green oak leaf and batavia; the frilly-leaved lollo rosso and others, with Little Gem enjoying a renaissance.

Capton Fruit Farm are now growing purslane, and peppery rocket, halfway between a herb and a salad leaf, for the restaurant. The salads that accompany or are part of many of our dishes vary according to season and availability.

Roger Phillips's beautifully photographed book, *Wild Food*, has led me to explore the hedgerows, too. Pennywort, succulent and round leaved, grows prolifically around Dartmouth, and in the spring there are violet leaves. Young hawthorn leaves and buds – 'bread and cheese' – have a nutty taste. I do take care not to over-pick, taking leaves only from areas where these plants grow in abundance, just enough to enjoy as part of a mixed salad.

Mushrooms: We are lucky in having in Nick Coiley a resident fungi hunter. His finds vary from year to year – in the best he brings in the fragrant funnel-shaped chanterelles and cèpes, the meaty beefsteak, or the bell-shaped ink-cap mushrooms. These are all more delicate and perishable than the hardy cultivated mushroom. I would recommend the beginner to go out with an expert and also to use one of the excellent guides such as Roger Phillips, although the more unusual mushrooms are now stocked by the larger supermarket chains.

Nuts: The fresher they are, the better. The high oil content of most nuts means that once shelled they have only a short shelf-life. It's rare, for instance, that you can buy a decent walnut these days, except in the shell. Ready-shelled walnuts quickly turn rancid.

Hazelnuts and almonds have more staying power but not limitless. I buy from the local wholefood store, which has a good turnover. Pine kernels, too, are usually fine, with their creamy sweet taste. Expensive, but lovely for all kinds of dishes.

Though it is worth making the effort, it is an undeniable fact that shelling fresh chestnuts is a tedious job. However, you can now buy very good prepared chestnuts in a shrink-wrapped pack from delicatessens. They are not cheap, but the quality is excellent. Tinned chestnut purée is useful and almost as good.

Oils and fats: To me, oil implies olive oil. In recipes where I've not specified the type of oil to use, my instinct would be to use a good, light flavoured and textured **pure olive oil**. Other cooks might prefer to use an almost flavourless oil instead, say, sunflower, safflower, grapeseed, or groundnut.

In much the same way, when I suggest that you use olive oil

in a dish, the kind you use is up to you. I would use an **extra virgin olive oil** with its heady strong olive flavour for grilling and to accent a mayonnaise. The more cautious may prefer to stick with the pure olive oil.

I keep a small pan of pure olive oil set aside for frying small batches of croûtons for fish soups, for example, or other ingredients that would benefit from the extra lift of olive oil. But in general, I prefer a limpid, light groundnut oil for deep-frying, which imparts no taste, leaves no residues of grease. Both oils are filtered frequently, and discarded the instant they carry any sign of taint or discoloration.

I save **goose**, **duck** and **chicken fat**, which all give superb flavour to sautéed potatoes, or snippets of fried bread to accompany other poultry dishes, or which can be used in making rillettes, and to seal other pâtés.

For hollandaise sauce, on asparagus, and for baking I use an **unsalted butter**, and for everything else a lightly salted butter. **Clarified butter** is obtained by warming the butter gently but completely then allowing it to cool and set. When set the butter can be lifted off the top and the milky whey (solids) thrown away. Clarifying enables the butter to be used at higher temperatures without burning.

Rice: It's important to use the right kind of rice for particular dishes. Basmati has a delicious distinctive taste and is the one I use predominantly as an accompaniment. Italian Avorio or Arborio rice gives risottos and other moist rice dishes a characteristic creamy richness. Round grain pudding rice plumps up, with a melting texture for sweet rice puddings and moulds.

Spices: Again, a whole new world has opened up with the wide choice of spices now available not only in specialist shops but in supermarkets as well. No need any more for the anonymous curry powders. It's much more exciting to create one's own marriages of spices, based on their full aromatic qualities, rather than sheer heat.

Spices retain more of their aroma when whole, but even so shelf-life is limited. Once ground, though, there's nothing to prevent the volatile oils escaping, taking the best of the aroma with them. Grind spices in small quantities, and only when you are about to use them. Then the full aroma is trapped in the food you cook. I keep a little electric coffee grinder solely for grinding spices.

We buy **saffron** in small packets of the threads which I think keeps its flavour better than the powdered saffron.

Tomatoes: Canned tomatoes, boosted perhaps with a little tomato purée, are better for cooking than watery, fresh ones throughout most of the year. It's only in the warmer summer months that tomatoes in this country have the right balance of acidity and sweetness and real tomatoey flavour to make them worth using.

Vanilla sugar: We keep two jars of vanilla sugar going in rotation; each holds about 2 kg/4½ lb caster sugar with eight vanilla pods buried in it. As one jar is emptied we move on to the second, refilling the first jar and leaving for about one month to enable the sugar to absorb the vanilla flavour.

Vinegars: Always, always, use wine vinegar, white or red, never harsh malt or spirit. Sherry vinegar and balsamic vinegar have a distinctive spiciness. I make some flavoured vinegars simply by steeping herbs or fruit in white wine vinegar. One of the most unusual is the Elderflower Vinegar on page 59. As well as adding interest to salad dressings, they are good for deglazing pans to make the basis for a quick sauce.

FOOD SAFETY

There has been much concern in recent years about the potential dangers of food poisoning from certain foods, such as eggs, unpasteurized cheeses, and calves' and ox brains. This simply underlines the importance of knowing your source of supply, buying wisely, and ensuring correct handling and storage of food in the kitchen, practising strict hygiene at all times.

Stocks & Basic Sauces

Well-made stocks are the foundation stones of a good kitchen. In a restaurant it is easy enough to have a constant supply of all manner of stocks, but the domestic kitchen is rarely geared up for constantly simmering vats of liquid – not enough staff for a start.

Stock cubes are a poor substitute. The freezer, or freezing compartment of the fridge, makes them quite unnecessary anyway. Stocks freeze well, and making about 2 litres/3½ pints of stock is little more time-consuming or irksome than making half that quantity. If freezer room is limited, boil the stocks briskly to reduce them by half or three-quarters before freezing, making a note of the reduction ratio on the label so that they can be suitably diluted when used.

Many sauces freeze well, too. The classic Bordelaise and Brown Sauces, which take time to make, but are great fun to tackle once in a while, can be frozen. The Brown Sauce is a good base for other sauces, too, a 'super-stock'. In the same fashion, tomato sauces can be varied in all kinds of ways through the addition of herbs, spices, wines and cream, so it is useful to keep a few conveniently-sized tubs of plain tomato sauce stashed away in the freezer.

Sauces are much simpler now than they used to be, and the strict rules about what sauce should go with what dish have been discarded. I am just as likely to use a light vegetable purée as a sauce, like the Mushroom Sauce for pasta on page 87, or the Leek and Watercress Sauce on page 156, as I am to use one of the classics.

The old habit of masking the entire contents of a dish with a heavy blanket of sauce is, thank heavens, dying out. It makes so much more sense to choose a sauce as an accompaniment rather than as a disguise, and to use only as much as is needed to balance the elements. The trend towards putting a small amount of sauce straight on to the plate and laying meat or fish on top is an intelligent one, as long as both sauce and flesh are worth displaying, as they should be.

The simplest sauces are often based on the cooking juices left behind in the pan. The fat is drained off, the pan deglazed with alcohol, vinegar or stock, or all three, then reduced and thickened finally with a little cold butter whisked in at the last moment, or with a splash of double cream.

Flour-based sauces have fallen out of favour, but I don't think that they should be dismissed out of hand. They do have their place, particularly in domestic cookery, but they are not paramount. I find that I use much less flour than I used to, reducing quantities to give thinner, lighter and less gluey sauces. The important thing to remember with any flour-based sauce is that it needs to be cooked sufficiently long to get rid of the taste of raw flour.

I love Hollandaise Sauce and its countless variations. Its reputation for being tricky and hard to handle is undeserved. And besides, it is so good with very plainly grilled or poached fish that it is worth mastering. Soubise Sauce is delicious, with the sweetness of slowly cooked onion. It is lovely with a poached egg for lunch, and is an ideal complement to roast lamb.

In fact, most of the sauces given in this chapter are exceedingly versatile and just the thing to dress up basic meat or fish. I can think of little better on a summer evening than a steak of perfectly fresh turbot or salmon, poached or grilled *à point* and served with a good sauce – a herby mayonnaise, a tomato and ginger sauce, or a lemon onion sauce, for instance. Or a piece of guinea fowl, charcoal grilled, with apple mayonnaise and a mushroom purée.

Note: Keep meat and poultry stocks and court bouillon for up to one week in the fridge and up to two months in the freezer. Keep fish stock for two days in the fridge and one month in the freezer.

CHICKEN STOCK

This is the most useful of all stocks, a good light base for soups and stews, and even light enough for some fish dishes. Use the same method for duck and other poultry stocks. If you want a darker, stronger stock, roast the bones in a hot oven for 20 minutes or so until browned, before simmering.

MAKES ABOUT 2 LITRES/3½ PINTS

900 g/2 lb raw chicken carcasses, with giblets and feet
(but no livers)
2 onions, sliced
2 carrots, sliced
2 sticks of celery, chopped
6 parsley stalks
1 sprig of thyme
3 bay leaves
1 tablespoon black peppercorns

Put all the ingredients into a large pan, and add 2.25 litres/4 pints cold water. Bring gently to the boil, skimming off any scum that rises to the surface. Cover and simmer steadily for 1 hour. Strain through a very fine sieve and leave to cool.

When cool, lift off the fat that has set on the surface; this can be saved and used for other dishes. Use or freeze the stock as required.

VARIATION

GAME STOCK

Substitute the carcasses of any game birds, such as pheasant, for the chicken. Necks or giblets can be added.

BEEF, LAMB OR MUTTON STOCK

A stock that is worth making in large quantities, then reducing and freezing in small ones, to be used when needed. For general use I don't bother to roast the bones, but if the stock is to be used for a brown sauce, or a Bordelaise, it is necessary to give it a stronger flavour and a darker colour. Spread out the bones on a roasting tray and roast in a preheated hot oven, somewhere between 190°C/ 375°F/gas mark 5 and 220°C/425°F/gas mark 7 depending on whatever else you may be cooking, for about 30 minutes until the bones are well browned, turning occasionally.

MAKES ABOUT 2 LITRES/3½ PINTS

1.4 kg/3 lb beef, lamb or mutton bones
2 onions, sliced
2 carrots, sliced
2 sticks of celery, chopped
6 parsley stalks
1 sprig of thyme
3 bay leaves
1 tablespoon black peppercorns

Put all the ingredients into a large pan and add enough cold water to cover. Bring to the boil, skimming off any scum that rises to the surface. Cover and simmer very gently for 2 hours. Strain through a very fine sieve and leave to cool.

When cold, lift off the fat that has set on the surface; this can be used for cooking meat or roasting potatoes. Use or freeze the stock as required.

FISH STOCK

Use the debris left from preparing firm white fish such as turbot, brill, sole or John Dory. Avoid bones from oily fish such as mackerel and herring, although salmon is fine.

MAKES ABOUT 2.25 LITRES/4 PINTS

900 g/2 lb fish trimmings
1 onion, sliced
1 stick of celery, chopped
4 parsley stalks
1 sprig of thyme
1 bay leaf
½ tablespoon black peppercorns

Put all the ingredients into a large pan and cover with cold water. Bring to the boil, skimming off any scum that rises to the surface. Cover and simmer very gently for 30 minutes. Strain through a very fine sieve and leave to cool. Use or freeze the stock as required.

COURT BOUILLON

*A court bouillon is simply a light stock, nothing more than flavoured
water, used usually for poaching fish. Overcooked tasteless fish boiled
to death in plain tap water has been one of the scourges of British
cooking. But fish that has been poached – that is, cooked in a liquid
that is barely simmering – in a delicate court bouillon is quite
another matter. I use this court bouillon for poaching skate wings in
particular, but it is also useful for cooking brains (see page 241).*

MAKES ABOUT 1.2 LITRES/2 PINTS

2 onions, sliced
2 carrots, sliced
2 sticks of celery, chopped
2 sprigs of thyme
1 bay leaf
1 small bunch of parsley stalks
2 tablespoons white wine vinegar
1 pinch of salt
2 teaspoons black peppercorns

Put all the ingredients in a pan and add 1.2 litres/2 pints cold
water. Bring to the boil, cover and simmer for 30 minutes. Taste
and adjust seasonings – it should be quite highly seasoned.
Strain through a very fine sieve and leave to cool. Use or freeze
the court bouillon as required.

HOLLANDAISE SAUCE

This most luxurious of sauces has a reputation for being tricky but once the technique has been mastered, it should pose no problems. Never be tempted to rush it.
Plain hollandaise can turn a grilled or poached dish into a magnificent treat. To ring the changes, add chopped fresh herbs or a handful of sorrel leaves shredded and cooked in butter.

MAKES 300 ML/½ PINT

3 egg yolks
2 tablespoons dry white wine
2 tablespoons lemon juice
225 g/8 oz unsalted butter, melted
salt
cayenne pepper

Put the egg yolks, wine and lemon juice in a bowl. Sit the bowl over a pan of simmering water, making sure that the base of the bowl does not touch the water. Whisk until the mixture is slightly thickened. Gradually add the melted butter, drop by drop at first then progressing to a slow trickle as the sauce thickens, constantly whisking with a balloon whisk. When all the butter has been added, the sauce should be shiny and thick enough to coat the back of a spoon. Season to taste with salt and cayenne pepper.

ORANGE HOLLANDAISE

The sharp juice of Seville oranges, with its aromatic citrus smell, is a superb addition to a Hollandaise Sauce that is to be served with fish, or with vegetables, especially broccoli.

When Seville oranges are in season, replace the lemon juice in Hollandaise Sauce with an equal quantity of Seville orange juice, and stir in 1 dessertspoon of the finely grated zest. Throughout the rest of the year, use 1 tablespoon lemon juice, 1 tablespoon orange juice, and 1 dessertspoon finely grated zest of a sweet orange.

BÉCHAMEL SAUCE

MAKES 750 ML/1¼ PINTS

50 g/2 oz onions, sliced
3 parsley stalks
1 bay leaf
1 sprig of thyme
600 ml/1 pint milk
50 g/2 oz butter
50 g/2 oz flour
salt
cayenne pepper

Put the onions and herbs in a pan with the milk and bring to the boil. Remove from the heat and leave the milk to infuse for 10 minutes. Strain.

Melt the butter in a pan and stir in the flour to make a *roux*. Cook gently, without colouring, for 5 minutes. Remove from the heat and gradually mix in the strained milk. Return to the heat and bring to the boil, stirring constantly to make a smooth sauce. Season to taste with salt and cayenne pepper. Simmer very gently, stirring, for 5 minutes. Taste and adjust seasonings.

LEMON ONION SAUCE

*This sharp, sweet sauce, based on an original from Colin Spencer, is
delicious with fish, brains or sweetbread fritters.*

MAKES ABOUT 300 ML/½ PINT

1 lemon
450 g/1 lb onions, chopped
25 g/1 oz butter or 2 tablespoons oil
salt
freshly ground black pepper

Pare the zest of the lemon in long strips with a potato peeler,
being careful to avoid the white pith. Place in a pan with the
onions and butter or oil. Cover tightly and cook over a gentle
heat, without browning, for 30 minutes, or until really tender.
Purée with the lemon juice in a food processor or blender. Add
salt and pepper to taste.

SOUBISE SAUCE

This is a very simple onion sauce that we serve with best end of lamb in the summer. For an excellent variation, which is again ideal with lamb, stir in a tablespoon of chopped fresh mint at the end.

MAKES 300 ML/½ PINT

75 g/3 oz butter
450 g/1 lb onions, chopped
1 tablespoon flour
300 ml/½ pint appropriate meat stock (depending on
the meat you are serving it with) or milk
freshly grated nutmeg
salt
freshly ground black pepper

Melt the butter in a pan and sweat the onions, without browning, for 15 minutes. Stir in the flour and gradually add the stock or milk, mixing well. Season lightly with nutmeg, salt and pepper. Simmer very gently for 15 minutes. Taste and adjust seasonings.

MESSINE SAUCE

*This is a creamy, delicate sauce, to serve with simply cooked fish
(maybe a poached turbot steak, or a fillet of brill) when a hollandaise
seems rather too rich for the occasion.*

MAKES 600 ML/1 PINT

50 g/2 oz butter
1 small onion or 2 shallots, chopped
½ tablespoon each chopped chervil, tarragon and
parsley
2 teaspoons flour
600 ml/1 pint single cream (or half single cream and
half milk)
juice of ½ lemon
2 teaspoons Dijon mustard
salt
freshly ground black pepper

Melt the butter in a pan and sweat the onion or shallots for 5
minutes, until tender. Add the herbs and cook slowly for a further 5 minutes. Stir in the flour and cook gently for 2 minutes.
Gradually add the cream or milk and cream. Flavour with
lemon juice, mustard, salt and pepper. Continue to cook over a
low heat for 5 minutes. Taste and adjust seasonings.

SAFFRON CREAM SAUCE

Saffron, worth so much more than just its own weight in gold, is a spice that we use a great deal. Our suppliers are the Saffron Flour Company, who used to pack their saffron in Kingsbridge, near Dartmouth. They've now moved to Plymouth and diversified into fish and chip shop requisites – batter bases and so on. But they've kept the name and the saffron.

MAKES ABOUT 750 ML/1¼ PINTS

65 g/2½ oz butter
50 g/2 oz shallots, chopped
65 ml/2½ fl oz dry white wine
40 g/1½ oz flour
600 ml/1 pint fish stock, see page 31
a scant ¼ teaspoon saffron filaments
150 ml/¼ pint double cream
lemon juice
salt
freshly ground black pepper

Melt 25 g/1 oz of the butter in a pan and sweat the shallots for 5 minutes, until tender. Add the wine and bubble until it is reduced to 2 tablespoons.

Melt the remaining butter in a separate pan and stir in the flour. Gradually add the stock, then the wine and shallot reduction. Simmer gently for 10 minutes, then stir in the saffron. Cover and let it infuse for 5 minutes over a gentle heat. Finally, add the cream, lemon juice, and salt and pepper to taste. Reheat gently if necessary.

PIQUANT CREAM SAUCE

A classic sauce for boiled ham, roast pork or tongue. The cooked roux
gives a nutty flavour as well as a pretty pale coffee colour.

MAKES 600 ML/1 PINT

8 shallots, chopped
4 juniper berries, crushed
75 ml/3 fl oz white wine vinegar
50 g/2 oz butter
50 g/2 oz flour
475 ml/16 fl oz chicken or beef stock, see pages 29, 30
75 ml/3 fl oz dry white wine
salt
freshly ground black pepper
150 ml/¼ pint double cream

Put the shallots, juniper berries and vinegar in a small pan and
boil hard to reduce until all but dry. Melt the butter in a separate
pan, stir in the flour to make a *roux* and cook until it is coffee-
coloured.

Heat the stock separately. Remove the *roux* from the heat and
gradually stir in the hot stock, wine, and salt and pepper to
taste. Add the shallot reduction. Return to the heat, bring to the
boil and simmer gently for 15 minutes. Strain and stir in the
cream. Taste and adjust seasonings, then reheat.

RHUBARB SAUCE

This is a simple sauce with a clear, sharp taste, which is perfect with oily fish such as mackerel or herring.

MAKES 300 ML/½ PINT

225 g/8 oz rhubarb, trimmed and cut into 2.5 cm/
1 inch lengths
1 small onion, finely chopped
juice and grated zest of 1 orange
4 tablespoons water
1 teaspoon finely chopped fresh root ginger
salt
freshly ground black pepper

Put all the ingredients in a pan, cover and cook over a low heat for about 30 minutes. Purée in a processor or blender and adjust seasonings.

BROWN SAUCE

*Brown Sauce is really a twice-cooked stock, bursting with the
concentrated extracts of meat bones, vegetables and aromatics. It is
the backbone of many classic meat sauces, such as the Brown Piquant
Sauce (see page 43). It's worth making it in large batches and then
freezing in 300 or 600 ml/½ or 1 pint containers, ready for
later use.*

MAKES ABOUT 1.2 LITRES/2 PINTS

450 g/1 lb chicken giblets (excluding the liver) and bones,
or beef bones, or both
175 g/6 oz dripping
450 g/1 lb onions, sliced
225 g/8 oz carrots, sliced
4 sticks of celery, sliced
½ head of garlic, chopped
3 bay leaves
2 sprigs of thyme
2 sprigs of marjoram
50 g/2 oz streaky bacon, chopped, or bacon trimmings
100 g/4 oz flour
1.75 litres/3 pints beef stock, see page 30
2 tablespoons tomato purée

Spread out the giblets and bones in a roasting tin and roast in a
preheated oven, 200°C/400°F/gas mark 6, for 15–25 minutes,
turning occasionally, until evenly browned.

Melt the dripping in a large pan and sweat the vegetables,
garlic, herbs and bacon for 30 minutes. Stir in the flour and
then the stock and tomato purée. Bring to the boil and add the
giblets and bones. Simmer for 2–3 hours, then strain.

BROWN PIQUANT SAUCE

This is a lively, sharp sauce that we might serve with calves' sweetbreads (see page 230), tongue or plain pork chops.

MAKES 300 ML/½ PINT

15 g/½ oz butter
50 g/2 oz shallots, chopped
50 ml/2 fl oz dry white wine
½ tablespoon white wine vinegar
300 ml/½ pint Brown Sauce, see page 42
1 teaspoon Dijon mustard
1 tablespoon chopped parsley
½ tablespoon chopped capers
½ tablespoon sliced gherkins
1 pinch of granulated sugar
salt
15 g/½ oz butter, chilled and diced

Melt the butter in a pan and sweat the shallots for about 5 minutes, until tender. Add the wine and vinegar, and boil hard to reduce until all but dry.

Add the Brown Sauce, simmer gently for 15 minutes, then strain. Stir in all the remaining ingredients except the butter. Taste and adjust seasonings, and reheat. Whisk in the chilled butter just before serving.

BORDELAISE SAUCE

*The Bordelaise Sauce is the king of steak sauces, though at The
Carved Angel we might be more likely to combine it with slices of
bone marrow.*
*To prepare these, put some marrow bones which have been sawn into
15 cm/6 inch lengths in a roasting tin and cook in a preheated oven,
220°C/425°F/gas mark 7, for 15 minutes.*
*With a thin knife, ease out the marrow from the bones and place in a
bowl of cold water. The water will soak out any blood. Drain and cut
the marrow into 6 mm/¼ inch thick slices. Add to the Bordelaise
and heat gently for 5 minutes – or you can heat through the marrow
by just letting it sit in hot Bordelaise. Do not overheat or the marrow
will melt completely.*

MAKES 600 ML/1 SCANT PINT

225 g/8 oz shallots, chopped
300 ml/½ pint red wine
1 sprig of thyme
1 bay leaf
600 ml/1 pint Brown Sauce, see page 42
salt
freshly ground black pepper

Put the shallots in a pan with the wine and the herbs. Boil hard
to reduce until all but dry. Add the Brown Sauce, season to taste
with salt and pepper, and simmer for 30 minutes. Strain and
adjust the seasonings.

MAYONNAISE

A good stiff mayonnaise made with olive oil is the ideal foil to cold lobster. For a sauce tartare to go with Grilled Pigs' Trotters (see page 235), leave out the extra virgin oil, and add instead a tablespoon each of chopped parsley, capers and gherkins, and a few pickled nasturtium seeds if you have them. To pickle nasturtium seeds, pick them while they are fairly dry, pop in a jar and cover with spiced vinegar. Store for two to three months before using.
If mayonnaises break or curdle, I usually manage to retrieve them by putting about a dessertspoon of cold water in a bowl and, little by little, whisking in the curdled mayonnaise. It is not normally necessary to add another egg yolk.

MAKES 750 ML/1¼ PINTS

4 egg yolks
juice of ½ lemon
600 ml/1 pint good quality olive oil
2 tablespoons extra virgin olive oil
salt
freshly ground black pepper

Beat the egg yolks with the lemon juice in a bowl. Gradually beat in the olive oils with a balloon whisk, a few drops at a time at first, increasing to a slow trickle as you continue. Season to taste with salt and pepper.

Mayonnaise can also be made very quickly in a processor or blender. Make in two batches, using half the ingredients in each batch. Put the egg yolks, lemon juice and a little salt and pepper in a processor or blender. Set the motor running and dribble in the oil slowly. Taste and adjust seasonings.

AÏOLI

This is the classic addition to a Southern French Fish Soup (see page 65), beaten in at the end of cooking to give a luxurious pungent finale. We also serve it as one of a pair of sauces – the other might be a Tomato and Chilli Sauce (see page 55) – to set off simple grilled fish.

MAKES 750 ML/1¼ PINTS

4–6 cloves of garlic
½ teaspoon salt
4 egg yolks
juice of ½ lemon
600 ml/1 pint olive oil
freshly ground black pepper

Pound the garlic with the salt to a cream in a mortar with a pestle. Beat in the egg yolks with the lemon juice. Whisk in the oil, a few drops at a time at first, as for an ordinary mayonnaise. Add pepper, taste and adjust seasonings.

Alternatively, put all the ingredients, except for the oil, in a processor or blender and mix well. Dribble in the oil while the motor is running. Taste and adjust seasonings.

HERB MAYONNAISE

*A green summer mayonnaise for cold fish, chicken or eggs. It is a
particular favourite with salmon or salmon trout, pastel green
against pastel pink. If you are making the mayonnaise in a processor
or blender, there is no need to chop the herbs finely first.*

MAKES A GENEROUS 300 ML/½ PINT

1 egg
juice of ½ lemon
300 ml/½ pint groundnut oil
salt
freshly ground black pepper
1 handful of soft herbs (parsley, chervil, chives, dill or
fennel, for example), finely chopped

Beat the egg with the lemon juice in a bowl. Gradually whisk
in the oil with a balloon whisk, a few drops at a time at first,
increasing to a slow trickle as you continue. Season to taste and
add the herbs.

Alternatively, break the egg into a processor or blender, and
then add the herbs, lemon juice and a little salt and pepper to
taste. Set the motor running and slowly trickle in the oil until
the mixture is thick. Taste and adjust seasonings.

APPLE MAYONNAISE

This is an unusually fruity mayonnaise, which I make to accompany
Quail in Aspic (see page 110), but which is also an admirable
addition to any summer buffet.

MAKES 750 ML/1¼ PINTS

3 large eating apples
½ quantity of mayonnaise, see page 45
lemon juice

Slice the apples – there is no need to peel and core them – and
put in a pan with 150 ml/¼ pint cold water. Cover, bring to the
boil and simmer for about 15 minutes until really tender. Rub
through a sieve. Leave to cool, then mix with an equal volume
of mayonnaise. Sharpen to taste with lemon juice.

CHINESE PLUM SAUCE

This is a fruity sweet and sour sauce, almost a ketchup, which is lovely with charcuterie such as a chicken galantine (see page 169), grilled poultry and cold meats. It keeps well in the fridge for up to a fortnight. A teaspoon of grated fresh root ginger can be added for extra zip.

MAKES 1.2 LITRES/2 PINTS

450 g/1 lb plums
1–2 red or green chilli peppers
150 g/5 oz caster sugar
100 ml/4 fl oz white wine vinegar
150 ml/¼ pint cold water

Halve the plums. Halve and seed the chillis. Put the plums, chillis and the remaining ingredients in a heavy-based pan. Cover and simmer very gently for about 20 minutes, until the plums are soft and collapsed. Rub through a sieve to remove stones and skins. Taste and adjust seasonings.

CUMBERLAND SAUCE

A classic sweet and sour sauce to serve with ham, tongue, and other cold meats. It is particularly nice with the Sweetbread Terrine on page 115. Keep any unused sauce in a tightly covered jar in the fridge for up to a month.

MAKES 450 ML/¾ PINT

1 lemon
1 orange
225 g/8 oz redcurrant jelly
50 ml/2 fl oz port
1 pinch of cayenne pepper

Pare the zest from the lemon and orange in long strips with a potato peeler, being careful to avoid the white pith. Shred finely and blanch for 1 minute in boiling water. Drain and pat dry with kitchen paper. Process the jelly with the port, the juice of the orange and lemon and the cayenne pepper in a processor or blender, until smooth. Stir in the shredded peel.

COURCHAMPS SAUCE

This is a surprisingly well-balanced sauce, considering the seemingly discordant list of ingredients. It is strongly flavoured, of course, but marvellous in small quantities with lobster and other shellfish. For a milder version that won't overwhelm a fish terrine, say, mix with equal quantities of mayonnaise.

MAKES 150 ML/¼ PINT

2 tablespoons brown crab meat (or meat from the head
of a lobster)
2 teaspoons anisette
1 teaspoon soy sauce
1 teaspoon chopped parsley
1 teaspoon chopped tarragon
1 teaspoon Dijon mustard
4 tablespoons olive oil
juice of ½–1 lemon
salt
freshly ground black pepper

Process all the ingredients except the lemon juice, salt and pepper in a processor or blender. Add the lemon juice, and salt and pepper to taste.

WALNUT AND
HORSERADISH SAUCE

Peeling the walnuts may seem an awfully fiddly task, but the final result makes it worth while if you do have the time. This is another sauce that is a delight with cold salmon trout or cold meats.

MAKES ABOUT 450 ML/¾ PINT

100 g/4 oz walnuts
300 ml/½ pint double cream, lightly whipped
1–2 teaspoons granulated sugar
4 tablespoons grated fresh horseradish
juice of 1 lemon
salt
freshly ground black pepper

Pour boiling water over the nuts. Leave to stand for a couple of minutes, then drain. When cool enough to handle, peel off the thin brown skin. Chop the nuts and stir into the cream with the remaining ingredients. Taste and adjust seasonings.

CHILLI OIL

A recipe calls for one fresh chilli pepper, but you will rarely be able to buy less than 100 g/4 oz, enough to set fire to a week or two of curries. What do you do with the rest of them?

They will keep tolerably well for a week in the vegetable drawer of the fridge, and can be frozen, but I find that the best way of preserving them is in oil. Slit green or red chillis in half and remove the seeds and stalks. Pack them into a jar, and cover with light olive oil, or a tasteless oil. Store in the fridge.

Both the chillis and the chilli-flavoured oil can be used as needed. The oil is good for grilling, stir-frying, in Rouille Sauce (see page 66) and sprinkled over a pizza, to jazz it up. It keeps almost indefinitely in the fridge.

BASIC TOMATO SAUCE
(PROVENÇALE SAUCE)

*I rarely buy tomatoes in winter since their flavour is so poor. For
sauces and soups you get a much better result from canned tomatoes.
This is a basic sauce that can be varied in many ways. For instance,
you might add a teaspoon (or more) of grated fresh root ginger or
orange rind to make a good sauce to accompany fish. Any sauce that
is not used immediately can be frozen.*

MAKES ABOUT 600 ML/1 PINT

65 ml/2½ fl oz olive oil
1 medium onion, sliced
3 cloves of garlic, sliced
5 basil leaves
1 sprig of marjoram
2 × 400 g/14 oz cans tomatoes, and their juice
salt
freshly ground black pepper
lemon juice (optional)
sugar (optional)

Heat the oil in a pan and sweat the onion, garlic and herbs for
10 minutes. Add the tomatoes, and salt and pepper to taste, and
simmer until thick. Pass through a *mouli légumes*, or whizz in a
processor or blender, then sieve. Adjust the seasonings, adding
a dash of lemon juice and a pinch of sugar to bring out the
flavour if necessary.

TOMATO AND CHILLI SAUCE

MAKES 450 ML/¾ PINT

1 tablespoon olive oil
50 g/2 oz onion, chopped
1 clove of garlic, chopped
1 × 400 g/14 oz can tomatoes, chopped, and their juice
½ chilli pepper, seeded and chopped
4 large basil leaves, chopped
salt

Heat the oil in a pan and sweat the onion and garlic for 5 minutes, without browning. Add the tomatoes, chilli, basil, and salt to taste. Simmer gently for 20 minutes. Pass through a *mouli légumes* or sieve. Taste and adjust seasonings. Reheat if necessary when needed.

GRELETTE SAUCE

This sauce is one of the great joys of summer. Offer it with the Fish Terrine on page 139, or deep-fried goujons of fish.

MAKES ABOUT 450 ML/¾ PINT

350 g/12 oz tomatoes, skinned, seeded and finely chopped
3 tablespoons double cream
1 tablespoon white wine vinegar
1 teaspoon Dijon mustard
1 teaspoon brandy
salt
freshly ground black pepper
½ tablespoon each chopped chervil, tarragon and parsley

Mix together all the ingredients in a bowl. Taste and adjust seasonings.

HERB VINAIGRETTE

A fresh green dressing for summer salads – green leaf, tomato or potato – which can be stored in the fridge, covered, for up to a week.

MAKES 450 ML/¾ PINT

65 ml/2½ fl oz white wine vinegar
1 level teaspoon salt
freshly ground black pepper
215 ml/7½ fl oz olive oil
65 ml/2½ fl oz hazelnut or walnut oil
1 handful of parsley and/or other soft herbs, such as tarragon, chervil and basil, finely chopped

Put the vinegar, salt, and pepper to taste in a bowl and whisk in the oils in a steady stream, until the mixture is well blended. Add the herbs, then taste and adjust seasonings.

Alternatively, process the vinegar, salt, whole herbs, and pepper to taste in a blender. Whisk in the two oils, then taste and adjust seasonings.

ELDERFLOWER DRESSING

A fragrant dressing, with the muscat scent of elderflowers. Use it to dress cold chicken or avocado salads, or to deglaze a pan after cooking roast chicken.

MAKES A GENEROUS 300 ML/½ PINT

3 tablespoons elderflower vinegar, see page 59
1 teaspoon caster sugar
150 ml/¼ pint groundnut oil
150 ml/¼ pint single cream
salt
freshly ground black pepper

Put the vinegar and sugar in a bowl and whisk in the oil in a steady stream, until the mixture is well blended. Add the cream, and salt and pepper to taste, and whisk again. Taste and adjust seasonings.

Alternatively, process the vinegar, sugar, and salt and pepper to taste in a blender. Whisk in the oil, then add the cream, taste and adjust seasonings.

ELDERFLOWER VINEGAR

This is one of the best ways to capture the heady, early summer fragrance of elderflowers. Use the muscat-scented vinegar to dress salads, or deglaze pans, or in the Elderflower Dressing (see page 58).

On a dry, sunny day, pick a generous bunch of creamy white heads of elderflower in their prime. Shake each one gently before you take it from the bush – if a shower of white cascades to the ground then that umbel is past its best. Leave it alone.

In the kitchen, shake the flowers again, to dislodge any stray bodies, trim off the stalks, then pack them fairly tightly into clean preserving jars, cover with fine white wine vinegar and seal well. Leave to steep in a dark cupboard for at least a month and up to a year. Strain through muslin, and bottle.

TAPENADE

Provençal Tapenade is a relish rather than a sauce, strong and forceful, and to be enjoyed in small quantities. If you don't use it all up at once it can be kept in a covered jar in the fridge for a week or more.
Spread it thinly on hot toast or on oven-baked slices of French bread. Or pack it into a small bowl and surround it with strips of raw vegetables and hard-boiled eggs, as a first course. It is excellent, too, with Grilled Goats' Cheese (see page 94).

MAKES 250 ML/8 FL OZ

24 black olives, stoned
8 anchovy fillets
50 g/2 oz canned tuna fish
1 tablespoon capers, drained
1 teaspoon Dijon mustard
lemon juice, to taste
1 tablespoon brandy
olive oil

Pound the olives in a mortar with a pestle until they are smooth. Add the anchovy, tuna and capers and pound again. Mix in the mustard, lemon juice and brandy. Finally, beat in enough oil to give a thick, unctuous paste. Spread a little on a corner of bread and taste – adjust the seasonings accordingly.

Alternatively, whizz together all the ingredients in a processor or blender.

PESTO SAUCE

It may seem strange to include a grilled tomato in Pesto Sauce, but it gives a marvellous flavour, balancing out the oiliness of the pine kernels and olive oil. It's an idea we picked up from Elizabeth David and which we have stuck with ever since.

As well as spooning this sauce over plain or spinach pasta, we occasionally omit the cheese and mix it with breadcrumbs to use as a topping for baked fish.

MAKES 300 ML/½ PINT

1 clove of garlic
salt
25 g/1 oz pine kernels
25 g/1 oz basil leaves
1 tomato, grilled
25 g/1 oz Parmesan cheese, freshly grated
freshly ground black pepper
olive oil

Put all the ingredients, except the salt, in a processor or blender and process, dribbling in enough oil to give a smooth, thick cream. Taste the sauce and add salt if necessary.

Alternatively, pound the garlic and salt in a mortar. Add the pine kernels, basil, and tomato and pound until smooth. Beat in the cheese and pepper, and enough olive oil to give a thick cream. Taste and add salt if necessary.

Soups

Soups are almost unfashionable now, or at least they seem to be when you scan restaurant menus. I'm not thinking so much of the chic consommés with a thousand and one bits and pieces floating round in them, but rather of the more traditional soups, thick and substantial.

Not that I've got anything against a superb consommé – I serve them on special occasions, as an elegant prelude to a large celebratory meal, such as New Year's Eve. They can be great fun to make, too, with little quenelles poached in the soup, tiny ravioli maybe, miniature spheres of carrot and potato, and the other frivolities that leap to mind. But, by and large, most of the soups made at The Carved Angel are really quite old-fashioned in style, with a preponderance of vegetable ones.

Even so, I do try to offer some soups that are a little bit unusual. The Banana Curry or the Brazil Nut and Lemon Soup are combinations that are immediately intriguing, and turn out to be quite delicious. Naturally, the starting point for any soup is the availability of good ingredients, so the season is the springboard for choice. We do a few cold soups in the summer. Cherry Soup is one of my favourites. The Spiced Pumpkin and all types of game are the autumn soups *par excellence*. Sorrel Soup is the one that I most look forward to making as spring gets properly under way.

Although I veer off for a while to experiment with other

kinds of fish soup, a thick clam chowder, perhaps, or a creamy Normandy-style soup, I always end up returning to the same substantial tomato and saffron Fish Soup that I have been making since my days at the Hole in the Wall. I've unintentionally neglected the range of meat soups at the restaurant. After all, a well-made oxtail soup is tremendous, and then there are those Victorian recipes for kidney soups, Brown Windsors and so on, soups whose reputations have been badly tarnished by sloppy production and a failure to pay attention to detail.

Soup is something that is easy to take for granted, forgetting how wonderful a good one can be. It's not until you have a bowlful of truly awful soup, probably served with packet bread, that you really appreciate your own home-made ones. All too often it seems that what is labelled 'home-made' on a menu, is actually 'home-made-out-of-a-packet', and as such a terrible travesty of the real thing. This is even more infuriating when one knows that a simple soup is so easy to make.

For me, a substantial, tasty soup is the perfect lunch dish. The only thing you need to complete the meal is good bread, with cheese and fruit to follow. In the middle of the day, I want a soup that is stimulating, uplifting and restorative, and I hope that most of our soups, with their pleasing appearance and well-founded flavours, fall into that category. At The Carved Angel we have a large white soup tureen, bought for 1/6d in Bath, which we use for the staff lunches – filled with good soup it always seems a lovely sight. The soup makes an easy, delicious lunch as a prelude to the busy time ahead.

Served in smaller helpings, soups transfer well to an evening meal. With the advent of blenders and food processors, there's really no need to thicken most soups with flour, so they won't weigh too heavily on the stomach.

A first-class soup needs to be freshly made and given some care and attention, whether you are following a particular recipe or just using up vegetables left over from the day before. Never be tempted to use soup as a dustbin – soups can be thrifty and economical but, like any other dish, they are only as good as what goes into them. Think before you throw in every scrap that lurks in the fridge.

A classy stock is very important, although you can get away without it if you have wonderful vegetables and herbs packed with flavour and as fresh as can be. But stock provides a backdrop to the main ingredients. Poultry stock, chicken or guinea fowl, is the most useful, not too domineering and light enough for delicate soups. You have to be a little more careful with a lamb stock, say, which has a more definite flavour.

I use both a blender, to break down the bits and emulsify, and a *mouli légumes*, or food mill, to get rid of any residual stringiness. The *mouli* is an immensely useful piece of equipment. My introduction to it came as a child, staying with a French family. I remember that they used it to make mashed potato, the most marvellous creamy purée with milk, butter and nutmeg, which was quite a revelation after the lumpy mash I was used to in England.

I don't make a lot of accompaniments specifically for soup, preferring usually to offer plenty of good fresh bread. The Fish Soup is a notable exception, always served with its garlicky croûtons and a bowl of fiery rouille. From time to time I will add a floating island of cheese-topped toasted or baked bread to a vegetable soup. On the whole, though, I like soups to be kept simple, finished off with no more than a swirl of double or soured cream and a sprinkling of herbs. A first-class soup needs no bolstering or disguise.

FISH SOUP

This is a thick, filling fish soup, really a meal in itself. We usually remove the haddock fillet before serving, but you could skin and flake it, then return it to the pan once the aïoli has been incorporated. As well as bringing a pungent, garlicky scent to the soup, the aïoli gives it a creamy texture. The accompanying rouille needs to be made very hot to cut through the richness. It's hard to gauge the exact number of chillis you will need – two of the spindly red Thai ones may be quite enough, though it'll probably take four of the larger green chillis to achieve the same strength.

The soup can be made in advance up to the point where the aïoli is added. Then, just before serving, whisk in the aïoli and bring to the boil.

Serves 4

4 tablespoons olive oil
1 small onion, finely chopped
2 cloves of garlic, finely chopped
1 stick of celery, finely chopped
½ cucumber, finely chopped
1 tablespoon chopped parsley
2 sprigs of thyme
2 or 3 sprigs of basil, dill or fennel
½ teaspoon saffron filaments
1 × 400 g/14 oz can tomatoes, chopped, and their juice
(or 450 g/1 lb fresh tomatoes, skinned and chopped)
¼ bottle of dry white wine
600 ml/1 pint fish stock, see page 31
lemon juice
salt
freshly ground black pepper
50 g/2 oz smoked haddock fillet
150 ml/¼ pint aïoli, see page 46

TO SERVE

Rouille, see below
Garlic Croûtons, see below
freshly grated Parmesan cheese

Heat the oil in a large pan and sweat the onion, garlic, celery and cucumber for 5 minutes. Add the herbs, saffron, tomatoes and wine and simmer for 5 minutes. Stir in the stock, a good squeeze of lemon juice, and salt and pepper to taste. Bring to the boil, cover and simmer for 10 more minutes, then add the fish. Cook for a further 5 minutes.

Remove the soup from the heat, take out the fish and whisk in the aïoli. Taste and adjust seasonings. Serve with Rouille, Garlic Croûtons and freshly grated Parmesan cheese.

ROUILLE

1 × 200 g/7 oz can pimentos, drained
1 clove of garlic
2–4 chilli peppers, seeded
2 tablespoons olive oil
salt, to taste

Whizz together the whole lot in a processor or blender. Taste and adjust seasoning.

GARLIC CROÛTONS

Cut four 1.25 cm/½ inch slices of white bread and remove the crusts. Fry in olive oil until a deep golden brown on both sides. Drain briefly on kitchen paper and rub one side of each slice with a cut clove of garlic. Cut the slices into 2.5 cm/1 inch squares with a serrated knife.

AUBERGINE SOUP WITH RED PEPPER CREAM

This soup looks enchanting as the red of the pepper cream contrasts with the sombre grey tones of the aubergine. The texture is pleasing and unusual, the flavours subtle. For a more demonstrative soup, spike the pepper cream with chilli, or Chilli Oil (see page 53), or a little left-over Rouille (see page 66).

SERVES 4–6

2 tablespoons olive oil
450 g/1 lb aubergine, peeled and chopped
1 small onion, chopped
1 large clove of garlic, chopped
900 ml/1½ pints chicken or lamb stock, see pages 29, 30
salt
freshly ground black pepper
Red Pepper Cream, see below, to serve

Heat the oil in a pan and sweat the aubergine, onion and garlic for 20 minutes, until tender. Purée with the stock, salt and pepper in a processor or blender. Taste and adjust seasonings. Return the soup to the pan and reheat when needed. Serve with Red Pepper Cream.

RED PEPPER CREAM

1 red pepper, quartered and seeded
2 tablespoons single cream
salt
freshly ground black pepper

Grill the pepper until the skin is blackened and blistered. Place in a plastic bag, seal and leave until cool enough to handle. Skin and purée with the cream. Season to taste with salt and pepper. Spoon on to the soup just before serving.

ARTICHOKE AND HAZELNUT SOUP

We make this soup when we have a few cooked artichokes left over, or when we've bought a basketful of globe artichokes at a good price. It's an excellent soup served hot or cold. The hazelnuts give a grainy texture and emphasize the already nutty flavour of the globe artichokes.

SERVES 6

6–8 globe artichokes
25 g/1 oz hazelnuts
1.2 litres/2 pints chicken stock, see page 29
salt
freshly ground black pepper
150 ml/¼ pint single cream

Wash the artichokes, pull off the stalks and cook in boiling salted water, uncovered, for about 40 minutes, until the bases are tender. While they are cooking spread out the hazelnuts on a baking tray and leave in a hot oven for 5–10 minutes, until they begin to brown. As soon as they are cool enough to handle, rub between the palms of the hands to remove the papery skins. Crush in a mortar with a pestle, or whizz in a processor or blender.

Drain the artichokes well. When cool enough to handle, remove the leaves, one by one at first, scraping the flesh off the bases of the larger ones. When the leaves become small and purple-white, grasp the crown of leaves in one hand, insert a knife between the crown and the base and ease the crown of leaves away. Scrape the soft part from the inner base of the crown.

Pull the choke away from the base in small clumps and discard, scraping off any lingering hairs from the base with a knife. Cut the base into quarters. Repeat with the remaining artichokes. Put the purée collected from the leaves, and the bases in a pan with the stock, hazelnuts, and salt and pepper to taste. Bring to the boil, cover and simmer for 5 minutes. Process briefly in a processor or blender, then pass through a fine *mouli légumes* or sieve.

Stir in the cream and adjust seasonings. Serve hot or cold.

BANANA CURRY SOUP

This recipe came from an Estonian woman who used to work with us at the Hole in the Wall in Bath. She had moved all over Europe during the war, finally ending up in Bath. This always seemed such a strange combination for an Eastern European to come up with. But she was a very good cook, and this was one of her best recipes.

SERVES 6

25 g/1 oz butter
1 small onion, chopped
½ teaspoon curry powder
900 ml/1½ pints chicken stock, see page 29
350 g/12 oz ripe, unblemished bananas, peeled and chopped
2 tablespoons lemon juice
salt
150 ml/¼ pint single cream

Melt the butter in a pan and sweat the onion for 5 minutes. Stir in the curry powder and cook for a further 30 seconds or so. Add the stock, bananas, lemon juice, and salt to taste. Bring to the boil, cover and simmer gently for 15 minutes. Process the soup in a processor or blender and stir in the cream. Taste and adjust seasonings, then return the soup to the pan and reheat to serve.

BRAZIL NUT AND LEMON SOUP

We first made this soup when we had a glut of brazil nuts left over one Christmas, and it seemed a good way of using them up. You could use other nuts instead – hazelnuts or walnuts, for instance, would give a similar grainy consistency, balanced by the fresh note of the lemon zest.

SERVES 6

25 g/1 oz butter
1 medium onion, sliced
1.2 litres/2 pints chicken stock, see page 29
100 g/4 oz shelled brazil nuts
zest of 1 lemon, cut into thick strips
salt
freshly ground black pepper
65 ml/2½ fl oz single cream

Melt the butter in a pan and sweat the onion, covered, for 15 minutes. Add the stock, nuts and lemon zest. Season to taste with salt and pepper, cover and simmer gently for 20 minutes. Process in a processor or blender until smooth. Return the soup to the pan and stir in the cream, check the seasoning and reheat to serve.

BORSCH

I'm very fond of beetroot and have been thrilled to see it making a comeback as a rather fashionable vegetable. We use it in several dishes as a vegetable accompaniment, or in a sauce for duck (see page 193), but the glowing claret-red of Borsch remains a firm favourite. Unstrained, this makes a filling lunch-time soup, or it can be strained to give a clear broth.

You can also use goose or turkey stock for this soup, which is a good one to make at Christmas when you have a bird. Make as for chicken stock (see page 29).

SERVES 6

2 tablespoons pork fat
1 small onion, chopped
1 stick of celery, chopped
1 clove of garlic, chopped
1.2 litres/2 pints chicken or duck stock, see page 29
275 g/10 oz raw beetroot, grated
100 g/4 oz cooking apple, peeled, cored and diced
1½ tablespoons lemon juice
1½ tablespoons white wine vinegar
salt
freshly ground black pepper
1 large dill-pickled gherkin, finely chopped
soured cream, to serve

Melt the pork fat in a pan and sweat the onion, celery and garlic for 15 minutes. Pour in the stock, bring to the boil, cover and simmer for 10 minutes. Add the beetroot, apple, lemon juice and vinegar, and season to taste with salt and pepper. Simmer gently for 15 minutes. Strain if you prefer a clear soup and check the seasoning.

Just before serving, add the gherkin and stir a generous swirl of soured cream into each bowl of soup. Serve hot or cold.

PEAR AND WATERCRESS SOUP

This soup is based on a recipe from the Time-Life Book of Soups –
*the combination of the scented sweetness of good pears with the
peppery watercress is a real success. Serve it hot when there's a nip in
the evening air, or cold on a balmy, early autumn day.*

SERVES 6

1 bunch of watercress
3 ripe pears, sliced
900 ml/1½ pints chicken stock, see page 29
salt
freshly ground black pepper
175 ml/6 fl oz double cream
juice of ½ lemon

Wash and pick over the watercress. Cut off the green leaves and
reserve. Place the watercress stalks and the pears in a pan with
the stock, and salt and pepper to taste. Bring to the boil, cover
and simmer gently for 15 minutes. Remove from the heat. Process the soup in small batches with the watercress leaves in a
processor or blender, then sieve or pass through a *mouli légumes*
to remove debris. Stir in the cream, lemon juice, and extra salt
and pepper if necessary. Serve hot or cold.

COURGETTE FLOWER AND BASIL SOUP

This is the prettiest speckled green and yellow soup. A local farmer grows courgettes and gives us the flowers. They fade quickly, within a few hours, and have to be used straight away while they are still vivid and sprightly.

SERVES 6

50 g/2 oz butter
1 medium onion, chopped
1.2 litres/2 pints chicken stock, see page 29
15 courgette flowers
25 g/1 oz basil leaves and stems
salt
freshly ground black pepper

Melt the butter in a pan and sweat the onion for 10 minutes. Add the stock and bring to the boil. Throw in the courgette flowers and basil, then season to taste with salt and pepper. Cover and simmer gently for 5 minutes. Process in a processor or blender, and sieve or pass through a *mouli légumes*. Return the soup to the pan, check seasoning and reheat to serve.

SPINACH AND COCONUT SOUP

This soup, with its Caribbean overtones, is based on a recipe in Roger Vergé's Cuisine of the Sun. *Coconut and spinach go very well together – but then coconut fits in with so many flavours, bringing hints of tropical climes to sweet and savoury foods alike.*

SERVES 6

25 g/1 oz butter
1 medium onion, chopped
1.2 litres/2 pints chicken stock, see page 29
450 g/1 lb fresh leaf spinach, well washed
25 g/1 oz creamed coconut, grated
salt
freshly ground black pepper
150 ml/¼ pint double cream

Melt the butter in a pan and sweat the onion, covered, for 10 minutes. Pour in the stock and bring to the boil. Add the spinach, coconut, and salt and pepper to taste. Cover the pan and simmer gently for 15 minutes. Process the soup in a processor or blender and sieve or pass through a *mouli légumes*. Return the soup to the pan, stir in the cream, and adjust seasonings. Reheat to serve.

SPICED PUMPKIN SOUP

With its gentle taste and bright orange colour, pumpkin makes a good base for a comforting autumn or early winter soup. The cumin steers it firmly away from blandness, towards the aromatics of the Orient.

SERVES 6

50 g/2 oz butter
1 medium onion, chopped
900 g/2 lb piece of pumpkin, skin and seeds removed, diced
1 teaspoon finely ground cumin seeds
1.2 litres/2 pints chicken stock, see page 29
salt
freshly ground black pepper
soured cream, to serve

Melt the butter in a pan and sweat the onion for 10 minutes. Add the pumpkin, cumin, stock, and salt and pepper to taste. Bring to the boil, cover and simmer gently for 30 minutes. Process in a processor or blender and adjust seasonings. Return the soup to the pan, reheat to serve, and float a dessertspoonful of soured cream on the surface of each bowl.

SORREL SOUP

The arrival of the first sorrel leaves means that summer is really on its way. This soup, with its clean, sharp flavour, comes as an early celebration of the new season.
By adding the sorrel to the soup at the last moment only, the brilliant green of the fresh leaves and their lively acidity are preserved. Be careful not to overheat the soup before serving since the green may turn to sludge brown.

SERVES 6

50 g/2 oz butter
1 medium onion, chopped
1 tablespoon cooked rice
1.2 litres/2 pints chicken stock, see page 29
salt
freshly ground black pepper
225 g/8 oz fresh sorrel, well washed and dried
150 ml/¼ pint double cream

Melt the butter in a pan and sweat the onion for 10 minutes. Add the rice, stock, and salt and pepper to taste. Bring to the boil and simmer gently for 15 minutes. Process the hot soup with the raw sorrel in small batches in a processor or blender. Sieve or pass through a *mouli légumes* to remove debris. Bring the cream to the boil in a pan and stir into the soup. Taste and adjust seasonings. If necessary, reheat briefly, without boiling, to serve.

CHERRY SOUP

Finding fresh morello cherries is no easy task, but when you are lucky enough to come across them, this soup is well worth making. We have one customer, Mrs Paget, who brings us fresh morello cherries from her garden in Birmingham, and we use them to make this marvellous recipe, which is a winner. The recipe originates from Victor Sassie, and it found its way to The Carved Angel via Jane Grigson.

SERVES 6

450 g/1 lb morello cherries
50 g/2 oz granulated sugar
1 bottle of Riesling
1 pinch of ground cinnamon
grated zest of 1 lemon
juice of 2 lemons
1 double measure of brandy
600 ml/1 pint soured cream

Stone the cherries over a pan, so that none of the juice is lost. Set the fruit aside, and add the stones and stalks to the pan with the sugar and wine. Bring to the boil and simmer for 5 minutes. Strain the liquid into a clean pan and add the cinnamon, lemon zest and juice. Bring back to the boil, then add the cherries and any juice they have exuded. Once again, bring back to a rolling boil. Remove immediately from the heat and allow to cool slightly before stirring in the brandy.

Pour the cream into a separate bowl. Whisk the hot liquid into the cream, a ladleful at a time, keeping back the cherries. Once half of the liquid has been incorporated to give a smooth mixture, tip in the rest with the fruit, in one fell swoop. Mix and chill well before serving.

Pasta

Pasta-making is great fun. With little equipment – our machinery in the restaurant consists of nothing more than an ordinary kitchen processor and a cheap, hand-cranked, domestic pasta machine – and a fair quota of imagination, anyone who cares to can turn out a panoply of brightly and naturally coloured and flavoured pastas. Then there's the pleasure of matching the pasta with a good and complementary sauce – the permutations are legion, and with care and enthusiasm, the end results will justify the work involved.

We now find that we seldom make plain pasta; the variations are so much more interesting that it makes an appearance only for the sake of contrast. We might, for instance, play on the theme of the colours of the Italian flag, the *Tricolore*, with spinach and lobster tagliatelle for the red and green and a band of plain white tagliatelle to complete it.

Green spinach pasta is now as commonplace as the white, but eyebrows are still raised by the mention of chocolate pasta (flavoured with cocoa, not sweetened chocolate), which bears the richness of game with great success. Green peppercorns add a powerful aromatic bite to pasta, herbs of all kinds give freshness and a subtle backdrop to a tomato-based sauce, and hazelnuts contribute a nutty rough texture. Practise with known quantities first to understand the techniques, before leaping forward to try your own variations.

When we first experimented with making our own pasta some years ago, it was not the immediate success we had anticipated. The initial attempts were pitiful – it was doughy and heavy, or plain unmanageable. We mixed the dough by hand; we mixed it in the big commercial mixer; ultimately it was the food processor that began to give us the best results.

Whichever method you use to make the dough, the trick is to get the right consistency – not too damp and not too dry. Using the processor, you should aim for a crumbly looking mixture that can be drawn together with your hand to form a ball which just holds together. Wrap it in clingfilm and let it rest for 30 minutes or so in the fridge, before attempting to roll it out. By that time the dough will feel moister and more cohesive.

The next thing to do is to clear plenty of space. You need room to hang the pasta to dry, maybe from the edges of the table or from kitchen units, as well as room to roll it out. Halfway through the process is not the time to start clearing away clutter.

A pasta machine of the humbler type is a good investment as, unless you've been rolling out pasta by hand for years, getting an even and adequate thinness to your dough before it dries out and turns brittle can be tricky.

Divide the dough into four balls. Keep three of them well covered with a clean cloth so that they don't dry out, and roll out the other on a lightly floured surface into a long rectangle a little narrower than the width of your machine. Set the machine to setting number one, the widest, and wind the dough through. Cover it and repeat with the other three balls of dough.

Return to the first sheet, turn the machine up one notch to setting number two – a little narrower – and pass it through again. Cover and repeat with the other three. Overhandling can toughen the dough, but by letting each sheet rest while you deal with the others, it has time to relax.

Repeat the rolling and winding through process, turning up one notch each time, until you reach setting number six. The dough should be thin and even, but not so thin that it lacks substance when cooked.

At the last stage we usually run the sheets of pasta through the cutters to make noodles. Sometimes we make the fine tagliarini (3 mm/⅛ inch thick), but most of the time we stick with the wider tagliatelle, 6–12 mm/¼–½ inch across. For lasagne, cut the sheets to fit the baking dish.

Hang out the pasta to dry in single layers, without any overlap, for 30 minutes or so, draped over the edge of the table, or slung over a clean broom handle supported by a couple of chairs. Once it is dry enough to stop sticking to itself, wrap as much as you need that day in clingfilm and keep in the fridge. The remainder can happily be frozen or left to dry out completely.

BASIC PASTA

SERVES 6–8 AS A FIRST COURSE OR LIGHT MAIN COURSE

450 g/1 lb strong flour
½ teaspoon salt
3 eggs
1 tablespoon oil

Sift the flour with the salt into a processor. Process with the eggs and enough oil to give a crumbly dough. Gather together the dough to form a ball, wrap in clingfilm and leave to rest in the fridge for at least 30 minutes.

If you don't have a processor, work the eggs into the flour and salt by hand, gradually adding enough oil to give a firm dough. Knead on a lightly floured surface until smooth and elastic, then wrap in clingfilm and leave to rest for at least 30 minutes.

Roll out the dough (see page 80) and cut into required shapes.

PASTA VARIATIONS

SORREL PASTA

SERVES 6–8 AS A FIRST COURSE OR LIGHT MAIN COURSE

450 g/1 lb strong flour
½ teaspoon salt
3 eggs
100 g/4 oz fresh sorrel, well washed and dried, tough stalks
trimmed away
1 tablespoon oil

Sift the flour with the salt into a processor. Process with the eggs, sorrel and enough oil to give a crumbly dough. Continue as for Basic Pasta.

PARSLEY OR BASIL PASTA

Excellent served with a simple fresh tomato sauce.

Substitute 100 g/4 oz parsley or basil for the sorrel in the Sorrel Pasta recipe.

HAZELNUT PASTA

Substitute 50 g/2 oz toasted and finely chopped hazelnuts for the sorrel in the Sorrel Pasta recipe.

GREEN PEPPERCORN PASTA

Substitute 1 tablespoon green peppercorns for the sorrel in the Sorrel Pasta recipe.

LOBSTER PASTA

Substitute 50 g/2 oz lobster coral for the sorrel in the Sorrel Pasta recipe.

BLACK SQUID PASTA

When cleaning squid, save a tablespoon of the tiny black ink sacs. Substitute for the sorrel in the Sorrel Pasta recipe.

BUCKWHEAT PASTA

We often serve buckwheat noodles with game.

Use half strong white flour and half buckwheat flour instead of all strong flour in the Basic Pasta recipe.

CHOCOLATE PASTA

Substitute 50 g/2 oz cocoa for 50 g/2 oz of the flour in the Basic Pasta recipe.

LOBSTER AND PARSLEY NOODLES WITH SCALLOP AND MUSSEL SAUCE

SERVES 6–8 AS A FIRST COURSE OR LIGHT MAIN COURSE

½ quantity of Parsley Noodles, see page 83
½ quantity of Lobster Noodles, see page 83
olive oil
salt
freshly ground black pepper

FOR THE SAUCE
50 ml/2 fl oz olive oil
1 small onion, chopped
1 clove of garlic, chopped
1 × 400 g/14 oz can tomatoes, chopped, and their juice
4 large scallops
15 g/½ oz butter
450 g/1 lb mussels, well scrubbed and bearded
50 ml/2 fl oz dry white wine
2 tablespoons chopped parsley
freshly ground black pepper
lemon juice

Drop the pasta into a very large pan (the bigger, the better) of boiling salted water. Stir with a wooden spoon to separate. Bring back to the boil. With very fresh pasta, this may be quite enough to cook it to the *al dente* stage. Pasta that has had more time to dry out may take 1 or 2 minutes to cook. Drain the pasta and run it quickly under the cold tap. Drain again and toss in a little oil to keep the strands separate. Set aside until needed.

To make the sauce, heat the oil in a pan and sweat the onion and garlic until soft and translucent. Add the tomatoes and simmer hard until the sauce is thick with no trace of wateriness. Dice the white part and coral of each scallop, melt the butter in a pan and sauté for 1 minute.

Put the mussels in a separate pan with the wine. Cover and shake over a high heat until all the mussels have opened. Discard any that steadfastly refuse to open. Remove the mussels from their shells and strain the mussel liquid through a muslin-lined sieve to remove the grit.

Add the scallops, mussels and parsley to the tomato sauce. Stir in the mussel liquid a little at a time, tasting frequently – it will be strongly salty, so add only enough to give flavour without overwhelming. Taste and then season with pepper and a dash of lemon juice.

When the sauce is ready, toss the noodles in olive oil in a large pan over a medium heat until piping hot. Season to taste with salt and pepper, and arrange on a warmed serving dish. Pour the sauce in the centre of the pasta.

SORREL NOODLES WITH GOATS' CHEESE GNOCCHI

SERVES 6–8 AS A FIRST COURSE OR LIGHT MAIN COURSE

1 quantity of Sorrel Noodles, see page 82
olive oil
25 g/1 oz butter
salt
freshly ground black pepper

FOR THE GNOCCHI
450 g/1 lb fresh goats' cheese, crumbled
50 g/2 oz butter, softened
3 level tablespoons flour
2 eggs
freshly grated nutmeg
salt
freshly ground black pepper

Drop the pasta into a very large pan (the bigger, the better) of boiling salted water. Stir with a wooden spoon to separate. Bring back to the boil. With very fresh pasta, this may be quite enough to cook it to the *al dente* stage. Pasta that has had more time to dry out may take 1 or 2 minutes to cook. Drain the pasta and run it quickly under the cold tap. Drain again and toss in a little oil to keep the strands separate. Set aside until needed.

To make the gnocchi, whizz together all the ingredients in a processor, or beat by hand until smooth. Chill for at least 30 minutes. Fill a piping bag with the mixture, and drop 2.5 cm/1 inch lengths of it into a pan of barely simmering water. Poach for 5 minutes, then lift out with a slotted spoon. Drain well.

While the gnocchi are cooking, toss the noodles in the butter in a large pan over a medium heat until piping hot. Season to taste with salt and pepper, and arrange on a warmed serving dish. Pile the gnocchi on top and serve immediately.

HAZELNUT NOODLES WITH MUSHROOM SAUCE

SERVES 6–8 AS A FIRST COURSE OR LIGHT MAIN COURSE

1 quantity of Hazelnut Noodles, see page 83
olive oil
25 g/1 oz butter
salt
freshly ground black pepper

FOR THE SAUCE
25 g/1 oz butter
1 small onion, chopped
1 clove of garlic, chopped
225 g/8 oz mushrooms, sliced
300 ml/½ pint milk
salt
freshly ground black pepper
freshly grated nutmeg

Drop the pasta into a very large pan (the bigger, the better) of boiling salted water. Stir with a wooden spoon to separate. Bring back to the boil. With very fresh pasta, this may be quite enough to cook it to the *al dente* stage. Pasta that has had more time to dry out may take 1 or 2 minutes to cook. Drain the pasta and run it quickly under the cold tap. Drain again and toss in a little oil to keep the strands separate. Set aside until needed.

To make the sauce, melt the butter in a pan and sweat the onion and garlic until tender. Add half the mushrooms, the milk, and salt and pepper to taste. Simmer for 5 minutes, then process briefly in a processor or blender and sieve. Return the sauce to the pan, and stir in the remaining mushrooms and nutmeg. Bring back to the boil and simmer for 3 minutes.

Toss the noodles in butter in a large pan over a medium heat until piping hot. Season with salt and pepper, and arrange on a warmed serving dish. Pour the sauce over the noodles.

PARSLEY NOODLES WITH CHICKEN, LEMON AND GRUYÈRE

SERVES 6–8 AS A FIRST COURSE OR LIGHT MAIN COURSE

1 quantity of Parsley Noodles, see page 83
olive oil

FOR THE SAUCE
zest of 1 lemon, cut into narrow strips
50 ml/2 fl oz dry white wine
100 g/4 oz cooked chicken, cut into strips
75 ml/3 fl oz soured cream
100 g/4 oz Gruyère cheese, grated
freshly grated nutmeg
salt
freshly ground black pepper

Drop the pasta into a very large pan (the bigger, the better) of boiling salted water. Stir with a wooden spoon to separate. Bring back to the boil. With very fresh pasta, this may be quite enough to cook it to the *al dente* stage. Pasta that has had more time to dry out may take 1 or 2 minutes to cook. Drain the pasta and run it quickly under the cold tap. Drain again and toss in a little oil to keep the strands separate. Set aside until needed.

To make the sauce, simmer the lemon zest in the wine for 2 minutes in a large pan. Add the chicken and simmer for a further minute. Next tip in the noodles, soured cream, Gruyère cheese, and nutmeg, salt and pepper to taste. Toss together until the pasta is piping hot. Taste and adjust seasonings and serve.

GREEN PEPPERCORN NOODLES WITH SMOKED HAM OR PORK FILLET AND CREAM

SERVES 4 AS A FIRST COURSE

½ quantity of Green Peppercorn Noodles, see page 83
olive oil

FOR THE SAUCE
25 g/1 oz butter
100 g/4 oz smoked raw ham, or pork fillet, cut into narrow strips
300 ml/½ pint double cream
freshly grated nutmeg
freshly ground black pepper
salt

Drop the pasta into a very large pan (the bigger, the better) of boiling salted water. Stir with a wooden spoon to separate. Bring back to the boil. With very fresh pasta, this may be quite enough to cook it to the *al dente* stage. Pasta that has had more time to dry out may take 1 or 2 minutes to cook. Drain the pasta and run it quickly under the cold tap. Drain again and toss in a little oil to keep the strands separate. Set aside until needed.

To make the sauce, melt the butter in a large pan and fry the ham or pork fillet until it begins to brown and frizzle. Add the cream, and nutmeg and pepper to taste. Simmer for 3 minutes, then taste and add salt if needed. Add the noodles to the pan and toss in the cream sauce until piping hot. Taste and adjust seasonings and serve.

Cheese & Eggs

Ten years ago somebody mentioned in passing that there was a woman at Blackawton, just outside Dartmouth, whose happy brood of free-range hens laid superb eggs. We got in touch with Gladys Hunt, and her first delivery was soon on our doorstep. Her eggs were quite special, with big orange-yellow yolks, the kind that people remember from a country childhood.

She still delivers to us twice a week, and the eggs are as good as ever. It is very easy to take eggs for granted, and to be lulled into thinking that one egg is much the same as another. I don't know exactly what it is that Gladys feeds to her hens, but there is no doubt in my mind that they enjoy a good diet, devoid of processed foodstuffs, and the freedom to scratch round in the open. As a result the eggs they lay have an intensely 'eggy' taste, rich yolks and clear whites, that can't be matched by battery eggs.

People often overlook the simpler egg dishes that can be so delicious when well made. A proper omelette, still moist in the centre, primrose yellow, streaked with brown, lifted by the addition of shreds of raw sorrel, is one of the very best of all dishes, whether as a light lunch or main course. Poached and scrambled eggs, dressed as grandly or plainly as suits the appetite and occasion, are a treat, all too often thrown to vegetarians as if they were compensation for meat deprivation. Lucky vegetarians.

All of a sudden quails' eggs have been transformed from a rare luxury to a fairly commonplace commodity, on sale in supermarkets as well as sassy delicatessens. Apparently, quails, once they get going, are prolific layers! The eggs look enchantingly pretty, more like the sugar eggs that you get at Easter than bona fide ones. They differ subtly from hens' eggs in taste, with a creamier texture. They are also harder to peel when boiled. The inner skin that lies between shell and egg is protectively tough, but once you've broken through it the shell can be eased off with a teaspoon slipped under the skin. But even if you think you've mastered the technique, it's still a good idea to pop a couple of extra eggs into the pan to allow for error.

I'm very lucky when it comes to cheeses. There is now a marvellous variety of cheeses being made, all within easy distance of the restaurant. This is a reflection of the progress in the cheese industry throughout Britain over recent years. All kinds of producers are springing up to make truly high-quality cheeses in small quantities. I can put together a balanced cheeseboard using just Devon and Somerset cheeses. We buy our cheeses from Ticklemore Cheese Shop in Totnes, who provide an excellent service. They make their own cheeses and sell local ones. Fifteen years ago I had to buy Brie, Roquefort and Camembert from importers. The choice of English cheeses was very limited and the quality poor.

Sharpham cheese, similar to a Camembert, is made just outside Totnes. Beenleigh Blue, a ewes' milk cheese in the style of Roquefort, comes from a farm only a mile or two further on. The same farmer also makes Harbourne Blue, with goats' rather than ewes' milk. I buy a mature farmhouse Cheddar with its characteristic nutty taste from Keens of Wincanton, in Somerset.

There are two notable exceptions on the locals-only cheeseboard. One is the Bron Haul cheese. It is made in small quantities in North Wales by my niece. She has a couple of house cows and makes and matures her own delicious Cheddar-style cheese. The other is the irresistible Bonchester from Scotland. It is a full-fat cheese, pale and wickedly creamy, with a distinctive flavour.

I limit the number of cheeses that we have at any one time on the cheeseboard. It is far better, both in a small restaurant and in a domestic setting, to concentrate on a few really spectacular cheeses, properly looked after so that they stay moist and clean tasting, than to indulge in a massive cheeseboard, which inevitably leads to a huge amount of waste, or a tatty, dog-eared display of scraps and crumbs after its first couple of outings.

At The Carved Angel, there are usually some half-a-dozen or so cheeses out at any one time, enough to be able to achieve a nice balance. There will be a couple of goats' cheeses (including the fresh young ones marinated with oil and herbs – see page 93), a hard cheese, a sheeps' milk cheese, a creamy cheese, and a blue cheese. And alongside there is always a basket of home-made biscuits.

MARINATED GOATS' CHEESES

I preserve local soft goats' cheeses in oil, with sprigs of aromatic herbs. After a week or two in their jars, they carry the scent of the herbs and the fruitiness of the oil. They are marvellous for grilling (see page 94), or just as they are.

The cheeses I use are about 50 g/2 oz each in weight and arrive fresh every week from a local goat farmer. Any reasonably young, small goats' cheese can be used, as long as it has not matured enough to develop a rind that will act as a barrier against the flavours of the herbs. My cheeses are still moist and so need draining overnight on kitchen towels to absorb the excess moisture. This may not be necessary with older, drier cheeses.

Once drained, put the cheeses into wide-necked jars with sprigs of rosemary and thyme, and a couple of bay leaves, and cover completely with olive oil. Cover with a tight-fitting lid and leave them for a good fortnight before using. They keep for up to three months in a cool place.

GRILLED GOATS' CHEESE WITH TAPENADE, OR PUMPKIN AND GINGER

Ready-marinated French and English goats' cheeses are often stocked by good delicatessens and cheese shops, though they are easy enough to marinate yourself. Although marinated cheeses are best for grilling, a firm, fresh goats' cheese can be used instead. Serve with a lightly dressed green or tomato salad, scattered with toasted pine kernels. In the autumn substitute pumpkin for the year-round Tapenade.

SERVES 4

WITH TAPENADE

4 slices of brioche or good bread
½ quantity of Tapenade, see page 60
4 small goats' cheeses, marinated in oil, see page 93
freshly ground black pepper

Toast the brioche or bread lightly on both sides. Spread with Tapenade. Slice the goats' cheeses and arrange over the Tapenade, covering completely. Grind a little pepper over the top, and grill for about 5 minutes, until nicely browned.

WITH PUMPKIN AND GINGER

4 slices of brioche or good bread
225 g/8 oz piece of pumpkin, weighed after removing skin and seeds
25–50 g/1–2 oz butter
1 teaspoon grated fresh root ginger
salt
freshly ground black pepper
4 small goats' cheeses, marinated in oil, see page 93

Toast the brioche or bread lightly on both sides. Cut the pumpkin into slices no more than 6 mm/¼ inch thick. Melt the butter in a pan and sauté the pumpkin gently with the ginger, and salt and pepper to taste, for 5 minutes, until tender. Arrange the pumpkin on the toasted bread. Slice the goats' cheeses horizontally and place on the pumpkin, covering completely. Grind a little more pepper over the cheese, then grill for about 5 minutes, until nicely browned.

BLUE CHEESE AND BANANA FILOS

*I use Beenleigh Blue cheese, similar to Roquefort, for these filo
triangles. They make delicious* amuse-gueules *with drinks, sweet
and salty at the same time. Or you could make them larger – divide
sheets of filo into four or even two strips instead of eight, and serve as
a first course with a dressed tomato and cucumber salad.*

MAKES 16 LITTLE TRIANGLES

25 g/1 oz blue cheese, finely diced or crumbled
1 firm banana, peeled and finely diced
freshly ground black pepper
lemon juice
4 sheets of filo pastry
50 g/2 oz butter, melted

Mix together the cheese and banana and season with pepper
and a dash of lemon juice.

Brush two of the sheets of filo generously with butter, and lay
one on top of the other. Keep the remaining filo covered with a
sheet of greaseproof paper, and over that a clean damp tea
towel, to prevent it drying out. Cut the double layer of buttered
filo into eight strips. Put a teaspoon of the cheese and banana
filling in the corner of one end of each strip. Fold into small
triangular parcels as shown in the diagram on page 379 for
Scallops in Filo Pastry. Place on a buttered baking sheet. Repeat
with the remaining filo and filling.

Brush the triangles with any remaining butter, and bake in a
preheated oven, 220°C/425°F/gas mark 7, for 5 minutes, until
golden brown. Serve hot or cold.

CHEESE BEIGNETS SOUFFLÉS

These airy little puffs of cheese-flavoured choux pastry can be served with drinks, or as a light first course. The batter mixture is best used as soon as it is made, but it's no disaster if it is kept for up to six hours. The beignets may not be quite 'soufflés' but they will still taste delicious. Serve with a Tomato and Chilli Sauce (see page 55) or Cucumber Pickle (see page 364).

SERVES 8

450 ml/¾ pint water
175 g/6 oz butter, diced
215 g/7½ oz flour, sifted
6 eggs
50 g/2 oz Gruyère cheese, grated
50 g/2 oz Parmesan cheese, grated
salt
freshly ground black pepper
oil for deep-frying

Put the water and butter in a pan large enough to take all the ingredients. Stir over a medium heat until the butter has melted, then bring the water to the boil. Immediately tip in the flour and beat vigorously until the mixture comes away from the sides of the pan. Remove from the heat and allow to cool slightly. Beat in the eggs one at a time, making sure that each one is thoroughly incorporated before adding the next. Finally, add the grated cheeses, and salt and pepper to taste.

Heat a pan of oil to 160°C/320°F. Using a pair of teaspoons or dessertspoons, shape the mixture into small egg shapes and deep-fry, a few at a time, for 3–5 minutes, until puffed and golden brown. Drain on kitchen paper and serve.

DEEP-FRIED BRIE OR CAMEMBERT IN BEIGNET BATTER

Deep-fried Brie or Camembert, coated in breadcrumbs, has become standard bistro fare. I actually prefer my Brie coated in crisp, puffed choux paste (see previous page), which I also find much easier to use. No leaking cheese oozing out of a half-empty shell!

SERVES 6 AS A FIRST COURSE

175 g/6 oz firm Brie, Camembert, Sharpham, or other soft cheese
½ quantity of Cheese Beignet Batter, see page 97
oil for deep-frying

TO SERVE
Tomato and Chilli Sauce, see page 55, or Leek and Watercress
Sauce made with chicken stock, see page 156

Chill the soft cheese, then cut into 6 portions – wedges or cubes. Using a palette knife, smear with a 6 mm/¼ inch thick layer of batter, making sure that there are no gaps for the melting cheese to leak through.

Heat a pan of oil to 160°C/320°F. Just before you commit the cheese wedges to the oil, give them a final check to make sure that they are properly covered. Deep-fry half of them until golden brown. Drain briefly on kitchen paper and keep them warm while you cook the remaining portions. Drain quickly and serve with a Tomato and Chilli or Leek and Watercress Sauce.

PIPÉRADE

Pipérade is a tomatoey scrambled egg dish from the Basque Country. It surprises me that it is not better known since it is quick and easy to make, and quite delicious as long as it is not overcooked. Serve as a first course, or as a light lunch dish with crusty bread and a green salad.

SERVES 4 AS A FIRST COURSE OR 3 AS A LUNCH DISH

2 tablespoons olive oil
100 g/4 oz smoked pork or ham, cut into narrow strips
225 g/8 oz red, green, and/or yellow peppers, sliced
75 g/3 oz onions, sliced
2 cloves of garlic, chopped
freshly ground black pepper
salt
1 × 200 g/7 oz can tomatoes, drained and chopped
basil leaves
6 eggs
chopped parsley

Heat the oil in a pan and fry the pork or ham gently for 2–3 minutes. Add the peppers, onions, garlic, pepper and a little salt. Fry slowly without browning until tender. Add the tomatoes and basil, and increase the heat. Simmer until thick.

Beat the eggs lightly with salt and pepper to taste. Pour into the thickened tomato and pepper sauce. Stir until the eggs are softly scrambled. Sprinkle with the parsley and serve immediately before the pipérade has a chance to overcook.

EGGS WITH WATERCRESS MOUSSELINE

A terrifically simple, cold, light luncheon dish, or a pretty first course. It is rich and glamorous, and needs a generous bed of fresh peppery watercress to offset the cream sauce.

SERVES 8 AS A FIRST COURSE OR 4 AS A MAIN COURSE

40 g/1½ oz watercress leaves
100 ml/4 fl oz single cream
100 ml/4 fl oz double cream
salt
freshly ground black pepper
1 bunch of watercress, trimmed
8 soft-boiled eggs, shelled
brown bread and butter, to serve

Process the watercress leaves and single cream in a blender until smooth. Lightly whip the double cream with salt and pepper to taste. Fold in the watercress purée to give a sauce of coating consistency. Taste and adjust seasonings.

Divide the whole watercress between four or eight serving plates, tucking it round in circles to form nests. Place one or two egg(s) in each 'nest' and coat with the watercress cream. Serve with brown bread and butter.

PUFF PASTRY OF QUAILS' EGGS AND ASPARAGUS WITH HERB AND CREAM SAUCE

The separate components of this recipe are simple enough. The tricky bit is getting them all to come together at the same time! Still, it really is worth juggling your timings to get it right. Should you be lucky enough to have a few wild cèpes (boletus edulis), cook them gently in a small amount of butter and use them instead of the asparagus tips – a suitably grand means of stretching a little luxury a long way.
If you have time, practise making the puff pastry containers with a piece of thickish paper. They are not as difficult as they first appear.

SERVES 4

100 g/4 oz puff pastry, see page 347
8 quails' eggs
225 g/8 oz green asparagus tips, weighed after trimming
1 egg, beaten
sesame or poppy seeds
½ quantity of Messine Sauce or Hollandaise,
see page 38 or 33
4 sprigs of watercress or chervil, to garnish

Roll out the pastry on a lightly floured surface to form a 20 cm/ 8 inch square, 4 mm/⅛ inch thick. Trim the edges and divide into four neat 10 cm/4 inch squares. Make the puff pastry twists as shown in the diagram on page 381. Place on a baking sheet, cover and leave to rest in the fridge for at least 30 minutes.

Bring a pan of water to the boil. Add the quails' eggs, bring back to the boil and simmer for 1½ minutes. Drain the eggs and run them under the cold tap. Shell carefully – the yolks will still be slightly runny – and place in a bowl of cold water.

Tie the asparagus in a bundle and cook in boiling salted

water until just tender – about 5 minutes. Drain and keep warm. While the asparagus is cooking, brush the pastry with the beaten egg and sprinkle with sesame or poppy seeds. Bake in a preheated oven, 240°C/475°F/gas mark 9, for 5–7 minutes, until golden brown and risen.

Remove from the oven and, using a small, sharp knife, cut out the small square in the centre of each pastry, leaving border, sides and base intact. Lift off the squares and set aside in a warm place to use later as the lids.

Place each pastry case on a warmed serving plate and keep them warm while you reheat the quails' eggs in hot water for 1 minute and heat the sauce thoroughly. Drain the eggs well, drying briefly on kitchen paper. Sit two in each pastry case together with the asparagus tips, and coat with sauce. Alternatively, pour a little sauce into each pastry case and sit the eggs in it. Arrange the asparagus tips on each plate and coat with more sauce.

Cover with the pastry lids and garnish with the watercress or chervil.

Charcuterie

It is perplexing that a tiny strip of water such as the English Channel should prove, in certain instances, a quite insurmountable barrier. Though we cross it in our millions every summer to revel for a week or two in the pleasures of the Continent, among which the edible pleasures form no small part, the skills of the French charcutier and *traiteur*, or their Italian, Spanish or German counterparts, seem to find the crossing well nigh impossible.

We do import a handful of salamis and cured hams, but it is rare to find a butcher or owner of a delicatessen who makes a range of cooked meat products that can compare with those found in the smallest of shops across the Channel. Even our own indigenous products, such as brawn and potted meats, have been devalued by commercialization.

And so we miss out on some of the best of convenience foods. Either we do without or accept the garish, factory-made pâtés, which are crowned with a garland of cranberries glued in position with rubbery aspic. But there is a third alternative – to try your hand at making your own charcuterie at home.

It is often easier than you might imagine, and immensely satisfying, too. Much of the charcutier's skill lies in transforming cheap cuts of meat into products that are delicious to eat and will keep for a week or more with no need for extraneous additives. Patience is the key – marinating and slow gentle cooking are essential processes, but even so, neither demands the cook's constant attention.

Once the basic skills have been mastered, a whole world of possibilities opens up. Charcuterie is a flexible discipline. A plain terrine, for instance, can be altered radically by the addition of a few wild mushrooms, by a line of quails' eggs or by sherry-soaked chicken livers hidden in the centre to be revealed as the first slices of the terrine are cut. Bands of herb-speckled green side by side with delicate pink, flashes of muted apricot, green pistachios, red pepper, all lending their flavours and blending to create something uniquely personal.

Once the work is done you have what is, in effect, a convenience food. Ballotines, galantines, terrines and so on are made to last and, indeed, will improve in flavour with a day or two's 'maturation' in a cool place. For longer keeping, a week and even up to a fortnight, they need to be thoroughly sealed in clarified fat – butter or rendered fat from the meat maybe. Concentrated butter, which is butter with almost all its water and salt content removed, is perfect for the job and is available from supermarkets.

Many of the following recipes make great centrepieces for buffets, large gatherings and memorable picnics. Besides looks and taste, they have the added advantage of being easy to slice and serve, with no fiddly carving. All you need add is good bread, a couple of relishes or chutneys, salad, cheese and wine.

THE BRINE TUB

Many of the recipes in this section, and here and there throughout other chapters, call for pickled or brined meats, usually pork or beef. Submerging meats in a spiced brine is a hand-me-down from the days before fridges and freezers. The salt in the brine preserved the meat until it was to be used.

These days the need for preservation is largely obsolete, and the once secondary effects of brining are of much greater interest to the cook. The process emphasizes and develops the flavour, giving meat a mildly spiced savouriness.

Not so long ago most butchers would have kept a brine tub. These days it is a less common practice. If you can track down a butcher who still does his own brining, make the most of it. He will probably be very happy to brine hands of pork, trotters or silverside to order. I'm lucky in having an old-fashioned butcher, Luscombe's, not far away from me in Totnes. They normally keep pieces of belly pork, ox tongues and brisket in their tub, and I often buy pickled meats straight from them.

Even so, I do make a brine occasionally if we are going to make a galantine of suckling pig or something similar. After boning the pig, a week in a brine tub gives it a very good flavour and colour before cooking.

Suggested Brining Times
Pigs' trotters: 4 days
Belly of pork: 1 week
Ox tongue: 2 weeks
Suckling pig, boned: 1 week

BASIC BRINE

2.8 litres/5 pints cold water
350 g/12 oz salt
175 g/6 oz granulated sugar
50 g/2 oz saltpetre (available from chemists)
3 sprigs of thyme
1 teaspoon black peppercorns
1 bay leaf
4 whole cloves
1 teaspoon juniper berries
small chip of nutmeg

Place the water, salt, sugar and saltpetre in a large pan. Bring to the boil, stirring until the salt, sugar and saltpetre have dissolved. Skim off any scum that rises to the surface and add the remaining ingredients. Remove from the heat and allow to cool completely before using.

When absolutely cold, strain into a clean stainless steel bowl or bucket, or a well-scrubbed earthenware crock, which is big enough to take all the brine and with plenty of space left over for the cuts of meat that are to follow. Keep the brine tub in a cool place – larder or fridge.

Submerge the pieces of meat in the brine solution. Pickle for the time suggested in the chart on page 105, turning every day.

BALLOTINE OF DUCK

At first glance this seems a frighteningly complicated dish to tackle. Don't be put off. It is great fun to make. As you cut the first slices and see the elegant mosaic formed by the strips of meats, green pistachios, orange apricot, and farce studded with peppercorns, the sense of achievement is tremendous. The first mouthful will immediately confirm that this was time well spent.

SERVES 10 AS A FIRST COURSE

1 large duck, with giblets
450 g/1 lb pickled belly of pork, see The Brine Tub, page 104
1 carrot, quartered
1 onion, quartered
1 stick of celery, sliced
1 bouquet garni
225 g/8 oz chicken livers, trimmed and quartered
1 bunch of parsley, chopped
50 ml/2 fl oz port
50 ml/2 fl oz brandy
1 clove of garlic
1 pinch of chopped thyme
salt
freshly ground black pepper
100 ml/4 fl oz dry white wine
1 teaspoon green peppercorns
50 g/2 oz dried apricots
50 g/2 oz pistachio nuts, shelled
extra duck fat or butter
1 egg white

Bone the duck as shown in the diagram on page 382 and trim the skin from the belly of pork. Set aside the duck liver and the fat, and put the rest of the giblets, the duck carcass, and the skin from the belly of pork into a pan. Add the carrot, onion, celery and bouquet garni. Pour in 1.2 litres/2 pints cold water, bring to the boil, skimming off any scum that rises to the surface, and simmer gently for 2 hours. Strain and return to the heat. Boil briskly until the stock has reduced by half. Set aside.

Lay the boned duck skin-side down on a board. Remove half the leg and breast meat from the skin. Cut the breast meat and half the belly of pork into thin strips. Cut the duck liver and half the chicken livers into strips and mix into the duck and belly of pork, together with half the parsley, and the port and brandy. Pile it all on to the duck skin, cover and leave to marinate for 4 hours.

Mince the duck fat and the reserved leg meat with the remaining belly of pork, chicken livers and parsley, and the garlic and thyme. Season with salt and pepper to taste and add the wine and peppercorns, to give a thick *farce*. Cut the apricots into strips. Pour boiling water over the pistachios, leave for 10 seconds, then drain and refresh under the cold tap. Skin.

Now take the duck skin, and tip the mixture that has been marinating with it into a separate bowl. Spread the skin out on a tray, skin-side down. Leaving a 2.5 cm/1 inch border around the edges, spread half the *farce* over the flesh. Cover this with lengthways strips of pork, duck and apricot, interspersed with the marinated livers and sprinkled with the pistachios. Cover with the remaining *farce*.

Roll up the ballotine but not too tightly – the skin will appear floppy but will shrink when cooked and could burst if too tight. Sew up the edges neatly and firmly with button thread.

To cook, season the ballotine. Melt a little duck fat or butter in a flameproof casserole into which the ballotine fits neatly and brown it all over. As you brown the duck, pierce the skin all over with a very fine needle to release fat. Pour over the reserved stock, and bring to the boil. Cover and cook in a preheated oven, 140°C/275°F/gas mark 1, for 2 hours. Turn the ballotine over after 1 hour. Leave to cool in the stock overnight.

Next day, lift off the duck fat and set aside. Lift the duck out of the jellied stock. Snip and extract all the thread, then wrap the duck in foil and keep in the fridge. Beat the egg white to loosen. Heat the stock until it begins to liquefy, then whisk in the egg white and bring to the boil. Remove from heat and strain through a muslin-lined sieve. Taste and adjust seasonings, and leave to cool.

Serve the duck in thin slices with a little of the jellied stock and some spiced fruits (see pages 368 and 371).

QUAIL IN ASPIC

*This is a terrific party piece, pretty to look at, and excellent to eat too.
Like the Ballotine of Duck (see page 107), it appears rather more
complicated at first glance than it really is. However, taken step by
step, you'll find that it falls easily into place. Make the day before or
first thing in the morning, allowing plenty of time for it to set
properly. Then all that is left to do when the time comes is to turn it
out and garnish with a few extra herbs. Serve with an Apple
Mayonnaise (see page 48), and a simple apple and celery salad.*

SERVES 12 AS A FIRST COURSE

8 × 150 g/5 oz quails
1 egg
1 tablespoon finely chopped tarragon
200 ml/7 fl oz double cream
salt
freshly ground black pepper
1.75 litres/3 pints good chicken stock, see page 29
1 egg white
3 tablespoons Madeira
15 g/scant ¾ oz leaf gelatine (8 sheets), soaked, see page 301
6 quails' eggs, hard-boiled, shelled and halved
12 sprigs of chervil
2 tablespoons chopped parsley or chervil

Sever the quail legs and bone them – you should have between
175 and 200 g/6 and 7 oz of meat. Process with the whole egg
and the tarragon in a processor or blender until you have a
smooth paste. Add the cream, and salt and pepper to taste, and
process for a further 30 seconds. Rub through a sieve. This is the
quenelle mixture.

Leaving the gut in place, season and roast the quails in a
preheated oven, 220°C/425°F/gas mark 7, for 10 minutes,
until just cooked. Allow to cool for 30 minutes, then remove

the breasts and skin them. Slice thinly against the grain and set aside.

Pour the stock into a pan and add the quail carcasses and leg bones. Bring to the boil and simmer gently for 30 minutes. Strain into a shallow pan, and season with salt and pepper. Bring back to the boil, then turn down to a scant simmer. Using two teaspoons, shape the quenelle mixture into small ovals and drop into the stock. Cover the pan and poach very gently for 5 minutes. Lift out the quenelles with a slotted spoon and drain on kitchen paper. Cover with clingfilm and set aside.

When the stock has cooled, whisk in the egg white. Return to the heat and bring gently to the boil, whisking occasionally. Simmer for 5 minutes, then strain through a muslin-lined sieve. There should now be about 1.2 litres/2 pints of stock. Add the Madeira and adjust seasonings. Stir in the gelatine. This is now the aspic.

And so to the final assembly: make sure that all the separate components – quail breasts, quenelles, aspic and eggs – are cool. Pour a thin layer of aspic over the bases of twelve 250 ml/8 fl oz dariole moulds or one larger single mould. Lay a halved egg, cut side down, in each, and a sprig of chervil, then surround with the breast slices and quenelles. Sprinkle with chopped parsley or chervil and cover with the remaining jelly (which should by now be almost set), filling the moulds. Tap gently against the work surface to expel any trapped air. Chill in the fridge for at least 4 hours, or overnight, to set completely.

When ready to serve, run the metal moulds under the hot tap for 2 or 3 seconds. Turn out on to serving plate(s), and serve with the Apple Mayonnaise and a lightly dressed apple and celery salad.

RILLETTES

Virtually every charcutier in France sells rillettes, a coarse pork paste,
which is often made on the premises. Many of the commercial French
rillettes are excellent too, as long as the texture is not too smooth.
There are countless variations, whether in the seasoning, texture or in
the meats used. Goose, duck and rabbit rillettes are all made on the
same principle, using half pork and half poultry or rabbit meat.
It is one of the best introductions to charcuterie, as easy as pie to
make (probably rather easier, in fact), quite delicious, and sure to be
appreciated by children and grown-ups alike.
Serve with good bread, pickled gherkins, and olives.

MAKES AROUND 900 G/2 LB

900 g/2 lb belly or neck of pork, brined for 4 days if possible
450 g/1 lb pork fat
2 cloves of garlic, crushed
6 parsley stalks
2 sprigs of thyme
2 bay leaves
freshly ground black pepper
150 ml/¼ pint chicken stock, see page 29

Cut the belly or neck of pork into matchstick-sized pieces. Place
in a casserole or roasting tin with the remaining ingredients,
cover and cook in a preheated oven, 160°C/325°F/gas mark 3,
for 3 hours. Drain off the fat through a fine sieve and reserve.
Pound half the meat in a mortar with a pestle until reduced to a
paste or process in a processor or blender and sieve. Tear the
remaining meat apart with two forks to give fine shreds. Put
the two meats into a bowl and carefully pour the reserved fat
from cooking over them, leaving sediment and juices behind.
Mix well, taste and check seasoning, then pack into small pots
or a single terrine, and leave to cool. Cover and store in the
fridge for 24 hours before eating. Rillettes will keep, covered in
the fridge, for up to ten days.

GALANTINE OF PORK WITH PARSLEY AND GARLIC

This jellied galantine turns a relatively cheap cut of pork into a real treat. It makes a good first course with the crisp sharpness of Cucumber Pickle (see page 364), or gherkins, or it can be served as part of a plate of charcuterie, with maybe a richer pâté, and a firm salami for contrasting textures and flavours.

SERVES ABOUT 10 AS A FIRST COURSE

1 hand of pork, brined for 4 days, see page 105
2 pigs' trotters
2 onions, sliced
2 carrots, sliced
2 sticks of celery, sliced
4 juniper berries, crushed
9 parsley stalks
1 sprig of thyme
2 bay leaves
12 black peppercorns
4 strips of lemon zest
½ bottle of dry white wine
salt
freshly ground black pepper
4 tablespoons chopped parsley
1–2 cloves of garlic, very finely chopped

Skin and bone the hand of pork, discarding the bones. Put the meat, skin and trotters into a flameproof casserole with the onions, carrots, celery, juniper berries, parsley stalks, thyme, bay leaves, peppercorns, lemon zest and wine. Add enough cold water to cover. Bring to the boil, skimming off any scum that rises to the surface. Simmer very gently for 2–2½ hours, until the meat is tender. Take the meat and skin out of the stock. Set the trotters aside for another occasion (see the recipe for Grilled Pigs' Trotters, page 235). Strain the stock, and boil briskly until reduced by half.

Dice the meat and the skin, and season to taste with salt and pepper. Mix with the chopped parsley and the garlic. Pack loosely into a 1.2 litre/2 pint terrine lined with clingfilm. Taste the stock and adjust seasonings. Pour enough stock over the meat to cover. Leave overnight to set. Serve sliced with Cucumber Pickle.

SWEETBREAD TERRINE

*Tender lambs' sweetbreads are what is really called for in this terrine,
though larger calves' ones can be substituted if needs be. The sorrel
gives the surrounding* farce *a pretty contrasting colour and a
pleasing sharpness, against the creaminess of the sweetbreads. When
sorrel isn't available, use mushrooms, to give a quite different but
delicious flavour to the terrine.
Serve with a small, lightly dressed salad, and Spiced Oranges or
Plums (see pages 368 and 371).*

SERVES 10–12

350 g/12 oz belly of pork or salt pork
1 good handful of sorrel, shredded, or 100 g/4 oz mushrooms,
sliced and cooked in 25 g/1 oz butter
2 eggs
1 tablespoon flour
freshly grated nutmeg
salt
freshly ground black pepper
100 g/4 oz fat bacon, rinds removed, stretched with the
back of a knife
450 g/1 lb cooked lambs' sweetbreads, thinly sliced,
see page 229

Chop the belly of pork or salt pork roughly, discarding any bits
of bone. Mix with the sorrel or cooked mushrooms, the eggs,
flour and seasonings. Process briefly in small batches in a processor or put through a mincer, to give a rough *farce*. Line a 1.2
litre/2 pint terrine with the bacon, letting the ends dangle over
the side. Spread a layer of the *farce* over the base, and follow
with a layer of sweetbreads. Repeat until all the mixture is used
up, ending with a layer of *farce*. Flip any floating ends of bacon
over the top, and cover loosely with foil.

Stand the terrine in a roasting tin half-filled with water and bake in a preheated oven, 140°C/275°F/gas mark 1, for 2 hours, or until the sides shrink slightly from the terrine. Take out of the tin of water and allow to cool. Find a piece of wood or a saucepan that will fit neatly on top of the terrine. Weigh this down with weights from the scales, or cans, and leave to cool.

Serve sliced with a lightly dressed salad and Spiced Oranges or Plums.

SAUSAGES AND SALAMIS

A proper old-fashioned butcher's shop should be able to supply you with natural sausage casings. We buy what are known as 'hog's pudding' casings from Luscombe's in Totnes, and have on occasion bought 'ox middles' from the enterprising delicatessen in Dartmouth.

'Ox middles' are the larger intestines from beef carcasses. Similarly, hog's pudding casings are the large intestines of pigs. They arrive fully prepared by the butcher, preserved in a brine solution which just needs to be rinsed off before use. The easiest way to do this is to stretch one end of the casing over the spout of the cold tap, with the rest lying in the sink or bath. Turn on the water, and let it flush through the full length for a couple of minutes. Rinse the outside too, and then they are ready to use.

We have just got round at last to buying a sausage-filling attachment for the mincer and for us it really is worth the comparatively enormous cost. Filling sausage casings by hand is a lengthy process, although not difficult.

For the smaller sausages, use a piping bag, fitted with the widest nozzle, to fill the casings. It is easiest to work with shorter lengths of casing, about 1 metre/3 feet long, knotting one end firmly, then wrinkling the open end and most of the length up over the nozzle. Pack the casings well, leaving no air bubbles, and knot the far end tightly when full.

For larger sausages, salamis and chorizos, say, which will be left to dry rather than cooked immediately, use a wide funnel and/or a wide piece of rigid plastic tubing, forcing the filling down hard into the casing with a pusher. It is important to pack it down really solidly before knotting and hanging the sausages up in an airy, dry place, as the meat will shrink as it dries (see page 386).

RABBIT OR GAME SAUSAGES

Since I usually serve these sausages as a first course, I tend to make
them fairly small, around 10 cm/4 inches long. For a main course
you will probably want to make them larger, 15 cm/6 inches maybe.
They're good with a fruity sauce, tart cranberry or apple sauce
perhaps, and red cabbage or a Celeriac Purée (see page 258).

MAKES ABOUT 12

40 g/1½ oz crustless white bread
100 ml/4 fl oz milk
25 g/1 oz butter
75 g/3 oz onions, chopped
225 g/8 oz boned rabbit or game
100 g/4 oz fat pork
100 g/4 oz lean pork or veal
2 eggs
1 tablespoon chopped parsley ⎫
2 sprigs of thyme ⎬ or 3 juniper berries, crushed
2 sprigs of marjoram ⎭
salt
freshly ground black pepper
about 3 metres/3 yards of 225 g/8 oz sausage casings
1 egg, beaten
fine breadcrumbs

Tear the bread into small pieces and place in a pan with the
milk. Bring slowly to the boil and simmer gently, stirring, until
the bread and milk have amalgamated smoothly to give a thick
panada. Leave to cool.

Melt the butter in a pan and sweat the onions, without
allowing them to colour, for about 5 minutes, then leave to
cool. Pass the meats through a mincer or process in a processor
coarsely, without reducing to a paste. Mix in the panada,
onions, eggs, herbs or juniper berries, and salt and pepper to
taste.

Fill the casings firmly with the sausage mixture (see pages 117 and 386). Knot or tie with string or thread at 10 cm/4 inch intervals to make the individual sausages.

To cook, heat a large pan of salted water until the surface trembles. Do not let it boil. Poach the string of sausages for 10 minutes. Remove from the heat and leave to cool in the cooking water. Lift out and chill until ready to use.

Cut into individual sausages and skin, then dip them into the beaten egg, and roll them in the breadcrumbs. Grill or fry, turning frequently, until they are nicely browned.

SALAMI

*Dried sausages, salami and chorizo, are best made during the
autumn, winter and early spring while the weather is cool. Once
Easter has come and gone, and summer starts to emerge, it is already
too warm for the sausages to mature properly.*
Quatre-épices *is a mixture of four spices, much used in charcuterie
in France, though it is excellent with fresh pork dishes as well. The
exact proportions vary considerably, but we usually use the quantities
given in Jane Grigson's* Charcuterie and French Pork Cookery*:
7 parts pepper or allspice; 1 part nutmeg; 1 part cloves; 1 part
cinnamon. Grind the spices in a strong electric coffee or spice grinder,
to get the warmest aromatic blend. Any not used immediately can be
stored in a tightly-closed jar.*
*Both the salami and the chorizo can be happily frozen once they have
dried sufficiently. Leave them hanging on a hook for much longer
than six weeks and they end up too dry and tough to enjoy.*

MAKES 3 × 30 CM/12 INCH SALAMIS

900 g/2 lb lean pork
450 g/1 lb lean beef
50 g/2 oz sea salt
2 teaspoons granulated sugar
1 teaspoon saltpetre (available from chemists)
225 g/8 oz pork fat
1 teaspoon freshly ground black pepper
2 tablespoons black peppercorns
2 teaspoons *quatre-épices*, see above
1 teaspoon ground nutmeg
1 measure rum or brandy
1 tablespoon garlic purée
about 2 metres/2 yards of sausage casings

Dice the lean meats finely. Mix together the salt and sugar. Put
the meat into a bowl with the saltpetre and about four-fifths of

the salt and sugar mixture. Dice the pork fat finely and mix with the remaining sugar and salt in a separate bowl. Cover both bowls and leave in a cool place overnight.

Next day mix the contents of the two bowls together and add all the spices and flavourings. Pack the casings very tightly with the meats (see pages 117 and 386), knotting or tying *twice* at 30 cm/12 inch intervals. Cut between the pairs of knots to give individual salamis, and hang in a cool, dry, airy place, with plenty of space round each one for the air to circulate. Dry for five to six weeks.

CHORIZO

Orange, spicy chorizo is Spain's national sausage, eaten both raw and cooked. We serve it thinly sliced, together with our own salami, cream cheese streaked with herbs, and a bowl of black olives.

MAKES 3 × 30 CM/12 INCH SAUSAGES

1 small sweet red pepper
1 small red chilli pepper
450 g/1 lb lean shoulder of pork
225 g/8 oz fat belly of pork
75 ml/3 fl oz red wine
1 level tablespoon salt
1 pinch of granulated sugar
1 pinch of saltpetre (available from chemists)
¼ teaspoon *quatre-épices*, see page 120
¼ teaspoon cayenne pepper
1 large clove of garlic
about 2 metres/2 yards of sausage casings

Remove the stalks and seeds from the pepper and chilli and discard. Chop the pepper and chilli roughly, and pass through a mincer with the lean and fat porks. Add the remaining ingredients and mix thoroughly. Pack the casings tightly (see pages 117 and 386), knotting or tying *twice* at 30 cm/12 inch intervals. Cut between the pairs of knots to give individual chorizos, and hang in a cool, dry, airy place, with plenty of space round each one for the air to circulate. Dry for four to six weeks. At four weeks they will have an excellent fresh taste and by six they will have matured to a deeper flavour.

Fish

I find the complete about-turn in attitudes to fish since the early 1970s quite amazing. In those days you had fish either grilled with a *maître d'hôtel* butter, or poached with a cream sauce. The permissible combinations were rigidly adhered to, and we ate sole véronique, or one of the other stereotypes, all delicious enough when well made, but demanding little imagination.

Nowadays, however, the cooking of fish has taken on a marvellous exuberance – there has been a torrent of new recipes and ideas. The British are discovering that not only are there a huge number of ingredients that you can put with fish, quite apart from the standard ones, but that there is a whole host of types of fish, offering enormous variation in taste and texture.

Turbot, Dover sole and salmon are no less valued than they ever were, but we have learnt to appreciate fish like sea bass, monkfish, shark and red mullet as well. It is a great liberation for chefs and restaurateurs, especially for those of us situated in coastal towns, with access to the catches straight from the fishing fleets, or the rods and nets of amateur fishermen.

I imagine that it is the increase in foreign holidays that has made British restaurant-goers so much more adventurous. Walk into a fish restaurant or, better still, a fish market on the Continent, and the wide range of fish, bright, shiny and fresh, is a real eye-opener. Wherever you are in Spain, for instance, the fish looks marvellous. I spend my holidays in a village near a small town on the Costa Dorada called Villanova, which has a thrilling fish market. None of the stallholders there would dare to sell anything but perfectly fresh fish, or no shopper would consider buying it. You never see fish in Spain in the appallingly tired, stale condition that you see all too often in this country.

But, slowly, the quality of fish in Britain is improving. Certainly, the choice here at Dartmouth has improved terrifically in the past fifteen or so years. But we are right beside the sea, and so, of course, we ought to have good fish, and there is no excuse for anything other than the best.

All this new interest is reflected in the price. Only five years ago, porbeagle shark was very cheap indeed, but now it commands a price comparable with that for all the prime fish, turbot and sole, and so on. Even squid has shot up in price.

When I buy fish the first thing I look for is firmness of texture and a bright eye. There should be a generally fresh, sprightly look about it, and nothing unpleasant about the smell. In fact, there should be virtually no smell at all, at most an intimation of the clean open sea.

Sometimes we even get fish that is almost too fresh, if there is such a thing! Salmon, for instance, needs relaxing for a day before using. A steak cut from an absolutely fresh salmon, straight out of the water, tends to become distorted as you cook it. The same goes for the larger Dover sole, though it seems to cause hardly any problem with smaller ones.

Nearly all our fish is local. The salmon is fished a little further up the river, around Dittisham, from March to August. There are about eighteen people, mostly locals, who have licences. One of our suppliers, Patrick Keene, had to wait a good three years to get a licence; the number is strictly limited in order to protect the salmon. The only other freshwater fish we get are salmon trout, the occasional shad, and a few eel from Slapton Lake.

Mostly, it is sea fish, nearly all according to their season.

John Dory, sea bass and red mullet are very much summer fish for us. Dover sole is at its best in summer and autumn – there is far too much roe if you take them in the spring. Monkfish, brill and turbot are year-rounders.

We buy some of our fish direct from fishermen like Patrick Keene, and the rest comes from either our local fish shop, Market Fish, or from the travelling fishmonger, Mark Lobb. He has a stall in the twice-weekly market, and in between times does the rounds of local villages, delivering last week's orders, taking orders for the following week. Our last source is the amateur fisherman, sometimes small boys with a few whitebait or the rare lobster caught inadvertently on a line put over the edge of the Embankment outside our front door. Their faces are a delight as, wide-eyed, they see the lobster weighed, representing untold wealth. The more serious adult fishermen bring in plenty of bass, and the occasional turbot of anything up to 9 kg/20 lb weight.

I've dabbled with home-smoking but as a rule we buy in smoked salmon and eel. There are happy moments when the price of local salmon comes down sufficiently to make it worth sending some over to Newton Abbot to get it smoked professionally. Jackson's, a small firm there, are reliable and experienced smokers. Far too many of the new breed of smokeries fail to understand that oversmoking ruins good ingredients.

I salt herring and mackerel here at the restaurant, to serve with soured cream or in a sweet and sour sauce, as part of a dish of fishy hors d'œuvre. Alongside the herring, there may be some squid fried briefly with lemon, parsley and garlic, and a ceviche or kilaw of firm white fish or salmon.

When The Carved Angel first opened I would hardly have dared put any of those delicious marinated raw fish dishes, like gravad lax, ceviche and kilaw (with coconut) on the menu, but today few customers think twice about ordering them. It's lovely to feel so unrestricted, to be able to draw on Chinese or Indian influences, to be able to mix old and new ideas on the same menu. So many exciting ingredients, used judiciously, are superb with fish – samphire, coriander, green peppercorns, ginger, sorrel . . .

Although I find myself steaming fish much more than I used to, the main methods employed here are grilling, oven poaching and baking. Personally, I like a nice piece of bass, grilled until the skin is crisp and crunchy, a lovely contrast to the softer flesh underneath. With an Orange Hollandaise (see page 34), a Herb Mayonnaise (see page 47) or gingered Tomato Sauce (see page 54) alongside, who could ask for anything better?

MONKFISH AND
CUCUMBER BROCHETTES

These are the most delightfully fresh summery kebabs – the cucumber retains its crunch, lovely against the softer but still firm cubes of monkfish.

FOR EACH SERVING

150 g/5 oz monkfish
5 cm/2 inch piece of cucumber
1 teaspoon chopped dill
1 tablespoon olive oil
2 teaspoons lemon juice
salt
freshly ground black pepper
1 bay leaf, halved

Cut the monkfish into 2.5 cm/1 inch cubes. Halve and seed the cucumber then slice into 7 mm/¼ inch semi-circles. Mix the monkfish and cucumber with the dill, oil, lemon juice, and salt and pepper to taste. Thread on to a skewer, alternating monkfish and cucumber and slipping the bay leaf halves in among the rest.

Place under a preheated medium grill for about 4 minutes on each side, turning once, until the monkfish is just opaque throughout. Serve immediately.

RED MULLET WITH ANCHOVIES AND ORANGE

The gamey flavour of the red mullet, larded with salty anchovies, is softened by the tomato and orange sauce. The result is a dish that is bursting with definite, honest flavours. Keep vegetables simple – boiled or steamed potatoes and a green salad.

SERVES 4

4 red mullet, weighing about 225 g/8 oz each,
scaled and cleaned
8 anchovy fillets
seasoned flour
oil
100 ml/4 fl oz orange juice
4 tablespoons skinned, seeded and diced tomato
chopped parsley
1 orange, peeled and sectioned

With a sharp knife, make two deep diagonal slashes at an angle to the bone on either side of each mullet. Quarter four of the anchovy fillets and tuck a piece of anchovy into each slash. Chop the remaining anchovies roughly. Dip the fish into the seasoned flour to coat, brush with oil, then place under a preheated very hot grill for 5 minutes on each side. Place on a heated serving dish, and keep warm.

Pour the orange juice into the grill pan, adding the tomato and the rest of the anchovy fillets. Place over a direct heat, and stir. Let the juices bubble and reduce to make a sauce – the anchovies will dissolve in the heat. Pour round the mullet, decorate with the parsley and the orange sections and serve.

SEA BASS IN PASTRY
WITH SORREL AND MUSHROOMS

*The sea bass is a summer fish – the first few are brought into the
restaurant in April and May, but by July and August they are in full
flood, some small enough to serve whole for one diner alone, and
others reaching as much as 3.5 kg/8 lb or so in weight.
It is one of the finest of fish, with its firm, sweet flesh. Recently it has
become fashionable in many a restaurant, but we have always
thought of it as very much a local catch – a fish that amateur
fishermen might catch on holiday in Dartmouth, sometimes bringing
it back to sell to us.*

SERVES 4

50 g/2 oz fresh sorrel, well washed and dried
25 g/1 oz butter
1 shallot, chopped
100 g/4 oz mushrooms, chopped
salt
freshly ground black pepper
675 g/1½ lb sea bass, skinned and filleted
225 g/8 oz shortcrust pastry, see page 346
1 egg, beaten

FOR THE SAUCE
1 shallot, chopped
3 tablespoons fish stock, see page 31
50 ml/2 fl oz dry white wine
1 egg
50 g/2 oz fresh sorrel, well washed
salt
freshly ground black pepper
75 g/3 oz butter, melted and cooled until just warm

To make the stuffing, cut any tough stalks from the sorrel and discard. Shred the sorrel finely. Melt the butter in a pan and sweat the shallot until beginning to soften, then add the mushrooms, and salt and pepper to taste. Cook until tender, then increase the heat and bubble until the mushroom liquid has almost entirely evaporated. Add the sorrel and stir for a few seconds. Remove from the heat. Taste and adjust seasonings, then leave to cool.

Season the fillets of fish, then sandwich with half the stuffing. Spread the remainder on the top. Roll out the pastry thinly on a lightly floured surface, and wrap round the bass, enclosing the fish completely. Tuck the joins underneath. Lift on to a baking sheet and rest it in a cool place for 30 minutes. Brush with egg, and bake in a preheated oven, 230°C/450°F/gas mark 8, for 20 minutes, until nicely browned.

To make the sauce, put the shallot in a small pan with the stock and wine. Boil until almost dry. Spoon into a blender with the egg, sorrel, and salt and pepper to taste. Set the motor running and trickle in the melted butter a very little at a time to make an emulsion. To keep the sauce warm, pour it into a bowl, and set over a pan of almost simmering water, making sure that the base of the bowl is not immersed.

Serve the sauce with the Sea Bass in Pastry.

SEA BASS WITH
LETTUCE AND HERBS

*A simplified version, and a very successful one too, of a recipe from
Roger Vergé's* Cuisine of the Sun. *The lettuce acts as an insulator,
so the fillets of fish do need to be cooked for a few minutes longer than
you might expect.*

SERVES 4

4 × 175 g/6 oz fillets of sea bass, skinned
salt
freshly ground black pepper
1 tablespoon chopped dill
1 tablespoon chopped parsley
4 large lettuce leaves – Webb's or Iceberg
25 g/1 oz butter
100 g/4 oz chopped shallots
150 ml/¼ pint vermouth
150 ml/¼ pint double cream

Season the fillets with salt and pepper, then sprinkle evenly
with the herbs. Pour boiling water over the lettuce leaves to
blanch. Drain, then run them under the cold tap to refresh. Lay
the leaves out on a tray, and blot dry with kitchen paper. Lay
a fillet of fish on each leaf and wrap to make a neat parcel,
tucking the ends underneath.

Melt the butter in a large, flat, flame- and ovenproof pan and
cook the shallots gently for 5 minutes without browning. Lay
the fish parcels in the pan, add the vermouth, and salt and pepper to taste. Cover and cook in a preheated oven, 150°C/300°F/
gas mark 2, for about 15 minutes. When a sharp knife slips into
the fish with no resistance, lift the parcels out of the pan and
keep warm on a serving dish.

Add the cream to the cooking juices, and bring to the boil
over a direct heat. Reduce over a moderate heat until thick.
Check the seasoning and serve with the fish.

JOHN DORY WITH MUSHROOMS AND ORANGE

SERVES 4

4 John Dory, weighing about 450 g/1 lb each,
gutted and heads removed
150 ml/¼ pint dry white wine
salt
freshly ground black pepper
250 ml/8 fl oz double cream
chopped parsley

FOR THE STUFFING
2 oranges
50 g/2 oz butter
50 g/2 oz shallots, chopped
225 g/8 oz mushrooms, sliced
salt
freshly ground black pepper

Begin by making the stuffing: pare the zest from one of the oranges in thick strips, being careful to avoid the white pith. Drop into a pan of boiling water, bring back to the boil and cook for 2 minutes. Drain, then shred finely. Peel both the oranges, removing the pith, divide into segments and skin each segment. Reserve half the segments, the ones that are most perfect, to decorate the finished dish.

Melt the butter in a pan and sweat the shallots for 5 minutes. Add the mushrooms and cook for a further 5 minutes, until tender, then increase the heat and let the juices boil almost completely away. Add salt and pepper to taste, the orange zest and half the orange sections. Taste and adjust seasonings. Leave to cool.

Using a sharp knife, enlarge each of the 'pockets' of the fish (taking care not to cut right through) so that they can each take a quarter of the stuffing. Divide and pack in the stuffing, pressing it down firmly. Put the fish in a flame- and ovenproof dish with the wine. Season and bring to the boil, then cover with a lid or foil and bake in a preheated cool oven, 140°C/275°F/gas mark 1, for about 20–30 minutes until just cooked.

Transfer the fish on to a warmed serving dish, and lift off the upper layer of skin. Keep the fish warm. Place the cooking dish over a direct heat, and pour in the cream. Stir and reduce until thick. Taste and adjust seasonings. Pour round the fish, decorate with parsley and reserved orange sections and serve.

SALT COD WITH ALMONDS AND PINE KERNELS

We've recently been experimenting with salting our own cod. Baz
Mehew, who used to run the delicatessen on Newcomen Road, told us
how he salted fish. 'I just put a layer of salt in the tray, I put the fish
on top, cover it well with more salt, put it in the fridge for a fortnight,
then hang it up to dry.' A customer who is a marine biologist has
given us a rather more scientific outline with precise quantities, and
chef Alistair Little has vouchsafed his method.
Unfortunately, the weather has not been on our side. At first the cod
seemed to be drying out well, with a clean smell of the sea, but a
week of damp rainy weather and it began to yellow, and to develop a
more intrusive smell. In the end I had to give in, and throw it out.
We will try again, but for the time being I shall continue to use the
salt cod brought back from holidays in Spain. There is a shop in
Barcelona called La Casa del Bacalao, the House of Salt Cod. They
sell it in all shapes and forms – whole, grated, chopped and fillets –
as well as with garlic and chillis. They also hand out recipes for
cooking the cod, and this is one of them.

Serves 6

450 g/1 lb salt cod
seasoned flour
150 ml/¼ pint olive oil
50 g/2 oz toasted almonds
50 g/2 oz pine kernels
3 cloves of garlic
350 g/12 oz tomatoes, skinned
150 ml/¼ pint dry white wine
150 ml/¼ pint fish stock, see page 31
freshly ground black pepper
salt (optional)
chopped parsley

Soak the salt cod in cold water for 48 hours, changing the water every 12 hours. Drain well and dry on kitchen paper. Dip into the seasoned flour. Heat the oil in a frying pan and fry the cod for about 5 minutes, until nicely browned on both sides.

Process the almonds, pine kernels, garlic and tomatoes in a processor or blender to a purée. Add to the cod with the wine, stock and pepper. Heat gently until the surface of the liquid trembles. Do not allow it to boil, as this toughens the cod. Poach for 15 minutes until tender. Taste and adjust seasoning, adding salt if necessary. Scatter with the parsley to finish. Serve with slices of bread, fried in olive oil and then rubbed with garlic.

BRILL WITH PISTACHIO MOUSSELINE AND VEGETABLES

Serves 4

4 × 175 g/6 oz fillets of brill
50 g/2 oz carrots, cut into strips
50 g/2 oz mushrooms, sliced
150 ml/¼ pint dry white wine
25 g/1 oz butter, chilled and diced
sprigs of chervil, to garnish

FOR THE PISTACHIO MOUSSELINE
15 g/½ oz pistachio nuts, shelled
100 g/4 oz brill trimmed from the fillets, see below
15 g/½ oz chopped chervil
1 egg white
salt
freshly ground black pepper
150 ml/¼ pint double cream

Skin the brill fillets and trim any frill and a little off the tails to give 100 g/4 oz trimmings for the mousseline.

To make the mousseline, pour boiling water over the pistachios, leave for 30 seconds, then drain. Pull off the skins. Purée the fish trimmings with the pistachios, chervil and egg white in a processor or blender until smooth. Rub through a fine sieve. Season vigorously with salt and pepper. Gradually beat the cream into the mixture.

Spread the carrots and mushrooms on the base of a buttered flameproof dish, and lay the brill fillets on top. Either fill a piping bag fitted with a plain 1.25 cm/½ inch nozzle with the mousseline and pipe over the fillets, or spread the mousseline over the fish using a palette knife. Pour in the wine, cover with foil or a lid and cook in a preheated oven, 140°C/275°F/gas mark 1, for about 15 minutes until the fish is just opaque.

Remove the fillets to a warmed serving dish. Place the cooking dish over a direct heat, and reduce the juices by half over a fairly fast flame. Season, then whisk in the butter a few cubes at a time. Taste and adjust seasonings. Pour round the fish, garnish with chervil and serve.

KILAW

I first started making Kilaw many years ago – the original recipe came from Richard Cranfield when he worked here at The Carved Angel. He now runs the Mansion House Restaurant. Occasionally it appears on both our menus simultaneously, but over the years our recipes have changed. The basic coconut marinade is much as it was, but the various embellishments have developed along different routes. I now keep it very simple and serve it as a first course, adding diced red and green peppers only. But you could always enlarge it to main course status by adding tomato, cucumber, lettuce, avocado, tender raw peas or mangetouts, and so on.

SERVES 4 AS A FIRST COURSE

450 g/1 lb firm white fish fillets (brill, John Dory, turbot, Dover sole, for example), cut into strips
juice of 2 lemons
100 g/4 oz creamed coconut, grated
250 ml/8 fl oz warm milk
1 tablespoon finely grated fresh root ginger
½ teaspoon freshly ground black pepper
½ teaspoon ground turmeric
2 small cloves of garlic, crushed
salt
1 red pepper, seeded and diced
1 green pepper, seeded and diced

Spread the fish out in a shallow dish and pour over the lemon juice. Cover and leave in the fridge for 8 hours, stirring once or twice.

Dissolve the coconut in the warm milk, then add the ginger, pepper, turmeric, garlic and salt to taste. Leave to cool. Taste and adjust seasonings.

Drain the lemon juice from the fish, and pour over the coconut dressing, turning. Set aside for 2–4 hours – the longer time for the firm-fleshed fish such as turbot or Dover sole. Mix in the red and green peppers just before serving.

BRILL AND VEGETABLE TERRINE

I have made fish terrines in the past with a panada base, but now I prefer this rather lighter terrine. It can be made using other firm-fleshed fish such as turbot, sole or salmon.

SERVES 10

225 g/8 oz red peppers, halved and seeded
30 ml/1 fl oz olive oil
225 g/8 oz courgettes, sliced into 1.25 cm/½ inch rounds
225 g/8 oz head of Florence fennel
350 ml/12 fl oz Tomato Sauce, see page 54
11 g/scant ½ oz leaf gelatine (6 sheets), soaked,
see page 301
salt
freshly ground black pepper
12 fresh spinach leaves, well washed
30 ml/1 fl oz olive oil
225 g/8 oz brill fillet, cut into 1.25 cm/½ inch strips
¾ teaspoon saffron filaments

Brush the peppers with oil and bake in a preheated oven, 220°C/425°F/gas mark 7, for 20 minutes. Leave the peppers until cool enough to handle, then skin and cut into 1.25 cm/½ inch strips. Blanch the courgettes in boiling salted water for 5 minutes, then drain, refresh under the cold tap and drain again. Separate the fennel into leaves, discarding any bruised ones. Blanch in boiling salted water for 5 minutes, then drain, refresh, drain again and slice. Put the vegetables on a tray lined with kitchen paper to absorb the excess water and oil.

Heat the Tomato Sauce in a pan, add the gelatine and stir until it has dissolved. Check the seasoning. Blanch the spinach leaves in boiling salted water for 1–2 minutes, then drain, refresh and drain again. Leave to drain on kitchen paper. Line a 1.4 litre/2½ pint terrine with clingfilm and then with about two-thirds of the spinach leaves, keeping the rest for the top.

Heat the remaining 30 ml/1 fl oz of the oil in a large frying pan, add the brill and saffron, and season to taste with salt and pepper. Cook gently for 1 minute, then turn carefully and cook the other side for another minute. Lift out and drain on kitchen paper.

Put a few spoonfuls of Tomato Sauce in the terrine, then cover with a layer of vegetables, some more sauce, followed by fish, pressing down well each time. Repeat the layers until all the ingredients are used up. Top with the remaining spinach leaves and cover with clingfilm, pressing down gently. Leave to chill overnight. Turn out of the terrine, peel off the clingfilm and serve sliced into 6 mm/¼ inch slices with some mayonnaise and a crisp salad.

SALMON AND LOBSTER MOUSSE

*The lobster and the salmon together make a luxurious mousse, the
kind of thing that might be served as the centrepiece of a lazy
midsummer lunch. The recipe can also be adapted to make a feather-
light smoked salmon mousse. Leave out the lobster and the sherry
and substitute smoked salmon trimmings for the fresh salmon.*

SERVES 8

150 ml/¼ pint fish stock, see page 31
11 g/scant ½ oz leaf gelatine (about 6 sheets), soaked,
see page 301
350 g/12 oz salmon, poached
salt
freshly ground black pepper
100 g/4 oz cooked lobster
2 tablespoons dry sherry
lemon juice
450 ml/¾ pint double cream
150 ml/¼ pint egg white (approximately 4 large egg whites)

Warm the stock without boiling and add the softened leaf gelatine. Stir until it has completely dissolved. Leave the stock to
cool until tepid and the consistency of egg white.

Place the salmon in the bowl of a processor, season well with
salt and pepper, and pour in the stock. Whizz until smooth.
Alternatively, process in several batches in a blender. Dice the
lobster and sprinkle with the sherry. Stir into the salmon purée,
add the lemon juice and taste and adjust seasonings. The purée
should be quite strongly seasoned. Let it cool completely. Whip
the cream lightly and fold into the salmon. Whisk the egg
whites until they hold stiff peaks, and fold in as well. Pour into
a lightly oiled mould and leave to set in the fridge. Just before
eating, dip the mould briefly into hot water and turn out. Serve
with some dressed cucumber and a little chopped dill.

SALMON WITH SAMPHIRE

*This is a late spring and early summer recipe, when the wild salmon
are in season, and the tender young samphire is first covering the
sea-walls. Luckily it grows near the restaurant and I am able to pick
what I need (see page 365).*

SERVES 4

4 × 225 g/8 oz salmon steaks
freshly ground black pepper
1 good handful of rock samphire, well washed, see page 365
100 ml/4 fl oz dry white wine or champagne
150 ml/¼ pint double cream

Lay the salmon steaks in a buttered, shallow flameproof dish,
give a couple of twists of the pepper mill over the fish and
arrange the samphire on top. Pour over the wine or champagne, cover with a lid or foil, and cook in a preheated oven,
140°C/275°F/gas mark 1, for 15 minutes, until the fish is just
cooked. Drain the juices into a pan (keep the salmon and
samphire warm) and bubble over a high heat until they are
reduced by half. Add the cream and reduce again until the
sauce is very thick. Taste and adjust seasonings. Skin the
salmon and remove the bones. Arrange the salmon and
samphire on a warmed serving dish, and pour the sauce round
the fish.

GRILLED HERRINGS WITH APPLE AND HORSERADISH SAUCE

A homely recipe, maybe, but I love all those oily fish like herring and mackerel. This is a quick dish that we save for ourselves, for the staff lunch, rather than put on the menu. The hotness of the horseradish and the sharpness of the apple sauce balance the fattiness of the fish.

SERVES 4

25 g/1 oz butter
225 g/8 oz cooking apples, peeled, cored and sliced
2 teaspoons grated fresh horseradish
salt
freshly ground black pepper
4 herrings, weighing about 175–225 g/6–8 oz each, gutted
seasoned flour

Melt the butter in a pan and cook the apples gently for about 10 minutes, until soft. Mash to a purée. Stir in the horseradish, and salt and pepper to taste. Keep the apple purée warm.

Coat the herrings in the seasoned flour. Place under a preheated grill for about 5 minutes on each side until cooked through to the bone. Serve with the apple and horseradish sauce, and plain, boiled potatoes.

TURBOT WITH GINGER, LIME AND HOLLANDAISE SAUCE

Turbot is one of the finest of fish, and this recipe shows it off to full advantage with the sharpness of fresh lime and ginger, napped with buttery hollandaise.

SERVES 4

1 lime
4 × 175 g/6 oz turbot fillets
1 teaspoon grated fresh root ginger
salt
freshly ground black pepper
300 ml/½ pint Hollandaise Sauce, see page 33

Pare the zest from the lime in strips, being careful to avoid the white pith. Drop into a pan of boiling water and blanch for 1 minute. Drain well and shred. Peel the pith off the lime and divide into segments. With a sharp knife, strip the papery skin off each segment, leaving a bright green crescent.

Lay the fillets on a buttered ovenproof dish. Arrange the lime segments on the fish and scatter over half the shredded peel and all the ginger. Season with a little salt and pepper to taste. Cover the dish with a lid or foil, and bake in a preheated oven, 140°C/275°F/gas mark 1, for 15–20 minutes, until the turbot is just opaque throughout.

When cooked, spoon the Hollandaise Sauce on to the fillets and scatter the remaining peel over the top.

ELVERS

Elvers, silvery eel fry, are a rarely obtainable delicacy in this country for all but the lucky few living near a source such as the estuary of the River Severn. Even so, the cost is high, although redeemed by their richness – a little will go a long way.

They need only the briefest of cooking, dusted with flour and deep-fried like whitebait or cooked *'a la bilbaína'* as they do in Spain.

For four people, you will need around 225 g/8 oz elvers. Rinse and dry on kitchen paper or a clean tea towel. In a frying pan large enough to hold all the elvers, heat an even layer of olive oil with a halved dried red chilli, and a sliced clove of garlic. Infuse over a moderate heat for 5 minutes or so, then remove the chilli and garlic. Increase the heat, and add the elvers. Season generously with salt and pepper, and stir. Within seconds the elvers will turn white, and are ready to serve, with good crusty bread to mop up the juices.

EELS IN RED WINE WITH PRUNES

The firm flesh of the eel is a rare treat. This sauce, thick and plummy from the prunes, is at first glance an unlikely partner to fish, but it works with the positive flavour of the eel to give a rich succulent stew. Eels are usually brought into the restaurant live to ensure freshness – they deteriorate very quickly when dead. To deal with a live eel, grasp it firmly behind the head with a piece of kitchen paper or a clean tea towel. Then, using a sharp knife, decapitate it swiftly and gut it. If you buy eel ready prepared from the fishmonger, use it straight away.

SERVES 4

900 g/2 lb fresh eels, gutted
16 pickling onions
50 g/2 oz butter
2 thick rashers of green streaky bacon, cut into strips
1 tablespoon flour
600 ml/1 pint fruity red wine
1 bouquet garni
16 prunes
salt
freshly ground black pepper

Cut the eels into 5 cm/2 inch lengths. Bring a large pan of salted water to the boil and drop in the eel pieces. Blanch for 1 minute, and drain well. Leave to cool, then remove the skin.

Pour boiling water over the onions and leave for 30 seconds. Drain and run them under the cold tap, then peel. Dry on kitchen paper. Melt the butter in a pan and brown the onions with the bacon. Sprinkle the flour over the onions, and stir for 1 minute. Gradually add the wine, stirring until smooth, and then the bouquet garni. Bring to the boil and add the prunes, and salt and pepper to taste. Simmer for 30 minutes.

Add the pieces of eel to the pan. Cover and cook very gently, barely even simmering, for 15–20 minutes, until the eel is tender. Taste and adjust seasonings. Remove the bouquet garni before serving. Serve with croûtons fried in olive oil.

Shellfish

Our shellfish is nearly all caught locally. We have good supplies of lobster, crab, scallops, mussels and, more rarely now, prawns. We are lucky that the time lapse between sea and kitchen is so short – we get these shellfish at their very best, before their meat has time to lose any of its sweet, satisfying taste and texture.

It seems a shame to mask the delights of good shellfish with over-elaborate fiddling and fussing, so we tend to cook much of it very simply. When we get raw transparent prawns, we cook them briefly in boiling salted water, and serve them with nothing more than aïoli or a plain mayonnaise. There are few sights more pleasing than a plate piled high with rosy pink prawns. They seem to be so rare now, that I want to really be able to appreciate that exceptional firmness and sweetness – something you never get in ready-cooked prawns that have lingered too long on their journey to the table. Mind you, on the rare occasions when we are blessed with a surprisingly generous supply we may well splash out and cook them with a little cream and brandy.

Scallops and mussels are more plentiful, so we can afford to dress them up rather more, hence the predominance of recipes for these two in this chapter. Lobster, too, comes to us only a few hours out of the sea, and again we like to serve it at its purest, boiled or grilled with mayonnaise – to be honest, there's no better way to cook it. It is a wonderful sight, too, to see some-one really enjoying getting to grips with a lobster. Watching as they suck every bit of shell until there's nothing left in it at all. It is marvellous to think of people deriving such pleasure from something so simple.

LOBSTER MALLORQUINA

This is a recipe that dates back to my days at the Hole in the Wall. It is a good way of jazzing up a bought ready-cooked lobster, with a sherry and brandy soufflé topping, well seasoned but light enough not to overwhelm the delicate flesh.

SERVES 4

2 × 675 g/1½ lb lobsters, cooked
3 tablespoons dry sherry
salt
freshly ground black pepper
65 g/2½ oz butter
15 g/½ oz flour
150 ml/¼ pint single cream
lemon juice
brandy
2 eggs, separated
a few lobster eggs, if available

With a sharp knife, split the lobsters in half lengthways, and remove the flesh from the body, claws and tails, cutting it into scallops. Remove and discard the stomach sac in the head and the dark, thread-like intestine. Sprinkle with 1 tablespoon of the sherry, and salt and pepper to taste. Put the shells on to baking trays.

Make a *roux* with 15 g/½ oz of the butter and the flour, then add the cream a little at a time to make a sauce. Simmer for 5 minutes. Remove from the heat and season with the rest of the sherry, a squeeze of lemon juice, a dash of brandy, and salt and pepper to taste. Taste and adjust seasonings – it should be fairly strong as it will be softened by the addition of the eggs. Stir in the egg yolks.

Melt the remaining butter in a pan and warm the lobster meat gently in it. Whisk the egg whites until they hold stiff peaks and fold into the sauce. Pour a little of the sauce into the bottom of each shell, divide the lobster meat between them, and coat with remaining sauce. Sprinkle with a few lobster eggs, if using, and bake in a preheated oven, 230°C/450°F/gas mark 8, for 5–8 minutes, until golden brown. Serve immediately.

SCALLOPS WITH BACON
AND WHITE WINE

There is a natural affinity between scallops and bacon. The salt of one emphasizes the sweetness of the other. As with all good combinations, finding the right balance is where the real secret lies. There's just enough bacon here to lift the scallops without taking over.

SERVES 4 AS A FIRST COURSE OR 2 AS A MAIN COURSE

8 large scallops
freshly ground black pepper
50 g/2 oz butter
2 shallots, chopped
2 rashers of streaky green bacon, chopped
150 ml/¼ pint fish stock, see page 31
150 ml/¼ pint dry white wine
2 tablespoons chopped parsley
salt
4 slices of toasted brioche, to serve

Slice the white part of each scallop into three thin discs, cut the coral into two or three pieces, and season with pepper only. Melt the butter in a pan and cook the shallots gently for 5 minutes. Add the bacon and cook for a further 3 minutes, until the shallots are tender. Add the stock, wine, and parsley and simmer until reduced by half. Check the seasoning, and add salt if necessary. Finally, add the scallops to the pan, and cook briefly. As soon as they turn opaque remove from the heat. Serve with slices of toasted brioche.

SCALLOPS WITH WHITE WINE AND ARTICHOKES

Jerusalem artichokes make convivial companions for scallops. It is a pairing I first came across in Margaret Costa's Four Seasons Cookery Book *where she gives a recipe for a superb Scallop and Artichoke Soup. In this recipe they are cooked briefly together, co-stars in a delicate little ragoût.*

SERVES 4 AS A FIRST COURSE OR 2 AS A MAIN COURSE

8 large scallops
50 g/2 oz butter
175 g/6 oz Jerusalem artichokes, peeled and cut into batons,
and boiled in lightly salted water for 5 minutes
salt
freshly ground black pepper
50 ml/2 fl oz dry white wine
1 tablespoon chopped parsley
lemon juice
slices of toasted brioche or bread, or rice, to serve

Slice the white part of each scallop into three thin discs and cut the coral into two or three pieces. Melt the butter in a small pan, and add the artichokes, and salt and pepper to taste. Cook very gently until almost tender. Add the scallops and wine and cook slowly until the scallops turn opaque. Remove from the heat and add the parsley and a dash of lemon juice. Taste and adjust seasonings. Serve with slices of toasted brioche or bread or with rice.

SCALLOP MOUSSELINE WITH ARTICHOKE PURÉE

An elegant dish, this scallop mousseline – cut into the pretty green turrets and you reveal a centre of palest coral-pink. It tastes as elegant as it looks, too.
The mousseline could also be cooked as a terrine in a leaf-lined loaf tin instead of individual moulds. Increase the cooking time appropriately to compensate for greater volume. The artichoke purée can be made in advance and reheated as the mousseline is cooking. When Jerusalem artichokes are out of season, serve with an Orange Hollandaise, or a lighter Saffron Cream Sauce (see pages 34 and 39).

SERVES 8

FOR THE MOUSSELINE
375 g/13 oz prepared scallops
2 teaspoons salt
10 turns of the peppermill
1 egg
1 egg white
500 ml/17 fl oz double cream
about 24 fresh sorrel or spinach leaves, washed

FOR THE ARTICHOKE PURÉE
450 g/1 lb Jerusalem artichokes, peeled and diced
fish stock, see page 31
salt
freshly ground black pepper
lemon juice

Process the scallops with the salt and pepper in a processor or blender until smooth. Add the egg and the egg white and whizz for 1 more minute. Scrape into a bowl and chill for 30 minutes. Gradually beat in the cream to make a firm mousseline.

With a pair of scissors or a sharp knife, snip out any tough stalks in the sorrel or spinach leaves. Blanch spinach leaves for a few seconds only in a pan of boiling water. Refresh under the cold tap, drain well and pat dry with kitchen paper. Sorrel leaves are more pliable and would disintegrate in the boiling water, so wash and dry them well and use unblanched. Line eight buttered dariole moulds with the leaves. Fill with the mousseline. Tap each mould on the work surface a couple of times to settle the mixture.

Cover each mould loosely with a circle of buttered grease-proof paper, and stand them on a wire rack in a pan to keep them away from direct heat. Pour enough warm water into the pan to come halfway up the moulds. Heat until the water is just trembling, cover and poach for 10–15 minutes, until the mousseline is firm. Turn the moulds out on to individual plates and surround with hot artichoke purée.

To make the artichoke purée, place the artichokes in a pan with enough fish stock to cover. Bring to the boil and simmer for 20 minutes, until tender. Process the artichokes with enough of their cooking liquid in a processor or blender to give a thin purée. Sieve, and season lightly to taste with salt and pepper and a dash of lemon juice.

SCALLOPS IN FILO PASTRY WITH WATERCRESS SAUCE

*Filo pastry cooks to a crisp brownness in a matter of
minutes – just long enough to turn the scallops hidden inside opaque,
without toughening them by overcooking. The speckled green
watercress sauce can be made in advance, and reheated gently as the
scallop triangles bake. The idea is one I first came across at Clarke's
Restaurant in London, and it came originally from Nico Ladenis.*

SERVES 4

4 sheets of filo pastry
75 g/3 oz butter, melted
8 large scallops, whites sliced into 3 thin discs and coral cut
into pieces
chopped parsley
chopped dill
lemon juice
4 lemon wedges
4 sprigs of parsley

FOR THE SAUCE
15 g/½ oz butter
100 g/4 oz trimmed leeks, well washed and finely sliced
50 ml/2 fl oz fish stock, see page 31
salt
freshly ground black pepper
50 ml/2 fl oz single cream
25 g/1 oz watercress leaves

Cover the sheets of filo pastry with a sheet of greaseproof paper,
and over that a clean, damp tea towel – this prevents the pastry
drying out, and becoming brittle.

Take one sheet of filo and brush with melted butter. Cut in
half crossways. Lift one half and put on top of the other.

Arrange two of the sliced scallops in the centre, sprinkle with a little parsley and dill and a few drops of lemon juice. Fold in the two sides over the filling and roll up to make a neat parcel. Repeat with the other three sheets of filo and the remaining scallops, herbs and lemon juice to give four parcels. Lay each parcel seam-side down on an ungreased baking sheet and brush with melted butter. Bake in a preheated oven, 230°C/450°F/gas mark 8, for 10 minutes, until the filo parcels are golden brown.

To make the sauce, melt the butter in a pan and sweat the leeks gently until tender. Add the stock, and salt and pepper to taste, and simmer for 5 minutes. Process briefly in a processor or blender with the single cream and watercress to give a smooth sauce. Taste and adjust seasonings. If necessary, reheat gently without boiling. Divide between four plates and sit one filo parcel on each pool of sauce. Add a lemon wedge and a sprig of parsley and serve.

PUFF PASTRY OF SCALLOPS, MUSSELS AND LEEKS WITH SAFFRON

This method of making twisted puff pastry containers is much simpler than it first appears. Not only do they look pretty, but the soggy centre of vol-au-vents and the like is avoided. If you have little time to spare, then just cut rectangles of pastry and bake in a hot oven until risen and browned.
With the saffron sauce and shellfish, this makes quite a filling dish. Follow it with a light main course, or serve it as the centrepiece of a simple lunch or supper.

SERVES 4

225 g/8 oz puff pastry, see page 347
1 egg, beaten
25 g/1 oz butter
225 g/8 oz leeks, well washed and thinly shredded
8 large scallops, whites sliced into thin discs and coral cut into pieces
20 mussels, scrubbed, and opened in a pan over a high heat

FOR THE SAFFRON SAUCE
50 g/2 oz butter
50 g/2 oz shallots, chopped
150 ml/¼ pint dry white wine
25 g/1 oz flour
300 ml/½ pint fish stock, see page 31
1 very generous pinch of saffron filaments
lemon juice
salt
freshly ground black pepper
75 ml/3 fl oz double cream

Roll out the puff pastry on a lightly floured surface to form a 20 cm/8 inch square, 4 mm/⅛ inch thick. Trim the edges and divide into four 10 cm/4 inch squares. Make four twists as shown in the diagram on page 381. Place on a baking sheet, cover the pastry and leave it in the fridge for 30 minutes to relax. Brush with beaten egg, then bake in a preheated oven, 230°C/450°F/gas mark 8, for 7 minutes, until golden brown.

Remove from the oven and, using a small, sharp knife, cut out the small square in the centre of each pastry, leaving border, sides and base intact. Lift off the squares and set aside in a warm place to use later as the lids.

To make the saffron sauce, melt half the butter in a pan and sweat the shallots for 10 minutes, then add the wine and bubble until reduced to 2 tablespoons of liquid. In a separate pan, melt the remaining butter for the sauce and stir in the flour. Cook for 1 minute, then remove from the heat and add the stock little by little. Return to the heat, bring to the boil and simmer for 10 minutes. Add the saffron, reduction, a dash of lemon juice, salt and pepper to taste, and cream. Taste and adjust seasonings.

Melt the last 25 g/1 oz butter in a separate pan and cook the leeks briefly. Add the scallops, mussels and saffron sauce. Bring to the boil, then spoon into the pastry cases, top with the reserved pastry lids and serve immediately.

MUSSELS WITH SAFFRON

*The pairing of shellfish with saffron is one that reminds me
immediately of Provence, the seaside, and holidays. Here the mussels
are cooked directly on top of the tomato-saffron sauce, so be sure to
scrub and wash them thoroughly.*
This is equally good served cold, at room temperature, as hot.

SERVES 4

4 × 600 ml/1 pint measures of mussels
2 leeks, well washed
3 tablespoons olive oil
2 onions, chopped
2 cloves of garlic, chopped
2 sprigs of thyme
1 bay leaf
1 tablespoon chopped parsley
1 very generous pinch of saffron filaments
1 × 400 g/14 oz can tomatoes, drained
100 ml/4 fl oz dry white wine
juice of ½ lemon
salt
freshly ground black pepper

Scrub the mussels well and remove all their beards and
barnacles. Discard any that do not close when tapped against a
hard surface. Slice the white part of the leeks thinly. Save the
greens for soup or stock. Heat the oil in a large, wide, heavy-
based pan and sweat the leeks, onions, garlic, herbs and saffron
gently for 10 minutes, until the vegetables are soft. Add the
tomatoes, wine, lemon juice, and salt and pepper to taste. Bring
to the boil and simmer for about 5 minutes, until thick.

Add the mussels to the pan, cover and cook fast until they
open, shaking the pan to redistribute the mussels and prevent
the sauce from sticking. Within 5–10 minutes nearly all the

mussels should have opened. Discard any that stay steadfastly closed. Either serve immediately or leave to cool, removing top shells before serving.

MUSSELS STUFFED
WITH SPINACH

A Provençal recipe for mussels filled with spinach. The mussels can be prepared and stuffed in advance and finished off at the last moment. An excellent recipe for larger mussels – too small and it gets fiddly.

SERVES 4

4 × 600 ml/1 pint measures of mussels
50 ml/2 fl oz dry white wine
225 g/8 oz cooked spinach, squeezed dry
2 tablespoons thick Béchamel Sauce, see page 35
freshly grated nutmeg
salt
freshly ground black pepper
50 g/2 oz soft breadcrumbs
50 g/2 oz butter

Scrub the mussels well and remove all their beards and bar-nacles. Discard any that do not close when tapped against a hard surface. Pour the wine into a wide pan large enough to take all the mussels. Bring to a simmer and add the mussels. Cover and shake over the heat until all the mussels have opened. Any that steadfastly refuse to open after 10 minutes should be thrown out. Remove and discard the upper shell of each mussel.

Purée the spinach with the Béchamel in a processor or blender. Season with nutmeg, and salt and pepper to taste. Cover the mussels in their shells with this mixture, smoothing with a palette knife to give an even finish. Arrange the mussels in an ovenproof dish and sprinkle with breadcrumbs. Dot the butter over the mussels, then bake in a preheated oven, 220°C/ 425°F/gas mark 7, for 5 minutes. Whizz under a preheated grill to finish browning and serve straight away while the mussels are still bubbling.

CRAB SOUFFLÉ

This is a variation on the Soufflé Suissesse, a twice-cooked soufflé. The individual little soufflés can all be made in advance, and finished off with the cream and cheese in a hot oven at the very last minute. But do be careful not to overcook them second time round. Whip them out as soon as they are good and hot, and lightly browned. Any longer and they may well collapse.

SERVES 8

50 g/2 oz butter
25 g/1 oz flour
250 ml/8 fl oz fish stock, see page 31
1 teaspoon tomato purée
100 g/4 oz brown crab meat
100 g/4 oz white crab meat
1 tablespoon dry sherry
lemon juice
salt
freshly ground black pepper
3 eggs, separated
225 g/8 oz mushrooms, sliced
1 teaspoon grated fresh root ginger
450 ml/¾ pint double cream
25 g/1 oz Parmesan cheese, freshly grated

Melt half the butter in a pan, and stir in the flour. Cook for 1 minute, then, away from the heat, add the fish stock little by little. Return to the heat, bring to the boil and simmer for 10 minutes. Remove from the heat, stir in the tomato purée and the brown and white crab meat. Add the sherry, a generous dash of lemon juice to sharpen, and salt and pepper to taste. Mix in the egg yolks. Taste and adjust seasonings – it should be on the strong side as it will be diluted by the egg whites.

Whisk the egg whites until they are stiff and fold into the

soufflé mixture. Pour into eight well-buttered dariole moulds and stand them in a roasting tray filled with hot water to a depth of 2.5 cm/1 inch. Cook in a preheated oven, 190°C/375°F/gas mark 5, for 20–30 minutes, until just set. Leave to cool.

Melt the remaining butter in a pan and cook the mushrooms with the ginger for about 5 minutes, until tender. Divide between eight small gratin dishes, or spread out in one single ovenproof dish large enough to take all the soufflés. Turn the soufflés out on to the mushrooms, and pour the cream evenly over them. Sprinkle with Parmesan, and bake at 230°C/450°F/gas mark 8 for 6–8 minutes. Serve immediately.

Poultry & Game

Over the past five or six years there has been a marked change in eating habits, a move away from the heavier red meats to poultry and game when in season. It is particularly noticeable in the restaurant. Chicken and duck are always popular. The demand for steak, once an obligatory item on every menu, has declined dramatically.

This is a change that suits me well. I enjoy cooking and eating beef or lamb, say, but I find the extraordinary adaptability of chicken or duck, guinea fowl, rabbit, hare or pheasant terrifically exciting. The seasons set natural parameters. In summer months the charcoal grill comes into play, giving its smoky outdoors flavour to marinated chicken or guinea fowl. Autumn introduces the first of the game, gradually bringing stronger, earthier tastes and heartier dishes to the menu. Rich stews and casseroles replace the lighter dishes of the summer as the weather chills into winter. The last days of February see the end of the shooting season and, with luck, the first intimations of spring. Domestic fowl replace the game and fresh flavours start to oust the mellow winter comforters. And so, full circle, back to summer.

I always buy really good free-range chickens with lots of flavour. I have tried the maize-fed chickens but thought that they were rather disappointing. They certainly couldn't compare with the local chickens we were already buying. And as for the bland battery-reared chickens with their pappy flesh . . . the least said the better.

If the bird you start off with is of first-rate quality, then there is little to better a simple roast chicken with tarragon. Years ago I would have just mixed plenty of chopped tarragon with butter and smeared it over the skin before popping it in the oven. Now I find it pays to spend an extra five minutes on the preparation; I cut the wishbone out and push the herby butter under the skin, so that it sits right next to the flesh. As it cooks, the scent of the tarragon permeates the whole chicken.

A whole roast chicken is an ideal dish for Sunday lunch in the restaurant – the bird flamed with brandy and a sauce made with cream, stock and pan juices. I like chicken prepared in all sorts of ways – it responds so well to a seemingly endless cavalcade of flavours, from the spices of the East to the gentler creamy sauces of classic French cuisine.

It is often the unexpected arrival of some special ingredient that dictates the way we will be preparing the chicken that day. Last summer, for instance, Nick Coiley, one of the staff at The Carved Angel and a keen mushroom-gatherer, came across a small hoard of chanterelles growing near Old Mill Creek. There were not enough to put on the menu as a first course in their own right, but sufficient to accompany chicken in a creamy sauce. The recipe for Chicken in Jelly with Plums first entered the repertoire when we were faced with a surfeit of sweet, juicy purple plums.

Our local vet rears guinea fowl. Hung for a week or so, they develop an excellent flavour. Guinea fowl has a darker flesh than chicken, and tastes gamier though not as powerful as pheasant. It can be cooked in the same way as chicken – most recipes are interchangeable – and indeed can be used in many recipes which call for pheasant. Ideal if you are cooking for people who find well-hung game just too strong.

Every now and then I develop a particular taste for duck and it features heavily on the menu. Like so much of our meat, it comes from the trusty butcher's, Luscombe's, in Totnes. Their ducks have a good dryness and freshness. They don't carry too much fat – enough to keep the flesh tender as it cooks, but without giving it an unpleasant greasiness. We are also beginning to use Gressingham ducks, which have less fat and more lean meat.

Wild duck, mallard, often come off Slapton Lake, a curious freshwater lake that lies behind Slapton Beach, separated from the sea by a narrow strip of land. The ducks are just large enough to serve two generously and are very good indeed. I always hope that someone I know will be going up to Scotland in August for the start of the shooting season, and be kind enough to bring back a few grouse. Once or twice when I've been cleaning grouse I have found the heather flowers still there in their crops. This moorland diet of heather and berries gives them a special flavour. A rare treat.

Occasionally, there's a call from a huntsman about to set off pigeon-shooting. Would I care to take a few for the restaurant? The answer is invariably 'yes'. They are delicious. The legs are put aside to add to a game pie, and the rest is roasted rare so that the breast stays tender and pink, perfect as the central element of a warm salad.

Though pigeon sells well, there's been less enthusiasm for squabs when I've put them on the menu. Squabs are young, domesticated pigeons, about four weeks old. These ones were bred in Norfolk, though they have yet to make their mark in Britain it seems. I liked them, but maybe people are just too unfamiliar with them still. Nonetheless, I will try again, because they were too good to miss, with a very distinct true flavour, quite different from other poultry birds. It is always disappointing when you get excited about something new and delicious and you can't persuade your customers to try it, but it does bring out the pioneering spirit.

No such problems with pheasant, of course, again provided by a busy local shoot. Hares, on the other hand, are scarce in this area. In fact, a lot of the people down here won't shoot hares at all because they are so rare. So I have to get my supplies from further afield. Dealing with hare is, without doubt, a messy job. The sight can be off-putting, but I always think that it is worse for the onlooker than for the person tackling the hare. And it is certainly worth braving it out, since hare is marvellous value for money.

A single hare can provide a whole suite of meals, without ever becoming monotonous. Begin by cooking the saddle in cream or with grapes and brandy, perhaps. Then you can marinate the legs and shoulder overnight to make a classic *civet de lièvre* or jugged hare, or the more unusual Hare in Chocolate Sauce. Hare gives a superb flavour to game pies, too. All the debris, the head and the odds and ends left over from trimming the joints, can be boiled up to make a wonderfully warming soup. And finally there's the liver, which is just large enough to make pâté (as you would chicken liver pâté) for a light first course for two, three, or at a pinch, four people.

CHICKEN IN JELLY WITH PLUMS

Chicken thighs, cheaper and fuller-flavoured than the pale breasts, are the basis for this late summer fruited galantine. Serve it as a main course, or as part of a selection of charcuterie with spiced fruit (see pages 368 and 371), Apple Mayonnaise or Chinese Plum Sauce (see pages 48 and 49).

SERVES 4–6

8 chicken thighs, skinned and boned
450 g/1 lb plums, halved and stoned
1 shallot, finely chopped
1 tablespoon chopped parsley
1 tablespoon chopped tarragon
1 tablespoon brandy
4 tablespoons dry white wine
12 rashers of unsmoked streaky bacon, rind removed, stretched
with the back of a knife
salt
freshly ground black pepper
6 sheets of leaf gelatine (approximately
11 g /scant ½ oz), soaked, see page 301

Cut the chicken into neat strips. Mix with the plums, shallot, herbs, brandy and wine, and leave to marinate for 4 hours. Lift out the chicken and plums from the marinade.

Line a 1.2 litre/2 pint terrine with the bacon. Arrange a thin layer of chicken and plums on the base. Sprinkle with salt and pepper to taste, then cover with a single layer of gelatine, trimmed to fit without overlapping. Repeat until all the chicken, plums and gelatine are used up. Pour over the marinade. Cover the surface with foil and put on the lid.

Stand the terrine in a roasting tray filled with water to a depth of 2.5 cm/1 inch and bake in a preheated oven, 150°C/

300°F/gas mark 2, for 2 hours, until the juices run clear rather than pink. Lift out of the roasting tray and cool for 2 hours, then leave in the fridge to set. Just before serving, turn out and slice thickly.

PROVENÇALE CHICKEN WITH OLIVES, ANCHOVIES AND TOMATOES

This zippy tomato sauce with its olives, anchovies, and aromatic herbs brings all the heady flavours of Provence to the simplest of chicken dishes. It is best served with plain boiled rice, to soak up the delicious juice.

SERVES 4

FOR THE CHICKEN
2 cloves of garlic, sliced thinly
1 tablespoon thyme, finely chopped
1 tablespoon marjoram, finely chopped
1.4 kg/3 lb chicken, quartered
lemon juice
salt
freshly ground black pepper
2 tablespoons olive oil

FOR THE SAUCE
2 tablespoons olive oil
8 cloves of garlic, chopped
1 sprig of thyme
6 basil leaves
2 sprigs of marjoram
8 anchovy fillets, chopped
1 × 400 g/14 oz can tomatoes, chopped, and their juice
¼ bottle of dry white wine
24 small black olives, pitted

First make the sauce. Heat the oil in a pan and sweat the garlic and herbs for 5 minutes. Add the remaining sauce ingredients – the anchovies will dissolve in the heat – and simmer for 15 minutes. Taste and adjust seasonings.

While the sauce is busy simmering, prepare the chicken pieces. Mix the garlic with the herbs. With a sharp knife, make small slits in the flesh of the chicken and push herb-covered slivers of garlic deep into the cuts. Rub the skin with lemon juice and season to taste with salt and pepper. Heat the oil in a flameproof casserole and brown the chicken pieces. Pour over the hot sauce, cover and bake in a preheated oven, 200°C/400°F/gas mark 6, for 20–30 minutes, until the chicken is cooked. Serve with boiled rice.

CHICKEN WITH
ORANGE AND LEMON

*The sharpness of citrus juice and vinegar is softened by the sweet hint
of caramel and a last-minute dash of cream, to make a superb sauce
for tender grilled chicken and whole pieces of fruit. Serve with
nothing more than a few boiled new potatoes and a green salad.*

SERVES 4

90 g/3½ oz onion, chopped
4 tablespoons lemon juice
2 tablespoons orange juice
7 tablespoons chicken stock, see page 29
4 breasts of chicken or guinea fowl
1 tablespoon granulated sugar
4 tablespoons white wine vinegar
4 tablespoons double cream
salt
freshly ground black pepper

TO FINISH
1 orange
1 lemon

Mix the onion with the lemon and orange juices and stock in a
bowl to make a marinade. Pour over the chicken or guinea
fowl breasts, cover and leave in a cool place for 2 hours. Take
the chicken or guinea fowl out of the dish and transfer the
marinade to a small pan. Simmer gently, covered, for 20
minutes.

Put the sugar with 1 tablespoon cold water into a small pan
over a medium heat, stirring until it has dissolved completely.
Increase the heat and boil without stirring until it caramelizes
to a rich brown. Remove from the heat, tilt the pan away from
you at arm's length and add a dash of the vinegar. Swirl the

pan, and add the rest of the vinegar. Mix with the cooked marinade and process in a processor or blender. Return to the pan and add the cream, and salt and pepper to taste. Reheat and adjust seasonings.

Pare half the zest off the whole orange and lemon in long strips, being careful to avoid the white pith. Blanch in boiling water for 1 minute, and shred. Peel the fruit, taking off as much of the bitter white pith as you can. Separate into segments.

Grill the chicken or guinea fowl breasts for about 10 minutes on each side, until nicely browned and the juices run clear. Divide the sauce between four plates and arrange a chicken breast on each. Decorate with the orange and lemon segments and zest and serve immediately.

GRATIN SAVOYARDE

A delicious way of using up left-over chicken.

cooked chicken
Savoyarde Sauce, see below
50 g/2 oz soft breadcrumbs mixed with 25 g/1 oz melted butter

Tear the chicken into bite-sized pieces and spread in a thick layer in a gratin dish. Cover generously with the sauce and sprinkle over a thick layer of breadcrumbs. Bake in a preheated oven, 200°C/400°F/gas mark 6, for 20–30 minutes, until well-browned and piping hot. Serve immediately.

SAVOYARDE SAUCE

One of Elizabeth David's classic French sauces – a smooth velouté enriched with cream and flavoured with tarragon, cheese and mustard. It makes the perfect partner to Sunday's roast chicken (include the juices from the roasting pan in the stock), but can equally well be used to dress up the left-overs next day.

MAKES 600 ML/1 PINT

40 g/1½ oz butter
40 g/1½ oz flour
215 ml/7½ fl oz strong chicken stock (made by reducing 450 ml/¾ pint stock by half), see page 29
150 ml/¼ pint dry white wine
150 ml/¼ pint double cream
1 teaspoon chopped tarragon
salt
freshly ground black pepper
40 g/1½ oz Jarlsberg cheese, grated
½ tablespoon Dijon mustard

Melt the butter in a pan and stir in the flour to make a *roux*.
Cook gently for 1 minute. Remove the pan from the heat, and
gradually stir in the stock and wine. Finally, add the cream,
tarragon and a little salt and pepper to taste. Return to the heat
and simmer gently for 10 minutes, then stir in the cheese and
the mustard. Taste and adjust seasonings.

Serve with roast chicken, or use in a chicken gratin as above.

Fish Soup with Rouille and Garlic Croûtons

Puff Pastry of Quails' Eggs and Asparagus with Herb and Cream Sauce

Lobster Mallorquina

Pheasant Cooked in Red Wine with Pigs' Trotters

Dartmouth Pie

TOP: *Aubergine Loaf*
BOTTOM: *Aubergines with Pimentos and Lemon*

Ice Bowl with Champagne Sorbet; Rose Petal Sorbet; Geranium and Melon Ice Cream; Strawberry Ice Cream; Basil Ice Cream

TOP: *left to right: Whole Spiced Oranges; Rhubarb and Rose Petal Jam; Elderflower Vinegar; Spiced Apple and Medlar Jelly; Cucumber Pickle; Spiced Vinegar*
BOTTOM: *1eft to right: Pickled Samphire; Spiced Vinegar (two bottles); Marinated Goats' Cheeses; Spiced Damsons; Lemon Chutney*

CHICKEN WITH THREE SPICES

A mildly-spiced and aromatic dish that I first came across when I worked at the Hole in the Wall in Bath. Although I usually make it with chicken, it tastes lovely made with other white meats, too. Try using turkey, pork or veal. The spiced meat with its creamy sauce is delicious alone, but even better with slices of mango, or hot banana fritters.

SERVES 4

1 teaspoon whole cardamom pods
1 teaspoon whole coriander seeds
1 teaspoon whole cumin seeds
25 g/1 oz butter
100 g/4 oz onions, chopped
1 × 1.75 kg/4 lb chicken, quartered, or 4 boned chicken breasts
salt
freshly ground black pepper
150 ml/¼ pint chicken stock, see page 29
150 ml/¼ pint double cream
peeled and sliced mango, or banana fritters, see page 178,
to serve (optional)

Slit the cardamom pods and extract the black seeds. Grind to a fine powder in an electric coffee grinder with the coriander and cumin seeds. Melt the butter in a shallow flameproof casserole and sweat the onions for 5 minutes, until soft. Season the chicken with salt and pepper, and then rub in the spices. Add to the onions and fry without browning for 5 minutes, turning so that each piece is sealed all over.

Cover the casserole tightly and leave in a preheated oven, 150°C/300°F/gas mark 2, for 15–20 minutes, until the chicken is cooked and the juices run clear. Put the chicken pieces on to a warmed serving dish, cover and keep warm.

Lift the casserole back on to a direct heat, add the stock and reduce fast by half. Stir in the cream and reduce by half again. Taste and adjust seasoning, then coat the chicken with the sauce. Arrange the mango slices or banana fritters, if using, around the chicken and serve.

BANANA FRITTERS

SERVES 4

2 bananas, peeled
1 egg, beaten
breadcrumbs
oil for deep-frying

Cut the bananas in half, dip them into the beaten egg, then roll them in breadcrumbs. Leave in the fridge for 30 minutes to firm up. Heat the oil to 180°C/350°F and deep-fry until crisp and golden brown. Drain briefly on kitchen paper.

SPICED CHICKEN WITH PIMENTOS AND ALMONDS

*Cumin and coriander are featured here and in the recipe on page
177, but this dish couldn't be more of a contrast to the last. This one
is a variation of a Madhur Jaffrey recipe from her book* Indian
Cookery *and makes the most marvellous, fragrant curry. I use only
enough cayenne pepper to add a mere hint of heat, but if you prefer
more than just a tingle, increase the quantity to a ¼ or even ½ a
teaspoonful. Serve with a saffron-scented rice.*

SERVES 4

1 tablespoon whole coriander seeds
1 tablespoon whole cumin seeds
100 g/4 oz onions, chopped
2.5 cm/1 inch piece of fresh root ginger, sliced
3 cloves of garlic, sliced
25 g/1 oz blanched almonds
350 g/12 oz red peppers, seeded and sliced
½ teaspoon ground turmeric
1 pinch of cayenne pepper
2 teaspoons salt
7 tablespoons groundnut oil
850 g/1 lb 14 oz boned chicken, cut into finger-sized pieces
250 ml/8 fl oz cold water
2 tablespoons lemon juice

Grind the coriander and cumin seeds to a fine powder in an
electric coffee grinder. Mix with the onions, ginger, garlic,
almonds, peppers, turmeric, cayenne pepper and salt. Process
in small batches in a processor or blender until reduced to a
smooth paste.

Heat the oil in a large, heavy-based frying pan, and add the
paste. Fry, stirring constantly, for 10 minutes until most of the
water has evaporated, leaving a thick paste. Add the chicken,

water and lemon juice. Mix well, and bring to the boil. Taste and add extra lemon juice if necessary. Cover and cook very gently for about 15 minutes until the chicken is tender.

Serve with saffron rice.

BOURRIDE OF CHICKEN

The original Provençal bourride is a fish stew enriched at the last moment with garlicky aïoli. It is the same final touch that confers upon this chicken stew both its name and its marvellous flavour.

SERVES 4

350 g/12 oz leeks, well washed
3 tablespoons oil
225 g/8 oz carrots, sliced
225 g/8 oz onions, sliced
1 × 200 g/7 oz can tomatoes, drained and chopped
2 cloves of garlic, finely chopped
1.25 kg/2½ lb chicken, skinned and quartered
4 strips of orange zest
¼ teaspoon saffron filaments
2 sprigs of thyme
2 sprigs of marjoram
1 bay leaf
150 ml/¼ pint dry white wine
salt
freshly ground black pepper
4 tablespoons aïoli, see page 46
chopped parsley
croûtons fried in olive oil, to serve

Trim the green from the leeks, leaving just the white parts – you should have about 225 g/8 oz – and slice. Heat the oil in a flameproof casserole and sweat the leeks, carrots and onions for 5 minutes, then add the tomatoes and garlic. Stir well and add the chicken, orange zest, saffron, thyme, marjoram and bay leaf.

Simmer gently for 10 minutes, then add the wine, and salt and pepper to taste. Cover tightly, and bake in a preheated oven, 150°C/300°F/gas mark 2, for 25–30 minutes, until the chicken is tender. Lift the chicken on to a heated serving dish and keep warm. Stir the aïoli into the sauce and bring gently to the boil over a direct heat. Remove immediately from the heat, and taste and adjust seasonings. Pour over the chicken, and sprinkle with parsley. Fish out the bay leaf, and serve with croûtons.

GRILLED GUINEA FOWL WITH THYME, MARJORAM AND LEMON

Small guinea fowl split and grilled and eaten in the garden always seem to me to be the very essence of summer. They are delicious cooked on an outdoor barbecue, though you will lose the juices that go to make the light sauce. Make up for the loss by serving them with the Onion and Orange Confit on page 263. Spring chickens can also be cooked in this way.

SERVES 4

2 small guinea fowl, weighing 675–900 g/1½–2 lb each
1 tablespoon chopped marjoram
1 tablespoon chopped thyme
grated zest of ½ lemon
juice of 1 lemon
4 tablespoons virgin olive oil
salt
freshly ground black pepper
4 tablespoons chicken or guinea fowl stock, see page 29

Remove the legs and breasts of each of the guinea fowl, then trim off the winglets. Mix the herbs with the lemon zest. Make small cuts in the flesh of the guinea fowl and put in the herb mixture. Place in a shallow dish. Mix together the lemon juice and oil, and pour over the guinea fowl. Turn so that the pieces are evenly coated. Cover and leave in a cool place overnight.

Season the guinea fowl with salt and pepper and place under a preheated moderate grill for about 8 minutes on each side. Test with a sharp knife near the wing bone – when the juices run clear they are done. Lift out the guinea fowl and keep warm. Put the grill pan over a direct heat. Pour in the stock and bring to the boil, stirring and scraping up all the juices and brown residue. Serve with the guinea fowl.

GOOSE COOKED WITH
TOMATOES AND BRANDY

*All too often goose can be disappointingly tough and greasy. This
method of braising it slowly in the oven ensures that it stays tender
and moist. The initial browning draws out much of the fat, so the
goose won't be too greasy, either. But do make sure that you have, or
can borrow, a casserole or pan large enough (a preserving pan is
ideal) to take the whole bird before you decide to embark on
the recipe.*
*Render down the trimmings of fat and save for later use, perhaps for
sautéed potatoes or fried bread. Wings, feet, neck, and giblets should
be put aside to make the Goose Giblet Stew on page 244.*

SERVES 10–12

1 large goose, weighing about 5.5 kg/12 lb
salt
freshly ground black pepper
900 g/2 lb onions, sliced
15 cloves of garlic, sliced
2 sprigs of thyme
2 sprigs of marjoram
1 tablespoon chopped parsley
1 bottle of dry white wine
2 × 400 g/14 oz cans tomatoes, and their juice
3 tablespoons brandy

TO SERVE
Sugared Onions, see page 185
Chestnuts with Bacon, see page 186

Remove any fat from inside the goose, and trim off wings and
feet. Season well inside and out with salt and pepper. Find a
heavy flameproof casserole large enough to take the goose.
Brown the goose in the casserole, over a gentle heat at first until

the fat begins to run, then increase the heat to colour the skin evenly. Lift out the goose and set aside. Add the onions and garlic to the fat in the pan and fry for 5 minutes. Pour off excess fat, and add the herbs. Stir for a few more minutes, then return the goose to the casserole, breast down.

Add the wine, tomatoes, and salt and pepper to taste. Bring to the boil. Cover and cook in a preheated oven, 140°C/275°F/gas mark 1, for 1 hour. Turn the goose over and reduce the oven temperature to its lowest possible setting. Cook for a further 1½ hours, turning the goose breast down again for the last 30 minutes, until the juices run clear and the drumsticks are tender.

Lift the goose on to a serving dish, still breast down so that it remains moist. Keep warm. Skim off the fat and pass the sauce through a *mouli légumes*, or process briefly in a processor or blender and sieve. Pour into a pan, bring to the boil and reduce over a moderate heat until thick, stirring occasionally. Taste and adjust seasonings, and add the brandy. Carve the goose and spoon a little sauce over the hot meat. Surround with the Sugared Onions and Chestnuts, and pass the rest of the sauce separately.

SUGARED ONIONS

Both these Sugared Onions and the Chestnuts with Bacon that follow are delicious not only with goose, but also with game birds, or even with the Christmas turkey.

SERVES 10–12

900 g/2 lb pickling onions, skinned
25 g/1 oz goose fat or butter
salt
freshly ground black pepper
25 g/1 oz sugar
250 ml/8 fl oz red wine

Arrange the onions in a single layer in a shallow flameproof pan. Dot with goose fat or butter and season with salt and pepper. Cook over a medium heat, shaking the pan from time to time, until evenly browned. Sprinkle with the sugar and continue to cook until the sugar has melted into the fat. Add the red wine, bring to the boil, and cover tightly. Bake in a preheated oven, 150°C/300°F/gas mark 2, for about 15 minutes, until tender.

CHESTNUTS WITH BACON

SERVES 10

450 g/1 lb chestnuts
25 g/1 oz goose fat or butter
50 g/2 oz streaky bacon, cut into strips
chicken stock, see page 29
salt
freshly ground black pepper

With a sharp knife, slash the outer skin of each chestnut. Place in a pan with enough cold water to cover. Bring to the boil, and boil for 1 minute. Remove from the heat and, taking only two or three chestnuts out of the water at a time, when they are just cool enough to handle peel off the outer and inner skins. As the chestnuts cool they become harder to peel, so if necessary return the pan to the heat for a few minutes.

Melt the goose fat or butter in a pan and fry the bacon gently until just cooked. Add the chestnuts, enough stock to cover, and salt and pepper to taste. Bring to the boil, taste and adjust seasonings, then cover tightly and cook in a preheated oven, 150°C/300°F/gas mark 2, for about 15 minutes, until tender.

DUCK BREAST WITH GREEN PEPPERCORNS AND APPLE

Although you can now bring home prepared breasts of duck from both the butcher and the supermarket, a whole duck is often a better buy. Use the breasts straight away, save the plump legs for the next day's supper, make a good strong stock from the bones and debris, and render down the excess fat to use in duck dishes or for sautéed potatoes.

Duck breasts need the briefest of cooking times only – overcooking makes them tough and chewy. Pair with the sweetness of apple and the mild heat of green peppercorns and you can have an excellent meal in under half an hour. Halve quantities for a diner à deux.

SERVES 4

4 × 175 g/6 oz duck breasts, skinned
salt
2 teaspoons green peppercorns, crushed
25 g/1 oz duck fat or butter
1 tablespoon brandy
250 ml/8 fl oz strong duck or chicken stock, see page 29
250 ml/8 fl oz double cream
25 g/1 oz butter
2 Cox's Orange Pippins, cored and sliced

With a sharp knife, score the duck breasts, and sprinkle with salt. Press the peppercorns on to the breasts on both sides. Melt the duck fat or butter in a flameproof casserole and fry the breasts briefly on both sides to seal, then cover and cook in a preheated oven, 190°C/375°F/gas mark 5, for 5 minutes. Pour the brandy over the duck breasts, swirl the pan to heat the brandy gently, then ignite with a match. When the flames have died down, lift the duck on to a heated serving plate and keep warm. Add the stock and cream to the pan and bubble gently until reduced by two-thirds and thick.

Melt the butter in a separate pan and sauté the apple slices briefly. Slice the duck breasts thinly, across the grain. Pour a puddle of sauce on to each plate, and fan out the duck slices on top. Arrange the apple slices round the duck and serve.

DUCK LEGS WITH QUINCES

Another dish of duck with fruit, which is always a pleasing combination. This time I use the more robust legs, and scented quinces. If the duck comes complete with liver, dice it and sauté briefly, then serve on little squares of bread fried in duck fat, alongside the cooked duck.

SERVES 4

1 large or 2 small quince(s)
4 duck legs, trimmed of surplus fat
4 tablespoons brandy
salt
freshly ground black pepper
25 g/1 oz duck fat or butter
1 tablespoon flour
300 ml/½ pint red wine
300 ml/½ pint strong duck stock, see page 29
25 g/1 oz redcurrant jelly
1 strip of orange zest
juice of ½ orange
25 g/1 oz butter

Peel, quarter and core the quince(s). Put the trimmings into a pan with a generous 300 ml/½ pint cold water. Bring to the boil and simmer for 15 minutes. Strain and reserve the juices. Slice the quince quarters thinly and put into a shallow dish with the duck legs and the brandy. Turn to mix well, cover and set aside for 2 hours.

Lift out the duck legs from the marinade and sprinkle with salt and pepper. Melt the duck fat or butter in a pan and fry the legs gently for about 20 minutes, until evenly browned. Pour off nearly all the excess fat. Drain the brandy and juices from the quince slices and pour over the duck legs. Swirl to heat gently, then ignite with a match. When the flames have died down, put the duck legs into a casserole, leaving a little fat behind to make the sauce.

Sprinkle the flour into the fat in the pan, then stir in the reserved quince juice, wine and stock. Bring to the boil and pour into the casserole. Add the redcurrant jelly, orange zest and juice. Cover and cook in a preheated oven, 150°C/300°F/ gas mark 2, for 30–40 minutes, until the legs are cooked.

Melt the butter in a pan and fry the quince slices for 5–10 minutes, until tender. Arrange the duck on a warmed serving dish. Skim the sauce and taste and adjust seasonings. Strain the sauce, pour it over the duck, and surround with the quince slices.

DUCK STUFFED WITH HAM AND OLIVES

This is a very good rich winter dish for a small gathering of friends, or a family Sunday lunch. There's a fair amount of work involved in the preparation, but all that boning and sewing means that it is easy to carve once it reaches the table.

SERVES 4–6

1 duck, boned, see page 382
salt
freshly ground black pepper
40 g/1½ oz duck fat or butter
16 pickling onions, skinned
16 baby carrots
20 button mushrooms
300 ml/½ pint Brown Sauce, see page 42
2 tablespoons Madeira

FOR THE STUFFING
25 g/1 oz duck fat or butter
175 g/6 oz onions, chopped
175 g/6 oz cooked ham, finely chopped
175 g/6 oz mushrooms, finely chopped
18 black olives, pitted
1 duck liver, chopped
2 tablespoons brandy
¼ teaspoon ground allspice
salt
freshly ground black pepper

To make the stuffing, melt the duck fat or butter in a pan and sweat the onions for 5 minutes, until tender, then mix well with all the other stuffing ingredients. Leave to cool.

Spread the duck out flat, skin side down, and season well

with salt and pepper. Pile the stuffing on to the duck, and pat into a thick sausage shape. Enclose in the duck and sew up neatly, tucking the ends in and making sure that there are no gaps. Cover and leave in the fridge overnight.

Season the outside of the duck, melt the fat in a large pan and brown evenly. Lift out and set aside. Brown the onions and carrots in the same fat, then put into a casserole. Lay the duck on the bed of vegetables. Cover and cook in a preheated oven, 140°C/275°F/gas mark 1, for 1½–2 hours, until tender. Add the mushrooms about 15 minutes before the end of the cooking time.

Remove the duck to a heated serving dish and keep warm. Strain off the juices from the casserole and arrange the vegetables round the duck. Skim the fat off the juices, and pour into a pan. Simmer over a steady heat until reduced to 300 ml/½ pint. Add the Brown Sauce and the Madeira and simmer for a further 2 minutes. Taste and adjust seasonings. Pour a little sauce over the vegetables, and serve the rest separately. To serve, slice the duck thickly.

WILD DUCK WITH BLACKCURRANT AND BEETROOT SAUCE

The earthy sweetness of beetroot and blackcurrants marries well with the gamey taste of wild duck. Save the legs to use in a hot game pie, a confit, or the Duck Legs with Quinces on page 189.

SERVES 2

1 wild duck, for example, mallard
salt
freshly ground black pepper
2 tablespoons brandy
300 ml/½ pint duck, game or chicken stock, see page 29
25 g/1 oz redcurrant or apple jelly
50 g/2 oz blackcurrants, topped and tailed
50 g/2 oz cooked beetroot, grated
1 tablespoon crème de cassis

Sever the duck legs and set aside to use for another dish. Sprinkle the duck with salt and pepper, put in a roasting tin and roast in a preheated oven, 230°C/450°F/gas mark 8, for 20 minutes. Pour the brandy over the duck and swirl in the juices to warm. Ignite with a match. When the flames have died down, lift the duck on to a heated serving dish and keep warm.

Place the roasting tin over a direct heat and add the stock. Boil hard until reduced by half, scraping up all the meat juices. Add the jelly, blackcurrants, beetroot and cassis, stir and bring back to the boil. Reduce the heat and simmer very gently for 5 minutes. Taste and adjust seasonings.

Cut the breasts off the duck and carve into thin slices. Crush the carcass of the duck to extract any juices, and add to the sauce. Pour a puddle of sauce on to each plate, and arrange slices of meat in a fan shape on top of the sauce. Serve with game chips – slice some potatoes thinly on a mandoline, wash them in cold water, then dry and deep-fry.

PIGEON (OR VENISON) AND PORT PUDDING

This steamed savoury pudding is made in the same way as a traditional steak and kidney pudding. The long, slow cooking gives the rich flavours of game, port and mushrooms (use the darkest fleshed ones you can get) plenty of time to fuse and create a super gravy. The sweet acidity of redcurrant or quince jelly or the Spiced Apple Jelly (see page 372) is a particularly good accompaniment.

SERVES 4–6

FOR THE PASTRY
225 g/8 oz self-raising flour
100 g/4 oz shredded beef suet
1 tablespoon finely chopped parsley
1 pinch of chopped thyme
1 teaspoon salt
freshly ground black pepper
150 ml/¼ pint cold water, to mix

FOR THE FILLING
225 g/8 oz pigeon breast, sliced, or 225 g/8 oz venison, diced
seasoned flour
1 medium onion, sliced
100 g/4 oz mushrooms, sliced
150 ml/¼ pint port
150 ml/¼ pint game stock, see page 29
2 teaspoons Worcestershire sauce
salt
freshly ground black pepper

To make the pastry, sift the flour into a bowl and mix with the suet, herbs and salt and pepper. Add enough of the cold water to form a firm dough. Butter a 900 ml/1½ pint pudding basin generously. Roll out three-quarters of the pastry on a lightly floured surface, to a circle big enough to line the basin. Lift carefully into the basin, pressing the pastry into the corners so that it fits neatly and allowing a little overhang at the rim.

Toss the pigeon or venison in the seasoned flour, shaking off any excess. Fill the lined basin with alternate layers of onion, mushrooms, and meat, pressing down well. The filling will shrink a little as it cooks so it should be mounded up. Mix the port, stock and Worcestershire sauce, seasoning generously. Pour over the filling to three-quarters of the way up.

Roll out the remaining pastry to form a circle large enough to cover the basin. Brush the edges with water, and lay it over the filling. Trim off the excess pastry and press the edges together to seal. Cover the pudding with greased foil, and tie tightly in place with string, leaving long ends. Knot these to make a handle across the basin. Place the basin on a trivet in a large pan and surround with enough hot water to come halfway up. Cover and steam for 3½ hours. Check every 20 minutes or so that the pan has not boiled dry and keep topping up with boiling water.

To serve, turn out on to a warmed serving dish and cut at table.

PHEASANT COOKED IN RED WINE WITH PIGS' TROTTERS

*Pheasant has a tendency to be a dry meat. Even a young, tender bird
need to be protected with an ample jacket of pork fat or streaky
bacon if it is to stay moist when roasted. It is safer by far to casserole
pheasant of indeterminate age. The inclusion of pigs' trotters and their
stock in this casserole guarantees a wonderful succulence.
This usually makes my Christmas dinner. It is an ideal dish for two
people with hearty appetites and a love of sticky pigs' trotters and
well-hung pheasant.*

Serves 4

25 g/1 oz butter
12 pickling onions, skinned
100 g/4 oz pickled belly of pork, see page 104, or streaky bacon,
cut into strips
1 pheasant, trussed
salt
freshly ground black pepper
2 tablespoons brandy
2 cooked pigs' trotters, split in half, see page 235
12 button mushrooms
1 bouquet garni
300 ml/½ pint pigs' trotter stock, see page 235
300 ml/½ pint red wine

Melt the butter in a flameproof casserole and brown the
onions and belly of pork or bacon for 5 minutes. Remove from
the casserole. Season the pheasant with salt and pepper, then
brown in the butter for about 5 minutes. Return the onions and
pork or bacon to the pan. Pour over the brandy, swirl to heat
gently and ignite with a match.

When the flames have died down, tuck the trotters round the
pheasant and add the mushrooms and the bouquet garni. Pour

in the stock and the wine. Bring to the boil and adjust seasonings. Cover and cook in a preheated oven, 140°C/275°F/gas mark 1, for 30–50 minutes, depending on the age of the bird, until tender. Lift the pheasant on to a warmed serving dish, remove the trussing strings and surround with the vegetables and trotters. Discard the bouquet garni from the casserole. Skim the juices. Taste and adjust seasonings, then pour a little over the vegetables, and serve the rest separately.

PHEASANT IN PASTRY WITH PÂTÉ AND MUSHROOMS

*You could use chicken or guinea fowl in this pastry-wrapped terrine
with a fair degree of success, but I like it best made with pheasant,
which gives such a splendid flavour. The recipe looks lengthy and
involved, but it's worth taking your time over the preparation,
knowing that there's no fiddly carving to be done at the table.*

SERVES 4–6 AS A MAIN COURSE OR 8 AS A FIRST COURSE

1 pheasant
300 ml/½ pint pheasant stock, see recipe
salt
freshly ground black pepper
5 tablespoons Madeira
100 g/4 oz pickled belly of pork, see page 104,
or streaky bacon, diced
50 g/2 oz butter
1 small onion, chopped
100 g/4 oz mushrooms, finely chopped
350 g/12 oz shortcrust pastry, see page 346
50 g/2 oz liver pâté, made with chicken, goose, duck or
pheasant liver – home-made or bought
1 egg, beaten
150 ml/¼ pint Brown Sauce, see page 42
15 g/½ oz butter, chilled and diced

Take the legs and breasts off the pheasant. Remove the meat
from the thigh bones, and set aside. Use the carcass and bones
to make the stock (see page 29). Cut each breast into four thin
slices, season with salt and pepper and drizzle over 1 tablespoon of the Madeira.

Mince the thigh meat with the belly of pork or bacon, then
add 2 tablespoons of the Madeira, and salt and pepper to taste.
Melt the butter in a pan and cook the onion for 5 minutes,

without browning, until soft. Add the mushrooms and cook over a medium heat without browning, stirring constantly, for 5 minutes, until the mushrooms are cooked and the mixture is almost dry. Leave to cool.

Roll out the pastry on a lightly floured surface into a long oblong, roughly 23 × 15 cm/9 × 6 inches. Put half the mushroom *duxelles* mixture in the centre, flattening to form a thick layer. Cover with half the minced meats followed by half the slices of breast. Spread the liver pâté over the breast and continue building up layers with the remaining breast, then minced meats, and finally the last of the *duxelles*. Brush the edges of the pastry with beaten egg and lift them up and over the filling, wrapping it like a parcel. Press the edges together to seal and trim off excess.

Turn the pastry parcel over and place on a baking sheet. Use the pastry trimmings to decorate. Cover loosely and leave to rest in the fridge for at least 30 minutes. Brush with beaten egg, and bake in a preheated oven, 200°C/400°F/gas mark 6, for 20 minutes, until nicely browned. Reduce the heat to 150°C/300°F/gas mark 2 and cook for a further 10–15 minutes.

While the pheasant is cooking, make a sauce by boiling the stock until reduced by two-thirds. Stir in the Brown Sauce and remaining Madeira, simmer for 3 more minutes and add salt and pepper to taste. Finally, whisk in the chilled butter until incorporated. To serve, slice the pastry thickly, and hand round the sauce separately.

PHEASANT WITH CELERY

This is another old favourite that I learnt from George Perry-Smith at the Hole in the Wall. Pheasant, celery and port go together so well – a time-honoured combination that outlives the fleeting fashions of the food world.

SERVES 4

1 pheasant, trussed
salt
freshly ground black pepper
40 g/1½ oz butter
1 small head of celery, cut into 7.5 cm/3 inch lengths
2 rashers of streaky bacon, cut into strips
a generous 150 ml/¼ pint pheasant or chicken stock,
see page 29
300 ml/½ pint port
150 ml/¼ pint double cream

Season the pheasant inside and out with salt and pepper. Melt the butter in a flameproof casserole and brown the pheasant. Lift out the bird and set aside. Sweat the celery and bacon in the fat for 10 minutes. Return the pheasant to the casserole, breast side down. Add the stock, port, and salt and pepper to taste. Bring to the boil, then cover and cook in a preheated oven, 150°C/300°F/gas mark 2, for 30 minutes to 1½ hours, depending on the age of the bird. Arrange the pheasant and celery on a heated serving dish, remove the trussing strings and keep the bird warm.

Place the casserole over a direct heat and cook fast until the juices are reduced by half. Add the cream and reduce again by a third. Taste and adjust seasonings. Serve the sauce with the pheasant.

ROAST RABBIT WITH SPINACH STUFFING

Rabbit is a surprisingly neglected meat in Britain. It is a shame since young, domesticated rabbit, milder in flavour than wild but often more tender, makes a delicious family roast. Ask your butcher to leave in the liver, so that it can be added to the stuffing.

SERVES 4

1 rabbit
10 rashers of unsmoked streaky bacon, rinds removed
450 ml/¾ pint chicken stock, see page 29
1 tablespoon redcurrant jelly
lemon juice
15 g/½ oz butter, chilled and diced

FOR THE STUFFING
40 g/1½ oz butter
1 onion, chopped
450 g/1 lb fresh spinach, well washed
the rabbit liver, finely diced
salt
freshly ground black pepper

To make the stuffing, melt 25 g/1 oz of the butter in a large pan and sweat the onion for 5 minutes, until tender. Add the spinach, cover and cook for a further 5 minutes, until it has just collapsed. Melt the remaining butter in a separate pan and sauté the liver quickly. Add to the spinach and season well with salt and pepper. Leave to cool.

Fill the rabbit cavity with the stuffing and sew up or secure with wooden toothpicks. Sit the rabbit neatly in a roasting tin, tucking the legs underneath. Cover with the bacon. Roast in a preheated oven, 190°C/375°F/gas mark 5, for 45 minutes. Lift the rabbit on to a heated serving dish and let it rest in a warm oven while you make the gravy.

Set the roasting tin over a direct heat and add the stock, redcurrant jelly and a dash of lemon juice. Bring to the boil, scraping up all the residues. Boil until reduced by half, then taste and adjust seasonings. Strain quickly, and whisk in the chilled butter until incorporated. Carve the rabbit and serve with a spoonful of the stuffing and the gravy.

RABBIT WITH SAFFRON AND CUCUMBER

This is a dish that looks as good as it tastes, with its saffron-yellow sauce and garnish of cucumber and barely cooked tomato. It comes originally from Richard Olney's Simple French Food.

SERVES 4

1 rabbit, jointed, see page 384, with liver
salt
freshly ground black pepper
3 tablespoons olive oil
1 large onion, sliced
6 cloves of garlic, halved
½ teaspoon granulated sugar
1 tablespoon flour
½ teaspoon saffron filaments
300 ml/½ pint dry white wine
300 ml/½ pint chicken stock, see page 29
1 cucumber
40 g/1½ oz butter
225 g/8 oz tomatoes, skinned, seeded and chopped

Set the rabbit liver aside, and season the rabbit joints with salt and pepper. Heat the oil in a flameproof casserole and cook the rabbit gently with the onion and garlic for 10 minutes, until the onion is tender. Sprinkle the sugar and flour over the rabbit, and turn the meat and vegetables so that the flour is evenly distributed. Add the saffron to the casserole and then pour in the wine and stock. Cover tightly and cook in a preheated oven, 150°C/300°F/gas mark 2, for 40–50 minutes, until tender.

Lift out the rabbit and place on a heated serving dish. Keep warm. Pass the sauce through a *mouli légumes* or process briefly in a processor or blender and sieve. Taste and adjust seasonings, then pour the sauce over the rabbit.

While the rabbit is cooking, prepare the cucumber. Peel, and halve lengthways. Scoop out the seeds with a teaspoon or an apple corer. Slice into 6 mm/¼ inch thick crescents. At the last minute melt 25 g/1 oz of the butter in a pan and sauté the cucumber for 3 or 4 minutes, then add the tomatoes, and salt and pepper to taste and heat through briefly. Cut the reserved liver into strips and sauté in the remaining butter in a separate pan. Arrange the cucumber, tomato, and liver round the cooked rabbit and serve.

HARE IN CHOCOLATE SAUCE

We usually associate chocolate with puddings and sweets, but used in moderation it lends itself well to strong savoury dishes. In Italy and Spain it is often used to give an almost unidentifiable flavour to game dishes. In this recipe, it blends subtly with the pine kernels, candied peel and sultanas, to produce a delicious, mahogany brown sauce for hare. Serve with plain or parsley noodles.

If you only have the front and back legs of a single hare, and want to make this dish for two, halve all the ingredients except for the sugar and vinegar, but add only half of the caramelized vinegar syrup to the sauce – it's well nigh impossible to caramelize ½ tablespoon sugar on its own without burning it. You may find that you have to add a little extra stock.

SERVES 4–6

1 hare (front and back legs plus saddle), or the front and back legs of 2 hares, setting the saddles aside for roasting,
see page 384
seasoned flour
50 g/2 oz dripping
50 g/2 oz streaky bacon, cut into strips
1 onion, chopped
450 ml/¾ pint chicken stock, see page 29
salt
freshly ground black pepper
1 tablespoon granulated sugar
75 ml/3 fl oz white wine vinegar
50 g/2 oz candied peel, chopped
50 g/2 oz pine kernels
50 g/2 oz sultanas
50 g/2 oz bitter or bitter-sweet chocolate, grated

FOR THE MARINADE
450 ml/¾ pint red wine
1 onion, chopped
1 carrot, sliced
1 tablespoon chopped parsley
2 sprigs of thyme
1 bay leaf

Joint the hare. If you are just using legs, cut them all in half. Mix together all the marinade ingredients in a shallow bowl and pour over the hare. Cover and leave in a cool place overnight. Lift out the hare, drain well, and pat dry with kitchen paper. Strain and reserve the marinade. Dust the hare with seasoned flour, melt the dripping in a pan and brown the hare. Put the hare into a casserole.

Add the bacon and onion to the fat in the pan and fry for 5 minutes, then add the reserved marinade and the stock. Season to taste with salt and pepper and bring to the boil. Pour over the hare. Cover tightly and cook in a preheated oven, 150°C/300°F/gas mark 2, until tender – 45 minutes to 1½ hours, depending on the age of the hare.

Put the sugar with 1 tablespoon cold water into a small pan over a medium heat and stir until it has completely dissolved. Increase the heat and boil until it caramelizes to a rich brown. Remove from the heat, tilt the pan away from you at arm's length and add a little of the vinegar. Swirl the pan and add the rest of the vinegar. Pour into the casserole and add the remaining ingredients. Shake the casserole gently to mix, and return to the oven for a further 5–10 minutes. Taste and adjust seasonings and serve.

SADDLE OF HARE
COOKED IN CREAM

My favourite way with a saddle of hare – a real treat. It is a slightly simplified version of a recipe from Elizabeth David's French Provincial Cooking. *I serve it with a dish of Hot Grated Beetroot (see page 264) and a purée of celeriac and potatoes (see page 258). Cut the saddle of hare to include the ribs as well – that way you get two really substantial portions. Don't worry about the curdled appearance of the sauce before it is reduced. As it boils down it will regain an even, glossy appearance.*

SERVES 2

1 saddle of hare
2 shallots, chopped
300 ml/½ pint double cream
2 tablespoons white wine vinegar
salt
freshly ground black pepper
1 tablespoon redcurrant jelly

Skin the saddle – you will find that there are two layers. The first, the skin proper, is loose and easy to remove. The second is a thin, silvery membrane, which clings more tenaciously (see page 385). Put the skinned saddle into a casserole that fits it closely.

Scatter the shallots over the meat, and then pour in the cream and vinegar. Cover and cook in a preheated oven, 140°C/275°F/gas mark 1, for 1–1½ hours, until tender. Lift the saddle on to a heated serving dish and keep warm. Pour the sauce into a pan, add a little salt and pepper to taste, and the redcurrant jelly. Boil hard until the sauce has reduced and is thick.

Carve the saddle into long, thin slices, not forgetting the fillet underneath, and serve with the sauce.

SADDLE OF HARE WITH GRAPES AND BRANDY

A saddle of hare is the ideal joint of meat for two people, and is tender enough (provided the animal wasn't too elderly to begin with) to roast quickly at a high temperature. Add this cream and grape sauce as well, and you have an unashamedly luxurious meal ahead of you.

SERVES 2

1 saddle of hare, skinned, see page 384
salt
freshly ground black pepper
4 rashers of green streaky bacon, rinds removed
2 tablespoons brandy
150 ml/¼ pint game or chicken stock, see page 29
2 tablespoons port
150 ml/¼ pint double cream
24 black and/or white grapes, halved and pipped

Season the saddle with salt and pepper. Lay the bacon over the hare to protect the meat. Put the saddle into a roasting tin and roast in a preheated oven, 220°C/425°F/gas mark 7, for 15–20 minutes. Heat the brandy gently in a small pan, then pour over the hare and ignite with a match. When the flames die down, lift the saddle on to a heated serving dish and rest it in the warm oven, with the heat turned off and the door slightly ajar.

Add the stock to the roasting pan with the port, cream, and salt and pepper to taste. Bring to the boil and reduce hard until thick. Taste and adjust seasonings, then add the grapes.

Carve the saddle into long thin slices, not forgetting the fillet underneath. The meat should still be really pink. Stir any juices into the sauce. Serve the sauce with the slices of hare and the crisp bacon.

Meat

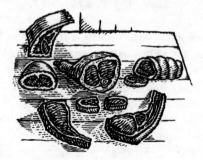

I deal mainly with three local butchers. There are two small family-run butchers here in Dartmouth. Shillabeer is the old established one where I buy beef and pork fillet, marrow bones and oxtail, and then there is Cutmore The Butchers – straight out of Happy Families – who have fresh lambs' sweetbreads in the summer.

Luscombe's are in Totnes, and are one of the best traditional butchers I know. They keep a proper brine tub, rear much of their own pork, and will get what they call 'long leg chickens', chickens which are kept for a week before gutting, to develop a deeper flavour.

The staff at all three butchers are highly skilled, and proud of that skill. They know how to cut and trim, and to prepare meat properly. Luscombe's have a huge wooden table right in the middle of the shop, where they do all the butchering of smaller joints, on demand. You get the best of both worlds here: precisely the cut of meat you need, neatly finished, and friendly personal service, too. It makes shopping a slower process, but it saves time and trouble later on in the kitchen.

It is a shame that not all butchers are like this. It pays good dividends to search out and patronize a professional butcher of this sort, one who is not merely set on beating the supermarkets at their own game. The initial preparation, if well done, minimizes work, cooking times and potential disaster.

I get most of our pork from Luscombe's. It is fatter than today's fashion dictates, so has a superb flavour, and is very tender. In fact, it bears scant resemblance to the tough, stringy pork many people are used to eating. It is a meat that has fallen into disfavour in recent years, partly because of this breeding out of taste, and the current enthusiasm for undercooked meats. When you do get hold of a well-reared piece of pork, its succulence can come as quite a surprise.

Luscombe's hams are also delicious – they cure them themselves and have them smoked down in Cornwall. We take one from them two or three times a year. Ham, too, has been appallingly degraded and devalued by commercialization. Those watery, thin slices of packaged ham have nothing in common with a dry, thick slice of traditional ham, with its deep layer of fat and glorious smell. Unfortunately, the cheap package ham seems to have made people deeply suspicious – I recently tried out on the menu a dish of superb ham with spiced apricots and a honey and cider sauce. It was a busy Sunday lunch, and not a single person ordered it.

There is always one steak or entrecôte on the menu, but I find that the demand for beef has dropped considerably. Even the Sunday lunchers tend less and less towards roast beef. It is a pity, since it is rare that a family these days can afford to cook the large joints of beef that made roast beef and Yorkshire pudding such a triumph. In a restaurant, on the other hand, if we could be sure of selling enough of it, it would be ideal. Although I don't feel strongly about veal, almost without thinking about it, I have stopped using it.

Local lamb is plentiful and of prime quality. I usually take the loin, to be boned and made into a neat tournedos, the best end, or the hind leg for steaks that may be plainly grilled, marinated first with a few herbs perhaps. Whenever I can, I buy laver, a Welsh seaweed, to serve with the lamb, maybe as croquettes or as a purée sharpened with orange. This is one of those perfect combinations, at least it is for those who like the taste and texture of the laver.

More unusual is the kid reared by Mr Martin from Gara Bridge, who supplies us with it in addition to goats' cheese (see page 218). Kid is a very mild meat, somewhere between lamb and veal, and is something that I look forward to. Like all meat, it does need to be hung for a week or so – not long enough to develop a gamey taste, but just enough time for the meat to relax. I use the forequarters, shoulder and belly for blanquettes or perhaps for an osso bucco-type dish. The hind legs are divided into larger joints to roast, some on the bone, possibly for a Sunday lunch, or boned with herbs and lemon to be served with a fruit jelly.

QUOORMA LAMB CURRY

This is a mild, aromatic curry, scented with the perfume of ginger, coriander and cardamom. What hotness it has comes from crushed black peppercorns, not the fiercer chilli peppers or powder.

SERVES 4

450 g/1 lb trimmed, boned shoulder of lamb
½ tablespoon grated fresh root ginger
salt
50 g/2 oz butter
2 onions, sliced
2 cloves of garlic, chopped
1 level teaspoon whole cardamom pods
1 teaspoon whole coriander seeds
1 teaspoon black peppercorns
1 level teaspoon whole cloves
50 g/2 oz creamed coconut, grated
50 g/2 oz double cream
½ teaspoon ground turmeric
1 teaspoon granulated sugar
25 ml/1 fl oz lemon juice

Cut the lamb into 4 cm/1½ inch cubes. Mix well with the ginger and a little salt. Melt the butter in a pan and sweat the onions and garlic for 5 minutes. Slit the cardamom pods and extract the black seeds. Grind to a powder in an electric coffee grinder with the coriander seeds, peppercorns and cloves. Sprinkle the spices over the onions and garlic and continue to cook for 1 minute.

Add the meat and the remaining ingredients to the pan. Mix well, cover, and cook very gently until the meat is tender – this may take anything from 30 minutes to 1 hour. Check occasionally and add a little water if it seems dry. Taste and adjust seasonings. Serve with rice.

LOIN OF LAMB STUFFED WITH KIDNEYS

The warm scent of the basil in the mousseline stuffing permeates the joint of lamb through and through. The filled roll of lamb is quickly cooked and easy to carve.

SERVES 5

2 lambs' kidneys
salt
freshly ground black pepper
25 g/1 oz butter
1 loin of lamb, boned
1 egg white
6 large basil leaves
100 ml/4 fl oz double cream
300 ml/½ pint lamb stock, see page 30
150 ml/¼ pint red wine

Skin and halve the kidneys and cut out the tough white core. Slice thinly and season to taste. Melt the butter in a pan and sauté the kidneys quickly, keeping them rare. Set aside.

Cut the fillet from the piece of lamb, weigh and add enough of the best trimmings from the loin to make up to 100 g/4 oz. Set this meat aside to make the mousseline. Turn the loin over, and very carefully trim off the skin and excess fat.

Chop the reserved 100 g/4 oz lamb roughly and process with the egg white and basil in a processor or blender until smooth. Rub through a fine sieve, then chill for 30 minutes. Beat in the cream. Add salt and pepper to taste, to form a mousseline. Stir in the sautéed kidneys.

Spread this mixture down the centre of the loin, and roll the meat round it. Tie with string at 5 cm/2 inch intervals along the length of the loin to secure. Leave to rest for at least 30 minutes in a cool place.

Sit the stuffed loin in a roasting tin, season with salt and pepper and roast in a preheated oven, at 230°C/450°F/gas mark 8, for 20 minutes. Lift the meat on to a heated serving plate and keep warm. Place the roasting tin over a direct heat to set the essence. Pour off excess fat. Add the stock and wine and bubble hard, stirring and scraping all the meaty residues into the liquids, until reduced by half. Strain. To serve, remove the string and carve the meat into 2.5 cm/1 inch slices. Pour a little of the sauce round it and serve the remainder separately.

BEST END OF LAMB WITH ROSEMARY CREAM SAUCE AND LAVER CROQUETTES

SERVES 2–3

1 best end of lamb
1 sprig of rosemary
salt
freshly ground black pepper
150 ml/¼ pint lamb stock, see page 30
150 ml/¼ pint single cream
½ teaspoon finely chopped rosemary
Laver Croquettes, see page 265

When buying your lamb, ask your butcher to remove the chine bone and nerve. Trim off the dry skin and the excess fat, leaving a thin layer next to the meat. Trim the cutlet bones so that they are all the same length. Score the fat in a diamond pattern to help it crisp up as it cooks. Press the sprig of rosemary well into the exposed meaty side of the joint. Allow to stand for 1 hour.

Put the lamb into a roasting tin and season with salt and pepper. Roast in a preheated oven, 230°C/450°F/gas mark 8, for 20 minutes. Lift the lamb on to a warmed serving dish and leave in the oven, with the heat turned off, door ajar, to relax for at least 5 minutes.

Pour off any surplus fat from the roasting tin, and set the tin over a direct heat. Add the stock, cream and chopped rosemary. Bring to the boil and let it bubble hard, stirring and scraping up all the meaty residues, until reduced by half. Strain, then taste and adjust seasonings. Carve the lamb, adding any juices in the dish to the sauce.

Serve with the sauce and Laver Croquettes, or ratatouille.

DARTMOUTH PIE

We found a sketchy recipe for Dartmouth Pie in Cassell's Dictionary
of Food. *It was more a description than a recipe, in fact – a mutton
pie with spices. We worked on the idea, fleshing it out with memories
of a venison and dried fruit pie that we used to make at the Hole in
the Wall, and this was the result. The well-spiced seasoning and
natural sweetness of the dried fruit give it an almost medieval air.
If you can't get real mutton, substitute well-hung beef or venison
rather than lamb – you need a meat that will stand up to the
concentrated flavours of spice and fruit.*

SERVES 6

900 g/2 lb mutton, trimmed
salt
2 level teaspoons black peppercorns
1 blade whole mace
1 level teaspoon whole allspice berries
5 cm/2 inch stick of cinnamon
2 teaspoons whole coriander seeds
dripping
450 g/1 lb onions, sliced
1 tablespoon flour
450 ml/¾ pint mutton or beef stock, see page 30
150 g/5 oz dried apricots
150 g/5 oz prunes, pitted
100 g/4 oz raisins
juice and grated zest of 1 orange (preferably a Seville orange)
225 g/8 oz shortcrust pastry, see page 346
1 egg, beaten

Cut the meat into 2.5 cm/1 inch cubes. Salt lightly. Grind the
peppercorns, mace, allspice, cinnamon, and coriander seeds to
a powder in an electric coffee grinder. Melt the dripping in a
large pan, brown the meat, then sprinkle with the spices. Cook

for 1 more minute and add the onions and the flour. Mix well, and pour in the stock. Stir and bring to the boil.

Put the fruit into a casserole and add the zest and juice of the orange. Tip in the contents of the pan and mix well. Cover tightly. Cook in a preheated oven, 150°C/300°F/gas mark 2, for 1½–2 hours, until the meat is very tender. Taste and adjust seasonings and leave to cool. Put the meat and vegetables into a deep 1.2 litre/2 pint pie dish, round a pie funnel.

Roll out the pastry on a lightly floured surface to 4 mm/⅛ inch thickness. Cut a 2.5 cm/1 inch strip long enough to go all the way round the edge of the pie dish. Brush the edges of the dish with water and lay the strip round the rim of the dish. Brush the strip with water and lay the remaining pastry over the pie, supported by the funnel, pressing down the edges to seal. Trim the edges, and make a hole in the centre to allow the steam to escape. Use the trimmings to make decorations, place on the pie and brush with beaten egg. Bake at 200°C/400°F/gas mark 6 for 30 minutes, until golden brown. Reduce the heat to 180°C/350°F/gas mark 4 and cook for a further 20 minutes. Serve immediately.

BLANQUETTE OF KID
WITH SORREL

*Mr Martin keeps goats for their milk, rather than their meat. He has
a huge business in goats' cheese and milk – we preserve his smaller
cheeses in oil with herbs and garlic.*

*Like lamb, kid is a spring meat, milky-pink with a
delicate flavour. We will roast some of the meat as whole joints, and
stew the shoulder with tiny spring vegetables in this pale blanquette.*

SERVES 6

900 g/2 lb boned kid, diced
2 tablespoons lemon juice
1 bouquet garni
salt
white pepper
lamb stock, see page 30
18 pickling onions
18 baby carrots
3 sticks of celery, cut into pieces about
2.5 cm/1 inch long
butter
flour
50 g/2 oz fresh sorrel, washed thoroughly,
shredded and thick stalks discarded
100 ml/¼ pint double cream
2 egg yolks

Put the kid into a pan with the lemon juice, and add enough
cold water to cover. Bring to the boil, then drain. Rinse the
meat in cold water to remove any scum. Place in a flameproof
casserole with the bouquet garni, salt and white pepper to taste
and enough stock to cover generously. Bring to the boil and
simmer very gently until just tender – about 45 minutes.

Meanwhile, pour boiling water over the onions and leave for

30 seconds. Drain and refresh under the cold tap. The skins should now come away easily. Add the peeled onions to the kid when it has been simmering for about 15 minutes. Follow with the carrots and celery 15 minutes later.

When the kid and vegetables are cooked, pour off the liquid and set the kid and vegetables aside. Strain the liquid through a muslin-lined sieve and measure. To each 600 ml/1 pint allow 25 g/1 oz butter and 25 g/1 oz flour. Melt the butter in a pan and stir in the flour. Cook for 1 minute, then remove from the heat and gradually stir in the cooking liquid. Return to the heat, bring to the boil and simmer for 15 minutes. Taste and season with salt and white pepper and, if necessary, a little extra lemon juice. Pour over the kid and vegetables, add the sorrel and mix well. Bring the whole lot back to the boil and simmer gently for 5 minutes. Remove from the heat.

Whisk the cream with the egg yolks in a large bowl until thoroughly amalgamated. Gradually beat in, spoonful by spoonful, about 300 ml/½ pint hot sauce from the kid. Now pour this mixture back into the casserole, shaking gently to mix completely. Serve immediately, or keep warm for up to 30 minutes in a cool oven, without boiling.

ESCALOPE OF PORK
WITH TAPENADE

*Tapenade, a paste of olives and anchovies, mustard and capers, brings
the bite of the South of France to this dish, mellowed by breadcrumbs,
and thick tomato sauce.*

SERVES 4

575 g/1¼ lb pork fillet, trimmed
½ quantity of Tapenade, see page 60
2 eggs, beaten
dry breadcrumbs
olive oil for frying
600 ml/1 pint thick Tomato Sauce, see page 54

Cut the pork at a slant across the grain into twelve slices. Spread
one side of each slice with Tapenade. Dip into the beaten egg
and coat in crumbs. Leave in the fridge for 30 minutes or so to
firm up.

Heat some oil in a pan and fry the pork escalopes for 5 minutes on each side, until nicely browned. Heat through the
Tomato Sauce, make a bed of sauce on a warmed serving dish,
and lay the escalopes on top. Serve with buttered noodles.

LOIN OF PORK WITH RHUBARB

*This is a dish we first tried when we had an abundance of rhubarb,
far too much to relegate to jams and puddings alone. The acidity of
the rhubarb counteracts the richness of the pork. In the autumn, we
use plums instead of rhubarb in this sauce, and the effect is similar.*

SERVES 8

1 wide strip of orange zest
1.75 kg/4 lb chine or best end of pork, chined and skinned – ask
the butcher to do this for you
chopped parsley
salt
freshly ground black pepper
450 ml/¾ pint dry white wine
450 ml/¾ pint stock made from the skin and bones, see page 30
225 g/8 oz granulated sugar
450 g/1 lb rhubarb

Blanch the orange zest in boiling water for 2 minutes. Drain,
and shred. With a sharp knife, make small cuts in the meat and
the fat along the bones, and push the orange zest and a little
parsley into the cuts with the handle of a teaspoon. Season with
salt and pepper. Sit the pork, fat side down, in a roasting tin and
pour over the wine. Leave in a cool place for about 4 hours,
basting occasionally. Add the stock to the tin and roast in a
preheated oven, 190°C/375°F/gas mark 5, for 1 hour. Turn the
pork over and roast for a further 30 minutes.

About 15 minutes before the pork is cooked, place the sugar
in a pan with 600 ml/1 pint cold water. Stir over a low heat
until the sugar has dissolved, then bring to the boil without stirring. Simmer for 5 minutes. Trim the rhubarb and cut into 5
cm/2 inch lengths. Drop into the sugar syrup, bring back to a
simmer and poach gently for 2–3 minutes until just tender but
not collapsing. Drain and keep warm.

Lift the meat on to a warmed serving dish and arrange the rhubarb round it. Strain the meat juices and skim off the fat. Moisten the pork with a little of the juices and serve the remainder separately.

CARRÉ OF PORK PROVENÇALE

SERVES 8

1.75 kg/4 lb chine or best end of pork, chined and skinned –
ask the butcher to do this for you
2 cloves of garlic, sliced
2 tablespoons chopped herbs (parsley, marjoram, thyme, basil,
1 sprig of rosemary, for example)
salt
freshly ground black pepper
450 ml/¾ pint red wine
450 ml/¾ pint stock made from the skin and bones, see page 30

FOR THE CRUMB TOPPING
100 g/4 oz soft white breadcrumbs
1 clove of garlic, very finely chopped
1 tablespoon chopped herbs

Trim the excess fat from the loin. With a sharp knife, cut small slits in the meat and, using the end of a teaspoon, push in the slivers of garlic and the herbs. Sprinkle with salt and pepper. Sit the pork in a roasting tin, fat side down, and pour over the wine. Leave in a cool place for 4 hours, basting or turning occasionally. Add the stock to the tin, and roast the meat in a preheated oven, 190°C/375°F/gas mark 5, for 1½ hours.

Mix together evenly the ingredients for the crumb topping. Turn the pork over, and press the crumb mixture firmly on to the fat. Skim some of the fat from the cooking juices, and use to baste the crumbs. Return the meat to the oven, and cook for a further 30 minutes, until the crumbs are nicely browned and crisp. Lift the pork on to a warmed serving dish and strain the cooking juices. Skim off the fat, and serve the juices as a sauce with the meat.

Offal

Offal and the extremities (pigs' trotters and ears, oxtail) are things that most people either have a passion for, or loathe beyond measure. I have a few customers who come here regularly to eat their fill of offal – one recently started a meal with grilled pigs' trotters, moving straight to the plate of mixed offal for his main course. Wine merchant Bill Baker is another keen offal man, though even he balked at the offer of half a grilled sheep's head!

On the whole, people are much more enterprising about what they will eat these days, although there are plenty who still have their reservations, or who would turn their noses up at the very thought of tackling sweetbreads, let alone a pig's trotter or grilled, crumbed ear. Little do they know what they are missing. On the Continent, these treats are rarely overlooked. Scan the display at a charcuterie in France and there is likely to be a tray of precooked trotters, neatly coated in breadcrumbs, just waiting to be taken home and grilled. Here in England, a demand for these odds and ends tends to be met with raised eyebrows and a bemused smile from the average butcher. You will have to do all the precooking yourself, but at least the price is low.

Offal and extremities fall neatly into two camps: those that demand long slow cooking, including tripe, oxtail, tongue, trotters and ears, and those that need very little at all – liver, kidneys, brains and sweetbreads, though the last two do need a fair amount of soaking and preparation.

Tongue, usually ox tongue, takes long, gentle simmering, and is worth every minute of it. Freshly cooked tongue has a superb taste and texture, both of which are quite absent in the dull packaged slices. Serve it hot or cold with a piquant sauce of some kind – the Chinese Plum Sauce on page 49 is just the thing with a plate of cold sliced tongue. I occasionally cook tripe, but maybe not often enough. It's hard to get uncured tripe and much of the prepared stuff doesn't really have a great deal of flavour.

In winter rich, slow-cooked oxtail stews are marvellous, with their thick savoury gravy. They need two hours in a low oven at the very least, and benefit from even longer cooking, until the meat collapses off the bone. Undercooked oxtail is a disaster, tough and unpleasant, so always allow plenty of time, or cook in advance and reheat thoroughly before serving (which has the added advantage that you can scoop off any congealed fat that has collected on the surface). Once the stew is under way, you only need to cast a glance at it every hour or so, giving it a quick stir, just to make sure that it isn't cooking too fast or drying out.

In total contrast, liver and kidneys require minimal amounts of cooking and are quite destroyed if they are overdone, toughening up and acquiring that unpleasant acrid taste. Calves' liver is best of all, so tender that it can be eaten with a fork. From time to time I can buy kids' liver, which is almost as good, sweet and mild. I keep the cooking simple – usually just cutting it into strips and frying briefly in butter with garlic, parsley and lemon as a first course. Fresh lambs' liver is pleasant enough, and can be used instead of calves' if necessary, but it isn't in the same class.

As with liver, calves' brains and sweetbreads are the best, but not always easy to lay your hands on, and more expensive than lamb or ox. Since they need to be soaked for some hours before brief cooking, and pressing (though you can get away with omitting this last stage), some forethought is required. Start preparation in the morning for the evening meal, or the night before if they are to be served for lunch.

CALVES' LIVER WITH GIN AND LIME SAUCE

*The ingredients list makes bizarre reading, but the final result,
forceful though it may be, is quite excellent with tender calves' liver.
The sauce hails from John Tovey's restaurant, Miller Howe.*

SERVES 4

575 g/1¼ lb calves' liver, sliced
1 tablespoon lemon juice
salt
freshly ground black pepper
butter for frying

FOR THE SAUCE
15 g/½ oz butter
1 small onion, chopped
2 tablespoons apricot jam
1 teaspoon tomato purée
450 ml/¾ pint beef stock, see page 30
juice and finely grated zest of 3 limes
1 tablespoon cornflour
2 teaspoons white wine vinegar
2 tablespoons gin
½ teaspoon Moutarde de Meaux
Worcestershire sauce
salt

To make the sauce: melt the butter in a pan and sweat the
onion for 5 minutes, until tender. Add the jam, tomato purée,
stock, lime zest and juice and bring to the boil. Mix together
the cornflour and vinegar, then add a tablespoon of the hot
liquid. Pour back into the pan and stir. Simmer for 5 minutes,
then strain and return to the pan. Add the gin, mustard,
Worcestershire sauce and salt to taste.

Season the calves' liver with the lemon juice, and salt and pepper to taste. Melt some butter in a frying pan and sauté the liver for 2–3 minutes on each side. The liver should still be pink on the inside. Serve with the sauce.

TO PREPARE SWEETBREADS

The sweetbreads we buy are either the very expensive calves' sweetbreads from the wholesale butcher, or the rather more reasonably priced lambs' sweetbreads from the summer lambs, which are sold by the local butcher.

Whichever sort you buy, sweetbreads need first to be soaked in cold water for about 2 hours to dissolve any bloody patches. Drain well then put the sweetbreads into a pan with enough chicken stock (see page 29) to cover and a little salt. Bring to the boil and simmer very gently until tender. The larger calves' sweetbreads will take about 30 minutes, while smaller lambs' sweetbreads need only 15 or so minutes. Test by piercing with a kitchen fork – the juices that run out should be clear rather than pink. Leave the sweetbreads to cool in the stock.

Calves' sweetbreads often have fat and sinew that will need to be removed, and sometimes the lambs' sweetbreads need to be trimmed of fat as well. Once the sweetbreads are cool and have been trimmed, if necessary, drain and lay them out on a tray. Put another tray on top and weight down with light weights or tins. Leave under the weights for 2–3 hours – this makes them easier to slice.

ESCALOPE OF CALVES' SWEETBREADS WITH PIQUANT SAUCE

SERVES 4

450 g/1 lb cooked calves' sweetbreads,
sliced, see page 229
2 eggs, beaten
soft breadcrumbs
clarified butter, see page 23, for frying
450 ml/¾ pint Brown Piquant Sauce, see page 43

Dip each sweetbread into the beaten egg and then coat in the breadcrumbs. Leave in the fridge for 30 minutes to firm up. Heat some butter in a pan and fry the sweetbreads for 10 minutes, until nicely browned on all sides. Reheat the Piquant Sauce thoroughly and serve with the sweetbreads.

A PUFF PASTRY OF SWEETBREADS AND MUSHROOMS WITH MARSALA

SERVES 4

175 g/6 oz puff pastry, see page 347
1 egg, beaten
1 teaspoon poppy seeds
225 g/8 oz cooked lambs' sweetbreads, see page 229
40 g/1½ oz butter
100 g/4 oz mushrooms, sliced
lemon juice
salt
freshly ground black pepper
50 ml/2 fl oz Marsala
50 ml/2 fl oz lamb stock, see page 30
25 g/1 oz butter, chilled and diced

Roll out the puff pastry on a lightly floured surface into an oblong about 40 × 15 cm/16 × 6 inches. Trim the edges and cut into four 10 × 15 cm/4 × 6 inch rectangles. Lay the pastry on a baking sheet and leave in the fridge to relax for 30 minutes. Brush with beaten egg and sprinkle with poppy seeds. Bake in a preheated oven, 240°C/475°F/gas mark 9, for 5–10 minutes, until well risen and golden brown. Split each rectangle in half, horizontally, to give a base and a lid, and place each base on a warmed serving plate. Keep bases and lids warm.

While the pastry is cooking, slice the sweetbreads. Melt the first lot of butter in a pan and sauté the sweetbreads and mushrooms for 5 minutes. Add a dash of lemon juice, and salt and pepper to taste. Stir in the Marsala and stock, increase the heat and bubble until reduced by a third. Taste and adjust seasonings then whisk in the chilled butter until incorporated. Spoon on to the four bases, top with the lids and serve.

OX TONGUE WITH PIQUANT CREAM SAUCE, BEETROOT AND CELERIAC

Luscombe's, the local butchers, keep a huge brine tub for curing pork, beef and ox tongue to order, though we do brine our own belly of pork and pigs' trotters.

A home-cooked tongue, with its velvety melting texture and meaty flavour, bears little resemblance to the tasteless, ready-sliced vacuum packs of tongue that have become all too commonplace. With the piquant sauce, celeriac and beetroot it becomes a dish for celebrations.

SERVES 6–8

1 brined ox tongue, see page 104
2 onions, sliced
2 carrots, sliced
2 sticks of celery, sliced
1 teaspoon black peppercorns
2 sprigs of thyme
6 parsley stalks
2 bay leaves

TO SERVE
Piquant Cream Sauce, see page 40
Celeriac Purée, see page 258
Hot Grated Beetroot, see page 264

Place the tongue in a large pan with the vegetables, peppercorns, thyme, parsley stalks and bay leaves. Add enough cold water to cover generously. Bring to the boil, cover and simmer very gently for 2–3 hours, until tender. Check by inserting a sharp kitchen fork after 2 hours. Leave to cool in the stock.

Lift the tongue out of the stock and remove the skin. The skin will peel off easily on the upper surface, though it may cling rather more tightly on the underside. Trim off any fatty bits and

small bones. Cut into 6 mm/¼ inch slices, starting at the root
end. Serve with the Piquant Cream Sauce, Celeriac Purée and
Beetroot.

GRILLED SHEEP'S HEAD WITH AÏOLI

A grilled sheep's or lamb's head is not something that everybody will appreciate, but if the thought of it doesn't upset you, then you really should try it. I first ate one in Spain, and enjoyed it immensely.

SERVES 2

1 sheep's or lamb's head
salt
freshly ground black pepper
1 clove of garlic
2 tablespoons parsley
1½ tablespoons olive oil
aïoli, see page 46

Ask the butcher to split a sheep's or lamb's head in two and remove the eyes. Season the cut and uncut surfaces with salt and pepper. Chop the garlic finely with the parsley and sprinkle it over the halves. Drizzle over the oil then place under a preheated hot grill for about 20 minutes on each side. Serve with aïoli.

GRILLED PIGS' TROTTERS
(PIEDS PANÉS)

Many people turn their noses up at the very thought of eating pigs'
trotters. Little do they realize that they are missing out on one of the
most delicious parts of the animal. Trotters have a savoury,
gelatinous texture, set off admirably here by the mustard and the
crisp breadcrumb coating.

SERVES 4

4 pigs' trotters, preferably brined for 4 days, see page 104
300 ml/½ pint dry white wine
2 onions, sliced
2 carrots, sliced
1 stick of celery, sliced
2 sprigs of thyme
1 bay leaf
6 cloves of garlic
2 strips of lemon zest
10 black peppercorns
salt
Dijon mustard
2 eggs, beaten
fine soft breadcrumbs

Trim the toenails from the trotters, and singe off all the hairs.
Put the trotters into a flameproof casserole with the remaining
ingredients, except the mustard, eggs and breadcrumbs. Bring
to the boil, skimming off any scum that rises to the surface,
then cover and cook in a preheated oven, 160°C/325°F/gas
mark 3, for 2 hours, until tender. Leave to cool.

Take the trotters out of the casserole and split in half lengthways. Pull out any bones near the surface. Spread the cut surfaces with the mustard, then dip into the egg and roll in soft
breadcrumbs. Leave in the fridge for 30 minutes to firm up.

Grill, turning once or twice, for about 10 minutes, until nicely browned. Serve with Cucumber Pickle (see page 364), or a nasturtium mayonnaise (see the introduction to mayonnaise on page 45).

ROAST KIDNEYS WITH CABBAGE AND FENNEL SEEDS

*We buy lambs' kidneys from Luscombe's in Totnes, who supply the
choicest local lamb. The kidneys are still encased in their natural
layer of fat, which just needs to be trimmed to form a neat, even
wrapping that will protect and baste the kidneys as they bake.
If you want to serve this as a main course double up the quantities.*

SERVES 4 AS A FIRST COURSE

4 lambs' kidneys complete with outer coating of fat,
neatly trimmed
salt
freshly ground black pepper
4 rashers of streaky bacon
50 g/2 oz butter
225 g/8 oz Savoy cabbage, shredded
½ teaspoon fennel seeds
150 ml/¼ pint double cream

Season the kidneys with salt and pepper, then place in a roasting tin and roast in a preheated oven, 230°C/450°F/gas mark 8,
for 12 minutes. Allow the kidneys to rest for 5 minutes.

Cut the bacon into strips, melt the butter in a pan and fry the
bacon. Add the cabbage, fennel seeds, and salt and pepper to
taste and cook quickly over a high heat until the cabbage is
tender. Arrange the cabbage on a warmed serving dish. Slice
the kidneys and arrange on the cabbage. Keep warm.

Pour off as much fat as possible from the juices in the roasting tin and place the tin over a direct heat. Tip the cream into
the tin, bring to the boil and check seasoning. Pour over the
cabbage and kidneys and serve immediately.

LAMBS' KIDNEYS WITH JUNIPER, MUSTARD AND CREAM

SERVES 4

8 lambs' kidneys
8 juniper berries
¼ teaspoon salt
freshly ground black pepper
25 g/1 oz butter
1 teaspoon Dijon mustard
150 ml/¼ pint double cream

Skin and halve the kidneys and snip out the inner cores. Slice each half in two, horizontally. Pound the juniper berries with the salt in a mortar with a pestle and sprinkle over the kidneys together with a generous twist of the pepper mill.

Melt the butter in a pan and sauté the kidneys gently for about 4 minutes, then add the mustard and the cream. Increase the heat and bubble the sauce until it thickens. Serve immediately.

OXTAIL WITH BEANS
AND VEGETABLES

The flouriness of the butter beans balances the richness of the oxtail,
but you could well use haricots, or other dried beans, in their place.

SERVES 4

100 g/4 oz dried butter beans
2 oxtails, cut in sections
seasoned flour
40 g/1½ oz dripping or lard
2 carrots, cut into batons
2 onions, quartered
2 sticks of celery, sliced into 2.5 cm/1 inch pieces
1 tablespoon flour
600 ml/1 pint red wine
600 ml/1 pint beef stock, see page 30, or water
1 bouquet garni
salt
freshly ground black pepper

Cover the beans generously with cold water and leave to soak
for 8 hours or overnight.

Trim the oxtails and roll them in seasoned flour. Melt the
dripping or lard in a pan, fry the oxtails for 10 minutes until
well browned, and place in a casserole. Drain the beans and
scatter over the meat. Add the vegetables to the dripping in the
pan and fry for 5 minutes, until lightly browned. Sprinkle with
the flour, stir to mix well then add the wine, the stock or water
and the bouquet garni. Bring to the boil, skimming off any
scum. Taste and adjust seasonings then pour over the meat.

Cover tightly and cook in a preheated oven, 140°C/275°F/
gas mark 1, for about 2 hours, until the meat is very tender and
falling off the bone. Check the seasoning once more, remove
the bouquet garni and serve.

OXTAIL WITH GRAPES

This stew, a marvellous combination of savoury meat and sweet, juicy grapes, is from Elizabeth David's French Provincial Cooking. *It is an autumnal dish to be made when the first chills are in the air and the ripest, most fragrant grapes are being gathered in.*

SERVES 4

225 g/8 oz fat bacon, diced
4 large onions, sliced
8 carrots, sliced
4 cloves of garlic, chopped
2 oxtails, cut in sections
1 bouquet garni
salt
freshly ground black pepper
1 kg/2¼ lb grapes, stripped from the stalk
1 large pinch of ground mace

Place the bacon in the base of a flameproof casserole and fry gently for about 5 minutes to release the fat. Add the vegetables, including the garlic, the oxtail pieces, bouquet garni, and salt and pepper to taste. Sauté for 5 minutes.

Crush 900 g/2 lb of the grapes lightly and add to the casserole with the mace. Cover and cook in a preheated oven, 140°C/275°F/gas mark 1, for 3 hours, until the meat is very tender and falling off the bone. Halve and pip the remaining grapes.

Lift the oxtail pieces out of the casserole on to a warmed serving dish and keep warm. Pass the sauce through a sieve or *mouli légumes*. Skim off as much fat as possible. If the sauce seems rather thin, reduce quickly until thick and unctuous. Taste and adjust seasonings. Pour over the oxtails, scatter with the remaining grapes and serve.

TO PREPARE BRAINS

We usually use ox brains, since these are easiest to obtain in Dartmouth. On happy occasions we have had the luxury of calves' brains.

To prepare either, soak in cold water for 1 hour. Carefully remove the outer skin with the blood-vessels in it. Soak the brains again in fresh cold water for at least 6 hours to remove the last traces of blood.

Make a court bouillon (see page 32) and leave to cool. Put the brains in a pan, pour over the bouillon and bring to the boil, then simmer very gently for 5 minutes. Remove from the heat and leave the brains to cool in their cooking liquid.

GRATIN OF BRAINS WITH SORREL

Crisp crumb against the smooth texture of the brains, together with the acidity of sorrel, is a favourite combination. Once the brains are cooked, this gratin takes no time at all to put together and finish.

SERVES 4

50 g/2 oz fresh sorrel, tough stalks snipped out, well washed and shredded
150 ml/¼ pint single cream
salt
freshly ground black pepper
1 set of cooked ox brains, sliced, see page 241
25 g/1 oz soft breadcrumbs

Process half the sorrel with the cream and a little salt and pepper to taste in a blender. Alternatively, chop half the sorrel finely and mix with the cream. Divide half the remaining sorrel between four small gratin dishes, about 15 cm/6 inches in diameter. Arrange the brains on top and cover with the last of the sorrel. Pour the sorrel cream over the top of each dish and scatter with breadcrumbs. Bake in a preheated oven, 240°C/475°F/gas mark 9, for 10 minutes, until golden brown – if the gratins look a little pale, whip them under a preheated hot grill to finish browning.

BRAIN FRITTERS WITH A TOMATO AND CHILLI SAUCE

Again, a good contrast between the textures of the batter and the brains, with a gentle kick from the chillied tomato sauce. Make the sauce and batter in advance, but leave the deep-frying until the very last minute.

SERVES 4

oil for deep-frying
1 set of cooked ox brains, sliced, see page 241
1 quantity of Tomato and Chilli Sauce, see page 55
Pickled Samphire, to garnish, see page 365

FOR THE BATTER
100 g/4 oz flour
2 tablespoons olive oil
salt
freshly ground black pepper
2 tablespoons chopped parsley
1 egg white

To make the batter, sift the flour into a bowl and make a well in the centre. Pour in the oil and add salt and pepper to taste, the parsley and 65 ml/2½ fl oz cold water. Mix well, gradually adding more cold water to give the consistency of thick cream. When you are ready to use the batter, whisk the egg white until it holds stiff peaks and fold into the mixture.

Heat the oil to 160°C/320°F. Dip the slices of brain into the batter and deep-fry until golden. Drain quickly on kitchen paper. Reheat the Tomato and Chilli Sauce thoroughly and spoon it on to a warmed serving dish. Arrange the brain fritters on top. Garnish with the Pickled Samphire.

GOOSE GIBLET STEW

*On the rare occasions when you cook a whole goose, be sure to save
the giblets and trimmings to make this homely, warming stew.*

SERVES 4–6

neck, giblets and trimmings from a goose
belly of pork, or streaky bacon (see recipe)
25 g/1 oz chopped onions
salt
freshly ground black pepper
3 tablespoons goose fat
4 carrots, sliced
1 large onion, sliced
1 small bunch of sweet herbs (parsley, marjoram, thyme, for
example), chopped
½ × 400 g/14 oz can tomatoes, and their juice
1.2 litres/2 pints goose or chicken stock, see page 29
225 g/8 oz green streaky bacon, chopped into
2.5 cm/1 inch pieces
225 g/8 oz cooked haricot beans
450 g/1 lb coarse boiling sausage

Skin the neck, reserving the skin, and chop the neck into six
pieces. Slice the gizzard and heart. Divide the wings in two.
Pass the liver through a mincer with an equal weight of belly of
pork or streaky bacon, the chopped onions, and salt and pepper
to taste. Mould it into a sausage shape on the neck skin and
sew up.

Season the chopped bits of neck, sliced gizzard, heart and
wings with salt and pepper. Brown for 5 minutes in the goose
fat then place in a flameproof casserole. Cook the carrots and
sliced onion in the same fat for 5 minutes until brown, and add
to the casserole with the stuffed neck, feet, herbs, tomatoes and
stock. Bring to the boil and add the bacon. Cover and simmer

gently for 2 hours. Finally, add the beans and sausage. Simmer for a further 30 minutes. Remove the thread from the neck sausage and cut the sausage into slices. Return to the casserole. Taste and adjust seasonings before serving.

Vegetables

Dartmouth is situated in a fertile area of keen home- and market-gardeners. Winters are mild and short and early springs coax the year's new crop of vegetables to maturity by late February or the first few days of March. Ivory-curded cauliflowers and tiny new potatoes herald the abundance that is to follow as days lengthen.

Whenever possible I use vegetables that are grown locally. With only a mile or two to travel from field to kitchen, they arrive in prime condition, having bypassed the damaging delays of long-distance travel and storage. Over the years I've built up valuable relationships with local growers, from Admiral Haynes, who grew sweet juicy tomatoes in his small garden, to the more commercial large-scale producers. At last I can buy courgettes a mere 7.5 or 10 cm/3 or 4 inches long with egg-yolk yellow flowers still intact, tiny broad beans and slender carrots tufted with feathery green fronds.

This wealth of Devonian vegetables boosted by more exotic imports from the Continent and further afield provides a constant source of delight and inspiration in the kitchen. Vegetable dishes of all kinds feature strongly on the menu, falling neatly into three groups.

Where they are to be served as a side dish, I prefer to cook them in the unfussiest of ways, plainly boiled or steamed perhaps, and subtly seasoned to complement rather than to distract attention away from the main dish.

Many of the more distinctive vegetable preparations are included as an integral part of a main course. Red cabbage is a natural companion for autumnal and wintry game. The Onion and Orange Confit goes beautifully with grilled meats and poultry, while the Spiced Onions might partner pâtés or terrines. When I find dark laver to mould into croquettes, I instinctively pair them with lamb.

Some of my favourite vegetable recipes are drawn from the Middle East and Mediterranean, lands where vegetables are never dismissed as the poor relations in the family of 'meat and two veg'. Enhanced with spices and herbs and dressed with fruity green olive oil, these marginally more elaborate combinations, and others of a similar nature, demand room to star in their own right. Adjusting quantities to fit the situation, I will serve them as a first course, individually or within a mixed vegetable hors d'œuvre, or as a main course to be enjoyed as much by meat-eaters as by vegetarians.

AUBERGINE LOAF

The coconut milk gives this Aubergine Loaf a Caribbean flavour – the inspiration comes from a recipe by Alice Wooledge Salmon in Homes and Gardens. *It makes a change from the much-loved combination of aubergine and tomato. We usually serve it as a first course, with a tomato sauce or salad, though it makes a marvellous partner with lamb.*

SERVES 8–10

350 g/12 oz aubergine, peeled and diced
½ tablespoon olive oil
2 cloves of garlic, chopped
2 eggs
250 ml/8 fl oz soured cream or plain yoghurt
1 pinch of ground cumin
salt
freshly ground black pepper
25 g/1 oz creamed coconut, grated

Steam the aubergine for 10 minutes, until tender. Heat the oil in a pan and cook the garlic gently until soft. Allow to cool slightly, then beat into the eggs in a bowl with the soured cream or yoghurt, cumin, salt and pepper to taste and coconut. Add the aubergine and stir. Pour into a greased 900 ml–1.2 litre/1½–2 pint mould, cover loosely with foil, and stand the mould in a roasting tin filled with warm water to a depth of 2.5 cm/1 inch. Bake in a preheated oven, 150°C/300°F/gas mark 2, for about 40 minutes, until just firm to the touch.

Turn out and serve hot, cut into thick slices, with a Tomato Sauce (see page 54), or leave to cool and serve with a tomato salad.

AUBERGINES WITH PIMENTOS AND LEMON

This is a superbly pungent dish, sweet and sour with a pleasing dash of bitterness from the lemon slices. It has too pronounced a flavour to offer as an accompaniment, but comes into its own as an hors d'œuvre, with good bread to mop up the juices. The recipe comes originally from Jane Grigson, but we've 'telescoped' the method to make it quicker and easier.

SERVES 8–10

50 g/2 oz brown sugar
5 tablespoons white wine vinegar
1 tablespoon currants
1 clove of garlic, chopped
salt
freshly ground black pepper
450 g/1 lb aubergines
100 ml/4 fl oz olive oil
225 g/8 oz onions, sliced
2 lemons, unpeeled, thinly sliced
2 red peppers, seeded and sliced

Mix the sugar with the vinegar, currants, garlic, salt and pepper to taste, and 150 ml/¼ pint cold water in a pan. Bring to the boil and simmer for 5 minutes. Set aside.

Cut the aubergines into 6 mm/¼ inch thick discs. Put them in a colander, sprinkle with salt and leave to drain for 30 minutes. Wipe dry. Pour the oil into one or two shallow baking dish(es) large enough to take the aubergine slices in a single layer. Spread the onions over the base of the dish(es), and cover with aubergine slices. Discard the ends of the lemons, and remove pips from the slices, then arrange lemon and pepper slices over the aubergine. Finally, pour the sugar syrup evenly over the dish(es). Cover with foil or a lid.

Bake in a preheated oven, 150°C/300°F/gas mark 2, for 1 hour, until the aubergine is tender. Lift the aubergine slices, still topped with lemon and pepper, on to a serving dish. If the juices are copious, reduce them by boiling hard in a pan over a direct heat until they are thick and syrupy. Taste and adjust seasonings then pour over the aubergine. This is best served just tepid, or at room temperature.

CARVED ANGEL CAPONATA

Caponata is a robust Sicilian aubergine and tomato stew, sweet and sour, with the salty tang of capers and olives. When I decided to include it in a plate of aubergine hors d'œuvre, I had to search round for a more elegant way of presenting it. This is what subsequently emerged – discs of aubergines topped with thick tomato sauce, and baked slowly to soak up the pungent flavours, without losing the crunch of the celery.

SERVES 8–10

2 medium aubergines
salt
3 tablespoons olive oil, plus extra to finish
2 medium onions, chopped
2 cloves of garlic, chopped
1 green pepper, seeded and diced
1 red pepper, seeded and diced
2 sticks of celery, chopped
1 tablespoon white wine vinegar
1 dessertspoon caster sugar
1 tablespoon tomato purée
freshly ground black pepper
18 black olives, halved and pitted
1 tablespoon capers, drained and rinsed

Slice the aubergines into 6 mm/¼ inch thick discs. Put them in a colander, sprinkle with salt and leave to drain for 30 minutes. Wipe dry.

Heat the oil in a pan and cook the onions and garlic gently for 5 minutes, without browning, until tender. Add the peppers and celery and cook for a further 5 minutes. Add the vinegar, sugar, tomato purée, and salt and pepper to taste. Stir, then add the olives and capers. Remove from the heat.

Top each aubergine slice neatly with the sweet and sour

mixture and arrange in a lightly oiled baking dish. Drizzle over and round the aubergines the extra oil – allow about 1 teaspoon per slice. Cover with foil and cook in a preheated oven, 150°C/300°F/gas mark 2, for 45–60 minutes, until the aubergine is tender. Leave to cool and serve at room temperature.

CARROTS WITH GINGER, LEMON AND HONEY

Adding a pinch of sugar and a dash of lemon to the cooking water of carrots is a well-known enhancer. This recipe goes several steps further, replacing sugar with honey and scenting the carrots with a waft of ginger. It's good enough to eat on its own, but goes well with grilled chicken too.

SERVES 6–8

1 lemon
1 tablespoon honey
2.5 cm/1 inch piece of fresh root ginger, sliced
50 g/2 oz butter
900 g/2 lb carrots, sliced thinly
salt

Pare the zest of the lemon in thin strips with a potato peeler, being careful to avoid the white pith. Squeeze the juice. Put the zest and juice into a blender with the honey, ginger, and 150 ml/¼ pint cold water. Process and strain.

Melt the butter in a large frying pan and sauté the carrots lightly. Add the contents of the blender, and salt to taste, bring to the boil, cover and cook gently for 15 minutes, until just tender. The carrots should absorb nearly all the liquid, but if necessary, uncover and boil hard to reduce to a buttery glaze.

CORN PANCAKES

These little pancakes, knobbly with nuggets of juicy sweetcorn, are an autumnal favourite. I usually serve them with game – pheasant, or quail perhaps.

SERVES 6

275 g/10 oz sweetcorn, cooked off the cob
65 g/2½ oz flour
1 egg
1 egg yolk
150 ml/¼ pint milk
100 ml/4 fl oz double cream
freshly grated nutmeg
salt
freshly ground black pepper
knob of clarified butter, see page 23, or goose fat

Chop the corn roughly. Sift the flour into a bowl and make a well in the centre. Beat together the egg and yolk and pour into the well. Pour in half the milk as well and stir, gradually drawing in the flour. Add the remaining milk and the cream and beat until smooth. Add the sweetcorn and season generously with nutmeg, salt and pepper.

Melt the butter or goose fat until just foaming in a heavy frying pan. Stir the batter, then drop dessertspoonfuls into the fat, leaving plenty of room between each one. Cook for about 3 minutes, until the underside is brown and it is just set on top. Turn and brown the other side for a further 3 minutes. Drain on kitchen paper, and keep warm while you cook the rest of the batter in the same way.

COURGETTE TERRINE

A slice of pale, green-streaked, creamy terrine laid alongside a salad of red tomatoes makes a delightful summer first course, or a light lunch. For more dressy occasions, bake it in dariole moulds lined with spinach leaves.

SERVES 8

450 g/1 lb courgettes
2 teaspoons salt
25 g/1 oz butter
2 eggs
300 ml/½ pint double cream
1 handful of herbs (parsley, tarragon and chervil or basil, for example), chopped
salt
freshly ground black pepper
fresh spinach leaves (optional)

Grate the courgettes and spread out in a colander. Sprinkle with the salt and leave to drain for 30 minutes. Rinse the courgettes and dry on kitchen paper or a clean tea towel. Melt the butter in a pan and cook the courgettes gently, without browning, for 5 minutes, until tender. Leave to cool.

Beat the eggs with the cream and add the herbs and a generous amount of salt and pepper. Stir in the courgettes. If using spinach leaves to line the moulds, pour boiling water over them, let them sit for 10 seconds then drain and refresh under the cold tap. Line a 1.2 litre/2 pint terrine with clingfilm or individual dariole moulds with the spinach leaves, then fill with the courgette mixture. Cover with foil.

Sit the terrine or the moulds in a roasting pan filled with warm water to a depth of 2.5 cm/1 inch and bake in a preheated oven, 140°C/275°F/gas mark 1, for 45 minutes to 1 hour for the terrine, 20 minutes for the moulds, until just firm to the touch. Allow the terrine to stand for 5 minutes, then turn out and serve hot. Alternatively, cool in the terrine and serve with a tomato salad.

GRATIN OF COURGETTES AND TOMATOES

This is one of those timeless Elizabeth David dishes. I've been making it for years now and it never fails to please me as much as it did the very first time.

SERVES 6 AS A FIRST COURSE
OR 4–5 AS A LIGHT LUNCH DISH

900 g/2 lb courgettes
2 teaspoons salt
75 g/3 oz butter
450 g/1 lb tomatoes, skinned, seeded and diced
2 tablespoons roughly chopped basil or parsley
2 cloves of garlic, chopped
freshly ground black pepper

FOR THE TOPPING
50 g/2 oz soft breadcrumbs
25 g/1 oz butter

Slice the courgettes 6 mm/¼ inch thick. Spread the slices out in a colander, and sprinkle with the salt. Leave to drain for 1 hour. Rinse and dry on kitchen paper or a clean tea towel.

Melt the butter in a pan and fry the courgettes for 5 minutes, until browned and tender. Lift out and set aside. Add the tomatoes, herbs, garlic, and pepper to taste to the pan, and simmer gently until thick and pulpy. Return the courgettes to the pan and mix well. Taste and adjust seasonings.

Spoon the courgette and tomato mixture into an ovenproof serving dish, in a layer about 4 cm/1½ inches thick. Sprinkle the breadcrumbs thickly over the top and dot with the butter. Bake in a preheated oven, 200°C/400°F/gas mark 6, for 25 minutes, until the topping is brown and crisp. Serve immediately.

CELERIAC PURÉE

SERVES 4

450 g/1 lb celeriac
100 g/4 oz potato
salt
50 g/2 oz butter
freshly ground black pepper

Peel the celeriac and potato and cut into 2.5 cm/1 inch cubes. Place in a pan and cover with cold, salted water. Bring to the boil and simmer for about 15 minutes, until tender. Drain well and purée in a processor or *mouli légumes*. Beat in the butter and season to taste. Serve immediately.

LEEKS IN RED WINE

Be prepared – this dish may not look too exciting, but looks belie the taste. The red wine mottles the leeks with an uneven purple tint, imparting its bouquet as it is absorbed. Serve the leeks cold, as part of an hors d'œuvre, or as a relish, or serve hot with duck or game.

SERVES 4–6

2 tablespoons olive oil
675 g/1½ lb leeks, well washed, dried, trimmed and
halved lengthways
250 ml/8 fl oz chicken stock, see page 29
150 ml/¼ pint red wine
salt
freshly ground black pepper

Heat the oil in a large pan and fry the leeks for 5 minutes, until lightly browned. Add the stock, wine, and salt and pepper to taste and bring to the boil. Cover and simmer very gently for 10 minutes, until the leeks are tender and most of the liquid has been absorbed. If the leeks are still swimming in liquid, lift them on to a serving dish and reduce the liquid by boiling rapidly until thick and syrupy. Pour over the leeks and serve hot or cold.

LEEKS PROVENÇALE

*The lemon and olives lift this leek and tomato ragoût out of the
ordinary. Make it as part of a cold vegetable hors d'œuvre, or serve
hot with a grilled steak.*

SERVES 4–6
2 tablespoons olive oil
675 g/1½ lb leeks, well washed, dried, trimmed and cut into
5 cm/2 inch pieces
2 cloves of garlic, chopped
juice and finely grated zest of 1 lemon
18 black olives, halved and pitted
1 × 400 g/14 oz can tomatoes, chopped, and their juice
salt
freshly ground black pepper

Heat the oil in a pan and sweat the leeks for 5 minutes. Add the
remaining ingredients to the pan and simmer, covered, for 15
minutes, until the leeks are tender and the sauce is thick and
pulpy. Taste and adjust seasonings. Serve hot or cold.

ONIONS IN SOURED CREAM

This is a simple and surprisingly delicious salad, one that I often serve among a trio of onion and leek hors d'œuvre.

Thinly slice onions. Cover with boiling water, then drain, cool and dry on kitchen paper. Dress with soured cream, and salt and freshly ground black pepper to taste.

SPICED ONIONS

*Baked with spices, vinegar and sugar, these onions are halfway
between a vegetable accompaniment and a pickle, and we serve them
accordingly with a dish of cold meats, or charcuterie, or as part of an
onion and leek selection. They keep well for up to four days, covered,
in the fridge.*

SERVES 6-8

900 g/2 lb pearl onions
2 tablespoons oil
½ teaspoon whole coriander seeds, toasted
½ teaspoon ground cinnamon
1½ tablespoons red or white wine vinegar
1 tablespoon dark muscovado sugar
25 g/1 oz sultanas
1 tablespoon tomato purée
250 ml/8 fl oz water
salt
freshly ground black pepper

Pour boiling water over the onions and leave for 1 minute.
Drain and run them under the cold tap to refresh. The skins
should now peel off easily. Dry the onions. Heat the oil in a pan
and fry the onions gently for 5 minutes. Grind the coriander
seeds as finely as possible in a mortar with a pestle or in an electric coffee grinder and add to the onions with the cinnamon.
Cook for a further 5 minutes, stirring.

Add the remaining ingredients to the pan, bring to the boil,
check the seasoning and then pour into an ovenproof dish
wide enough to take the onions no more than two deep. Cover
tightly and bake in a preheated oven, 140°C/275°F/gas mark 1,
for 1–1½ hours, until the onions are tender. Serve hot or cold.

ONION AND ORANGE CONFIT

Onion marmalades and confits, variously spiced and seasoned, have become immensely popular in recent years. Try this one with its subtle union of orange and caramelized onion, and mild balance of sweet and sharp, and you will quickly understand why. It is based on a recipe from French chef, Fredy Girardet, which appeared in Cuisine Spontanée. *Serve two tablespoons per person with grilled guinea fowl, chicken or lamb.*

SERVES 8

90 ml/3½ fl oz olive oil
1.25 kg/2½ lb onions, thinly sliced
25 g/1 oz caster sugar
1 carrot, cut into julienne strips
zest of 3 oranges, cut into julienne strips
50 ml/2 fl oz white wine vinegar
salt
freshly ground black pepper

Heat the oil in a flameproof casserole and fry the onions over a high heat until they begin to soften. Sprinkle the sugar over the onions and continue to cook until they begin to caramelize. Stir in the carrot and orange zest, then add the vinegar, and salt and pepper to taste. Mix thoroughly and place in a preheated oven, 140°C/275°F/gas mark 1, for 20 minutes, until tender. Taste and adjust seasonings. Best served hot.

HOT GRATED BEETROOT

SERVES 4

2 medium-sized raw beetroots
40 g/1½ oz butter
1 teaspoon red wine vinegar
salt
freshly ground black pepper

Wash the beetroots well and wrap in foil. Bake in a preheated oven, 150°C/300°F/gas mark 2, for 1 hour. Alternatively, boil the beetroots in lightly salted water for 1 hour, until tender. When they are cooked the skin can be rubbed easily from the root. Grate the cooked beetroot. Reheat thoroughly in the butter, sharpening with vinegar to taste. Season well with salt and pepper, and serve.

LAVER CROQUETTES

*I had to make a trip to an architectural antiques shop in South
Molton near Barnstaple, to buy a fitment for the kitchen. I found
what I wanted, and then discovered that it was market day. On one
of the fish stalls they were selling laver, that dark, delicious seaweed.
It was the nicest I'd ever seen, looking almost like wild spinach with
more texture to it than usual. It is common round the north Devon
and Welsh coastlines, but strangely we don't get it near Dartmouth.
Serve it as it is, warmed through and sharpened with the juice of a
lemon, with roast lamb, or stretch a small amount round a generous
number of people with these laver croquettes.*

MAKES ABOUT 16

50 g/2 oz butter
50 g/2 oz flour
300 ml/½ pint milk
6 g/scant ¼ oz leaf gelatine (3 sheets), soaked, see page 301
450 g/1 lb laver
juice of 1 orange
salt
freshly ground black pepper
1 egg, beaten
dry breadcrumbs
butter and oil for frying

Melt the butter in a pan and stir in the flour. Cook for 1 minute,
remove from the heat, then gradually beat in the milk to make
a smooth sauce. Return to the heat and simmer gently for 10
minutes. Cool slightly, then add the gelatine and stir until it has
dissolved. Leave until tepid. Stir in the laver and orange juice,
and salt and pepper to taste.

Chill until very thick and almost set. Roll heaped tablespoons of the mixture into croquettes, and chill again until
firm. Dip the croquettes into the beaten egg, then roll them in

the crumbs. Again, chill for 30 minutes or so to firm up. Then shallow-fry in half butter and half oil until golden, or deep-fry. Drain the croquettes on kitchen paper and serve.

CHESTNUT AND WALNUT PIE

This is a main course that I often cook for vegetarians, though meat-eaters always seem to enjoy it just as much. It is lighter than you might imagine, and slices well. Accompanied by Cumberland Sauce (see page 50), it would make a perfect centrepiece for a vegetarian Christmas lunch.

SERVES 6–8 AS A FIRST COURSE OR 4 AS A MAIN COURSE

175 g/6 oz chestnuts
1 tablespoon groundnut oil
1 small onion, chopped
1 stick of celery, chopped
1 clove of garlic, chopped
50 g/2 oz walnuts, chopped
50 g/2 oz cashew nuts (or brazils or almonds), chopped
1 egg
½ teaspoon each dried thyme and marjoram
1 tablespoon brandy
finely grated zest of ½ orange
salt
cayenne pepper
350 g/12 oz puff pastry, see page 347
1 egg, beaten, to glaze
Cumberland Sauce, see page 50, to serve

With a sharp knife, slash the outer skin of each chestnut. Place in a pan with enough cold water to cover. Bring to the boil, and boil for 1 minute. Remove from the heat. Take a couple of chestnuts out of the water and, when they are just cool enough to handle, peel off both the inner and outer skins. Peel the remainder a few at a time, returning the pan to the heat for a few minutes to loosen skins if necessary. Rinse out the pan and replace the chestnuts. Cover with water, bring back to the boil and simmer for about 20 minutes, until soft. Drain and chop.

Heat the oil in a pan and sweat the onion, celery and garlic for 5 minutes, until soft. Remove from the heat and add the chestnuts, walnuts and cashews. Mix in the egg, herbs, brandy, orange zest, and salt and cayenne pepper to taste.

Roll out the pastry on a lightly floured surface to a large oblong 6 mm/¼ inch in thickness. Lift carefully on to a baking sheet. Trim to even up edges. Pile the filling down the centre of the oblong. Brush the edges of the pastry with beaten egg and bring them together over the filling, to enclose completely. Pinch the edges to seal firmly. Trim off any excess and use the trimmings to decorate. Leave to rest in the fridge for 30 minutes. Brush with beaten egg and bake in a preheated oven, 220°C/425°F/gas mark 7, for 10 minutes, then reduce the heat to 160°C/325°F/gas mark 3 and cook for a further 20 minutes. Serve hot, sliced thickly, with Cumberland Sauce.

NUT LOAF

There's nut loaf and there's nut loaf. It can be, and all too often is, leaden and worthy. This is the other kind, light and delicious with a herb or vegetable filling at its heart. One of our girls made this for a staff lunch and it was so good that I now make it for vegetarian customers, accompanied by a tomato or onion sauce or a leek purée.

SERVES 6–8

FOR THE LOAF
2 tablespoons olive oil or 25 g/1 oz butter
1 onion, chopped
225 g/8 oz pine nuts, finely chopped, or a mixture of pine nuts, ground almonds and grated cashews
4 tablespoons milk
100 g/4 oz soft white breadcrumbs
2 eggs
salt
freshly ground black pepper
freshly grated nutmeg

FOR THE STUFFING
175 g/6 oz soft brown breadcrumbs
100 g/4 oz butter, melted, or 6 tablespoons olive oil
juice and grated zest of ½ lemon
1 tablespoon each chopped marjoram and thyme
2 tablespoons chopped parsley
salt
freshly ground black pepper

TO LINE THE MOULD
butter
dried brown breadcrumbs, or ground or flaked almonds

To make the loaf, heat the oil or butter in a pan and sweat the onion for 5 minutes, until soft. Remove from the heat, tip the onion into a bowl and add the remaining loaf ingredients. Mix well.

Mix the stuffing ingredients in a separate bowl.

Butter either two 450 g/1 lb loaf tins, or one 900 g/2 lb tin, and coat the insides evenly with dried breadcrumbs, or ground or flaked almonds. Half fill the tin(s) with the loaf mixture, and then divide the stuffing mixture between them, spreading it evenly and leaving a good 1.25 cm/½ inch gap round the edges. Top with the remaining loaf mixture, and smooth over. Cover the tin(s) with foil and bake in a preheated oven, 190°C/ 375°F/gas mark 5, for 30 minutes. Turn out carefully, and serve hot or warm.

VARIATIONS

WATERCRESS STUFFING

Substitute the chopped leaves from 2 bunches of watercress for the herbs in the stuffing.

SORREL STUFFING

Substitute 100 g/4 oz shredded sorrel leaves for the herbs in the stuffing.

PIMENTO STUFFING

Chop one canned or home-skinned red pimento finely, and add to the stuffing mixture.

MUSHROOM STUFFING

Cook 100 g/4 oz chopped mushrooms in 25 g/1 oz butter with 1 finely chopped clove of garlic, and add to the stuffing mixture.

SPINACH WITH PINE KERNELS AND CURRANTS

This is good enough to serve as a first course with triangles of fried bread or brioche, but it goes just as well with roast or grilled meats.

SERVES 4

50 g/2 oz butter
25 g/1 oz pine kernels
450 g/1 lb fresh spinach, tough stalks removed, well washed
25 g/1 oz currants
salt
freshly ground black pepper

Melt half the butter in a pan and fry the pine kernels until golden brown. Melt the remaining butter in a large pan. Add the spinach and cook over a high heat for about 5 minutes, stirring with a wooden spoon until tender and most of the liquid has evaporated. Add the currants, pine kernels, and salt and pepper to taste, and cook for another 2 minutes. Adjust seasonings and serve.

RED CABBAGE

*I like this served with hare, pigeon or roast pork. I will sometimes
cook a whole hand of pork buried deep in the cabbage. The pork gives
the juices a rich gelatinous quality.*

SERVES 6

1 small red cabbage
2 onions, sliced
2 cooking apples, cored and sliced
salt
freshly ground black pepper
2 tablespoons caster sugar
2 tablespoons port
2 tablespoons red wine vinegar
6 rashers of streaky bacon, rind removed, diced
1 bouquet garni
grated zest of 1 orange

Quarter the cabbage, cut out the tough core, and shred finely.
Place in a flameproof casserole with all the other ingredients
and mix well. Bring to the boil, check seasonings, then cover
tightly and cook in a preheated oven, 140°C/275°F/gas mark 1,
for 2–3 hours, until the cabbage is meltingly tender. Remove
the bouquet garni before serving.

MUSHROOMS ARMÉNIENNES

*This dish of whole mushrooms bathed in a red wine reduction made
regular appearances on the cold table at the Hole in the Wall in Bath.
It can be eaten hot, but is best served at room temperature.*

SERVES 6

1 tablespoon olive oil
4 rashers of streaky bacon, rind removed, chopped
675 g/1½ lb button mushrooms
4 cloves of garlic, chopped
salt
freshly ground black pepper
300 ml/½ pint red wine
3 tablespoons finely chopped parsley

Heat the oil in a large pan, and fry the bacon quickly. Add the
mushrooms, garlic, and salt and pepper to taste. Continue to fry
over a high heat for 5 minutes, until the mushrooms are half
cooked. Pour in the wine and bring to the boil. Cook rapidly for
a further 5 minutes, until the mushrooms are tender.

The wine should have reduced to a thick sauce by now – if
not, lift out the mushrooms with a slotted spoon, pile them into
a heated serving dish and keep warm. Boil the cooking liquid
until it has reduced and is syrupy. Taste the sauce and adjust
seasonings then pour over the mushrooms. Scatter the parsley
over the top.

BLACK-EYED BEANS
WITH MUSHROOMS

This recipe comes originally from Madhur Jaffrey's Indian Cookery, and is one I often turn to when vegans or vegetarians are expected at the restaurant. It is so good that we always cook at least four times the amount given below, so that there is certain to be plenty left over for the staff lunch. It's worth noting that although the quantity of beans may be increased fourfold, they require only 3.6 litres/6 pints of water, not the 4.8 litres/8 pints that you might expect.

SERVES 6

225 g/8 oz dried black-eyed beans
1.2 litres/2 pints cold water
6 tablespoons vegetable oil
1 teaspoon whole cumin seeds
2.5 cm/1 inch piece of cinnamon stick
150 g/5 oz onions, chopped
4 cloves of garlic, chopped
225 g/8 oz mushrooms
1 × 400 g/14 oz can tomatoes, chopped, and their juice
2 teaspoons ground coriander
½ teaspoon ground turmeric
1 pinch of cayenne pepper
1 teaspoon ground cumin
2 teaspoons salt
3 tablespoons chopped coriander or parsley

Pick over the beans, throwing out any stones or pieces of grit. Wash and drain. Put into a pan with the water, bring to the boil, cover and simmer for 2 minutes. Turn off the heat and leave to stand for 1 hour, still covered. Bring back to the boil and simmer for 20–30 minutes, until the beans are just tender. Remove from the heat and set aside.

Heat the oil in a flameproof casserole and add the whole cumin seeds and the cinnamon stick. Fry for 10 seconds or so, then add the onions and garlic and sauté for 5 minutes, until brown. Halve the mushrooms if large, otherwise keep them whole, and add to the casserole with the tomatoes, the remaining spices and the salt. Simmer gently for 10 minutes. Tip the beans into the casserole with their cooking water. Simmer, uncovered, for a further 30 minutes. Taste and adjust seasonings, sprinkle with coriander or parsley and serve with bread to mop up the juices.

SAFFRON RICE

This is a savoury rice, cooked gently so that the grains of rice absorb the aromas of saffron and garlic right to the core. It is important to use Italian Arborio or risotto rice, as it soaks up the liquids, becoming plump and meltingly tender without collapsing to a mush.

SERVES 6

2 tablespoons olive oil
1 onion, sliced
2 cloves of garlic, chopped
175 g/6 oz Arborio or risotto rice
1 × 400 g/14 oz can tomatoes, chopped, and their juice
scant ¼ teaspoon saffron filaments
25 g/1 oz currants
25 g/1 oz flaked almonds
salt
freshly ground black pepper

Heat the oil in a flameproof casserole and sweat the onion and garlic for 5 minutes, until soft. Add the rice, stir to coat evenly, then add the remaining ingredients and 150 ml/¼ pint cold water. Bring to the boil, cover and bake in a preheated oven, 150°C/300°F/gas mark 2, for 20–30 minutes, until the rice is tender. Taste and adjust seasonings. Serve hot or cold.

Ice Creams & Sorbets

What is it about ice creams and sorbets that is so appealing to children and adults alike? Perhaps it is the tingling shock of the cold as it hits the tongue, melting to release cool, fresh flavours. Whatever the reason, their eternal popularity is undeniable.

At The Carved Angel diners are offered a small scoop of a very light sorbet after the main course. This may be a wine or a melon sorbet – something pure, and not too sweet, to refresh and reinvigorate before deciding whether or not to indulge in a richer pudding. In fact, after two fairly substantial courses, this light sorbet, or a scoop of ice cream with a few raspberries or a slice or two of mango is often all that's needed to satisfy a craving for something sweet to round off the meal without overloading the stomach.

It always surprises me that so few people make their own ice cream, even though they obviously appreciate the difference in taste between an ice cream made with real cream and eggs, and the second-rate (or worse) commercial concoctions that have often never come into contact with either.

I derive immense pleasure from making ice creams and sorbets of all kinds, from the classic vanilla (so wonderful when made with first-class ingredients), strawberry and chocolate, to the more exotic and strange. The possibilities are limitless, and with basic methods understood, you can set about creating a range of flavours inspired by the season's best and most abundant produce.

I would advise anyone who has a particular fondness for ice cream, or whose family and friends are keen to tuck into it as frequently as possible, to invest in an ice cream churn or electric *sorbetière*. There are numerous versions on the market, some suspiciously cheap, others too expensive for most domestic households. But it is worth finding one that will suit both kitchen and pocket.

An ice cream churn gives ice creams and sorbets a fine, smooth texture. As the mixture freezes, it is constantly beaten so that the ice crystals are broken down with never a chance to set hard and large. It literally turns ice cream making into child's play. The only drawback is that you may get carried away, and end up with a freezer filled to the brim and overflowing with a hundred and one different flavours.

Even without special equipment, it is easy enough to make good ice creams and sorbets (see page 279). The texture will not be quite so fine. The process is more laborious and drawn out but still far from onerous. Do not be put off by these minor considerations. Your own home-made ice cream will be infinitely preferable to shop-bought, and once you get the hang of it you may soon find yourself hooked.

One of the obvious characteristics of ice cream is that it keeps well, and can be made in advance (though it is at its best on the day it is made), so always make more than you will need immediately, and keep several different flavours on the go. Try to use up within a month – keep longer and the texture begins to suffer. Freeze left-over egg white in small batches to be used for meringues, macaroons, soufflés and for clarifying stocks.

FREEZING ICE CREAMS AND SORBETS WITHOUT SPECIAL EQUIPMENT

Turn the freezer to its coldest setting. Pour the ice cream or sorbet mixture into a shallow freezing container and freeze. Have a look at it after 30 minutes or so. When the sides are beginning to set, whisk briskly, breaking up the frozen edges and pushing them towards the centre. Return to the freezer and repeat after another 30–45 minutes.

Return to the freezer once again. When the ice cream is just beginning to solidify, though not yet quite hard, take it out of the freezer and beat vigorously and quickly (a processor or electric mixer does the job best), until you have a relatively smooth slush. Put it back in the freezer to finish freezing. If you are ambitious and patient, repeat this last step once more.

CUSTARD-BASED ICE CREAMS

Made with a flavoured milk, thickened with egg yolks in a double boiler (or, for the brave, over a direct low heat, taking care not to overheat), these have a good body and a smooth texture. They are usually enriched further with double cream, and need churning or beating by hand as they freeze.

FRUIT FOOL-BASED ICE CREAMS

These are among the simplest of ice creams. The basic recipe calls for 450 g/1 lb soft fruit (strawberries, raspberries, blackberries, pineapple, mango) mashed or puréed with orange or lemon juice to taste, 175 g/6 oz caster sugar, and 300 ml/½ pint double cream. Mix well, making sure that the sugar has dissolved, and churn, or freeze and beat by hand as it sets.

PARFAITS (FROZEN MOUSSES)

These are usually based on a *meringue cuite* or an *Italian meringue*, which gives them an airy, soft texture. Once the ice cream mixture is made up and in the freezer, it calls for no more attention and can be served direct from the freezer. This means that it can be poured straight into a decorative mould, or piped on to clingfilm-lined trays in swirls and shapes before freezing. There's only one catch – to make the *meringue cuite* you do need to have either very strong arms to cope with the whisking, or an electric, hand-held whisk.

SORBETS

These are the most basic mixtures – a thin liquid, fruit juice or flavoured syrup, perhaps, sweetened to taste. As they contain no fat at all, they do need to be beaten fairly frequently as they freeze if they are to have a good texture. The best results are obtained with an ice cream churn or *sorbetière*. Hand-beaten sorbets can be made lighter and softer by folding in one or two stiffly whisked egg whites on the final beating. Sorbets made with wine, or generous quantities of alcohol, do not freeze solid, and have a softer texture. Serve straight from the freezer, as they melt quickly.

VANILLA ICE CREAM

*Cheap imitations have tarnished the lustre of real vanilla ice cream.
When properly made, with vanilla pod and double cream, it is one of
the greatest of classics, on its own, with a chocolate or strawberry
sauce, soft fruit or a hot fruit pie. For occasional variation, I use light
muscovado sugar, which gives a delicious caramel flavour.*

SERVES 4–6

1 vanilla pod
3 egg yolks
100 g/4 oz caster sugar
300 ml/½ pint milk
150 ml/¼ pint double cream

Slit the vanilla pod down its length. Beat the egg yolks with the
sugar in a bowl until pale and fluffy. Pour the milk into a pan
and add the vanilla pod. Bring slowly to the boil. Remove from
the heat and pour on to the egg yolks, stirring constantly. Set
the bowl over a pan of simmering water, making sure the base
does not touch the water, and stir for about 5 minutes, until the
custard is thick enough to coat the back of the spoon. Do not let
it boil. Stand the bowl in iced water to cool quickly. Remove the
vanilla pod.

When cool, add the double cream and mix well. Churn or
beat by hand as it freezes (see page 279).

Move the ice cream from the freezer to the fridge about 15
minutes before serving.

STRAWBERRY ICE CREAM

*This is a delicious way of using very ripe, well-flavoured fruit. For a
delightful summer dessert, fill meringue cases with the ice cream,
sliced strawberries or peaches, and rose petal cream (see page 309).
Other soft fruit in season such as redcurrants, raspberries and
loganberries also make very good ice creams, and can be served either
with suitable accompanying fruit or alone.*

SERVES 4

450 g/1 lb strawberries, hulled
175 g/6 oz caster sugar
juice of 1 orange
300 ml/½ pint double cream
lemon juice, to taste

Purée the fruit, sugar and orange juice in a processor or blender.
Pour into a bowl and whisk in the double cream. Taste, and if
necessary sharpen with a little lemon juice. Churn or beat by
hand as it freezes (see page 279).

Move the ice cream from the freezer to the fridge about 20
minutes before serving.

HONEY ICE CREAM

This is a lovely rich ice cream, with enough honey to give a good backdrop to the scented cardamom or lavender, without overwhelming. A plain honey ice cream, without the additions, makes an excellent alternative to vanilla ice cream as a partner to hot fruit tarts and other puddings.

SERVES 6

4 whole cardamom pods, or 6 sprigs of lavender flowers
600 ml/1 pint milk
175 g/6 oz clear honey
4 egg yolks
300 ml/½ pint double cream

Slit the cardamom pods, if using, and extract the seeds. Heat the cardamom seeds or the lavender with the milk, bringing slowly to the boil.

Whisk together the honey and egg yolks in a bowl and pour on the boiling milk, stirring constantly. Set the bowl over a pan of simmering water, making sure that the base does not touch the water. Stir for about 5 minutes, until the custard thickens and will coat the back of the spoon. Remove from the heat and strain. Leave to cool. Mix in the cream. Churn or beat by hand as it freezes (see page 279).

Move the ice cream from the freezer to the fridge about 20 minutes before serving.

GERANIUM AND MELON
ICE CREAM

The taste of this ice cream is beautifully balanced – a succession of melon, honey, milk, and scented geranium. I sometimes serve it in a solid ice bowl, splashed with the yellows and pinks of flowers embedded in the ice.

Serves 8

6 sweet geranium leaves
600 ml/1 pint milk
175 g/6 oz clear honey
4 egg yolks
225 g/8 oz Ogen or Galia melon flesh
300 ml/½ pint double cream

Place the geranium leaves in a pan with the milk. Bring gently to the boil. Whisk together the honey and egg yolks in a bowl and pour on the boiling milk, stirring constantly. Set the bowl over a pan of simmering water, making sure that the base does not touch the water. Stir for about 5 minutes, until the custard thickens and will coat the back of the spoon. Remove from the heat and strain. Leave to cool.

Chop the melon flesh roughly and purée in a processor or blender, then whisk into the custard. Mix in the cream. Churn or beat by hand as it freezes (see page 279).

Move the ice cream from the freezer to the fridge about 20 minutes before serving.

REDCURRANT ICE CREAM

SERVES 8

900 g/2 lb redcurrants
350 g/12 oz caster sugar
600 ml/1 pint double cream

Pass the redcurrants through a *mouli légumes*, or process in a processor or blender, or crush, and sieve.

Add the sugar and cream to the redcurrant juice, stirring until the sugar has completely dissolved. Churn or beat by hand as it freezes (see page 279).

Move the ice cream into the fridge about 20 minutes before you wish to serve it.

BASIL ICE CREAM

Basil ice cream sounds a bizarre notion, but think about it. Basil is one of the sweetest of herbs with no hint of bitterness or sharpness. The recipe and idea comes from Georges Blanc's The Natural Cuisine, and is inspired. It works wonderfully with lightly poached peaches.

SERVES 4

450 ml/¾ pint milk
1 vanilla pod
1 small bunch of basil, chopped coarsely
175 g/6 oz caster sugar
4 egg yolks

Place the milk, vanilla pod and basil in a pan and bring slowly to the boil. Whisk the sugar and egg yolks in a bowl until pale and thick, and pour on the boiling milk, stirring constantly. Set the bowl over a pan of simmering water, making sure that the base does not touch the water. Stir for about 5 minutes, until the custard thickens and will coat the back of the spoon. Remove from the heat and strain. Leave to cool. Churn or beat by hand as it freezes (see page 279).

Move the ice cream into the fridge about 10 minutes before you wish to serve it.

CHOCOLATE AND MOCHA ICED PUDDING

This is a terrifically rich and luxurious chocolate and coffee iced mousse, or parfait. The recipe was first given to us by a customer and was an instant hit. Some time later, food writer Geraldine Holt visited the restaurant and was thrilled to see it on the menu. It turned out to be a recipe she had created many years before!

SERVES 8–10

75 g/3 oz ground coffee
300 ml/½ pint milk
225 g/8 oz plain chocolate (Menier or Cocoa Barry, for example)
150 ml/¼ pint egg white (approximately 4 large egg whites)
175 g/6 oz granulated sugar
450 ml/¾ pint double cream, lightly whipped

Put the coffee into a pan with the milk and bring slowly to the boil. Break the chocolate into small pieces and place in a bowl large enough to take the milk as well. Strain the boiling milk through a muslin-lined sieve on to the chocolate. Squeeze the muslin to extract the last drops. Stir until the chocolate has completely dissolved. Leave to cool until tepid.

Place the egg whites and sugar in a bowl set over a pan of simmering water, making sure that the base of the bowl does not touch the water. Whisk for about 5 minutes, until the mixture starts to thicken. Remove from the heat and continue to whisk until the meringue is cool, stiff and very thick.

Fold the chocolate milk and the cream into the meringue – the final mixture should have the consistency of whipped cream. Line a mould or a tray with clingfilm. Fill the mould, or pipe whirls of the ice cream mixture on to the tray. Cover with foil or clingfilm and freeze.

This ice cream can be served straight from the freezer.

QUINCE PARFAIT

Quinces keep well enough for a week or so, but should you be faced
with a glut, don't let them go to waste. They are far too valuable and
rare a flavouring for both savoury and sweet dishes. The quince purée
given opposite can be frozen in small batches, to be used for sauces,
pies and tarts, as well as for this heavenly ice cream.
Other thick fruit purées can be used instead of the quince purée.

SERVES 6

2 egg whites
75 g/3 oz caster sugar
300 ml/½ pint double cream
dash of quince liqueur or brandy
300 ml/½ pint quince purée, see opposite
lemon juice

Place the egg whites and sugar in a bowl over a pan of gently
simmering hot water, making sure that the base of the bowl
does not touch the water. Whisk, with an electric beater if you
have one, for about 5 minutes, until you have a shiny, thick
meringue that just holds its shape. Remove from the heat and
continue to whisk until cold.

Whip the cream with the liqueur or brandy. Sharpen the
quince purée with a dash of lemon juice. Fold the cream and
purée into the meringue. Either fill a clingfilm-lined 450 g/1 lb
loaf tin with the mixture or pipe in swirls on a clingfilm-lined
tray. Cover with foil or clingfilm and freeze. Just before serving,
turn out of the mould and peel off the clingfilm. Slice thickly.
If piped, slide a palette knife or cake slice under each swirl
to loosen.

QUINCE PURÉE

Wash the quinces and wipe off the soft down. Slice roughly into a casserole. Cover tightly and bake in a preheated oven, 140°C/275°F/gas mark 1, for 1–2 hours, until very tender. Pass the quinces through the fine blade of a *mouli légumes*, or sieve. 450 g/1 lb quinces yields 300–450 ml/½–¾ pint purée.

STOCK SYRUP FOR SORBETS

This is the basic sugar syrup that we use when making all kinds of sorbets, and it has its uses in other puddings too. Since it keeps well for a month or more in the fridge in a screw-top jar, it is worth boiling up a generous quantity, especially in the summer when fresh fruit sorbets are doubly welcome.

MAKES 1.25 LITRES/2¼ PINTS

900 g/2 lb granulated sugar
1.2 litres/2 pints cold water

Put the sugar and water in a large pan, and stir over a medium heat until the sugar has completely dissolved. Bring to the boil, and simmer for 5 minutes. Leave to cool.

CHAMPAGNE SORBET

This is lovely for a special occasion. The alcohol in the champagne gives it a soft texture so it can be used straight from the freezer. If I am catering for a large party, I scoop it into champagne glasses before anyone arrives, and keep it chilled, glasses and all, in the freezer until called for.

SERVES 8–10

450 ml/¾ pint champagne
450 ml/¾ pint stock syrup, see page 290
150 ml/¼ pint cold water
juice of 1 lemon

Stir the champagne into the syrup, with the water and lemon juice. Churn or beat by hand as it freezes (see page 279). Serve straight from the freezer.

CRANBERRY SORBET

*A garnet-coloured sorbet which is refreshing with a trace of the
characteristic bitterness of cranberries. Its true, clear flavour is a real
pleasure round Christmas time, when the surfeit of rich and heavy
puddings becomes too much.*
*If you are beating the sorbet by hand as it freezes you might like to
fold in two stiffly beaten egg whites at the final stages, to give greater
volume and a softer texture.*

SERVES 8–10

450 g/1 lb cranberries
juice and grated zest of 1 lemon
juice and grated zest of 1 orange
1.2 litres/2 pints cold water
350 g/12 oz caster sugar

Pick over the cranberries and put in a pan with the lemon and
orange zests, and the water. Bring to the boil and simmer gently
for 10 minutes, until the cranberries have burst and collapsed.
Remove from the heat and add the lemon and orange juices
and the sugar. Stir until the sugar has completely dissolved.
Rub through a sieve. Churn or beat by hand as it freezes (see
page 279).

Move the sorbet into the fridge about 20 minutes before
serving.

POMEGRANATE SORBET

The pomegranate is a fruit that is used far too little in this country, though in the Middle East and Spain it appears frequently in both savoury and sweet dishes. Its juice makes an astringent, refreshing sorbet, a good way to round off a heavy meal. As with the Cranberry Sorbet, if it is to be made by hand, the addition of one stiffly beaten egg white lightens the texture.

SERVES 6

4–6 large pomegranates
300 ml/½ pint stock syrup, see page 290
juice of ½ lemon

Halve the pomegranates and squeeze on a lemon squeezer. You need 450 ml/¾ pint of juice in total. Strain the pomegranate juice and stir into the syrup with the lemon juice. Churn or beat by hand as it freezes (see page 279).

Move the sorbet into the fridge about 20 minutes before serving.

MELON SORBET

*Use the most fragrant melon you can find – Galia, Ogen, Charentais,
Cantaloupe, or whatever. Even nicer is to make up two separate
batches of sorbet, half quantities perhaps, one with an orange-fleshed
melon, the other with a green-fleshed melon. They look charming
together in a glass – pastel-peach against pale, almondy green.*

SERVES 8

625 g/1 lb 6 oz melon flesh
450 ml/¾ pint stock syrup, see page 290
juice of 1–2 lemons

Purée the melon flesh with the syrup and lemon juice to taste
in a processor or blender. Churn or beat by hand as it freezes
(see page 279).

Move the sorbet into the fridge about 20 minutes before
serving.

ROSE PETAL SORBET WITH CRYSTALLIZED ROSE PETALS

A pretty rose-scented sorbet, a reminder of an old-fashioned country garden on a sunny June afternoon. Scatter a few crystallized rose petals or fresh blue borage flowers over each serving to complete the effect.

I find that gum arabic, from specialist food shops and chemists, is easier to use than egg white for crystallizing supple flower petals. It has the same effect, but, once dissolved, is less thick and gluey. Use the rose petals to decorate cakes, cold soufflés, and other puddings.

SERVES 4–6

3 large, fragrant, dark red roses
300 ml/½ pint medium dry white wine
juice of 2 lemons
300 ml/½ pint stock syrup, see page 290
crystallized rose petals, see below, or fresh borage flowers

Separate the rose petals. Process them with the wine and lemon juice in a processor or blender. Stir into the syrup. Churn or beat by hand as it freezes (see page 279).

Serve straight from the freezer, and decorate with crystallized rose petals or with borage flowers.

CRYSTALLIZED ROSE PETALS

6 large, fragrant, dark red roses
1 teaspoon gum arabic
1 measure of vodka
caster sugar

Separate the rose petals. Dissolve the gum arabic in the vodka. Brush both sides of each rose petal with this solution, then dust with sugar. Leave to dry overnight on a foil-lined tray in a warm place (such as the airing cupboard). Keep in an airtight container for up to a week.

Puddings

I'm not really a great pudding eater, and yet this chapter has turned out to be the longest in the book. At home I usually finish a meal with fruit and cheese. Sunday is the only pudding day. The restaurant is closed in the evening and all day Monday, so Sunday afternoon marks the beginning of our weekend. It is the one time the staff and I have a chance to sit down to a quiet, more relaxed meal together, without having to rush back to work. We have time to talk, to linger and to treat ourselves to pudding, even if our choice is dictated by what is left uneaten by the customers.

I must admit, though, that I always order a pudding when I go out for a meal. I suspect that more and more people are following this pattern, replacing the daily dose of sugar and cholesterol with fruit, looking forward to richer puddings as something special, for high days and holidays.

Although I don't have a sweet tooth, I do enjoy making puddings a great deal – hence the length of this chapter. There's a particular pleasure in seeing someone's face light up as their plate of chocolate pudding, or slice of steaming Sticky Toffee Pudding is placed before them. This is a rare treat, a moment of indulgence, the grand finale to a couple of hours spent over delicious food, in comfortable surroundings and, one hopes, in good company.

Many of the puddings are quite classical. I do sometimes go

through a period when I concentrate on more modern notions, but I end up going back to the great standards, like the bavarois or charlotte. One taste, and I find myself thinking, 'Well, that really is quite delicious.' They have an enduring quality, and though one may give them a new twist, stamping one's own mark upon them, they survive precisely because they are so good.

Constructing one of the grander desserts for a special occasion does generate a sense of achievement – try the Zebra Cake or Coffee and Praline Charlotte. They do take time to put together but most of the work can be undertaken in advance. It is time well spent. That feeling of generosity and plenty induced by the sight of a truly splendid pudding is hard to beat.

The rich, substantial puddings are always popular, but there's more and more interest in the lighter, fruity desserts. Real jellies, for instance, are staging quite a come-back, shaking off their nursery image for a much more sophisticated one. The simple countryish French crémets and cœurs à la crème, moulded, drained creams, are as much dressing as you need give soft summer fruit.

And here in Devon in the summer we have the most marvellous soft fruit: tight, firm strawberries, finger-staining loganberries, black, white, redcurrants and velvet, dusky raspberries. They are too beautiful to hide away in the kitchen, so I like to have a huge shallow bowl filled with fruit set out on the side in the dining room, as lovely as any bowl of roses. During these months I want little else but soft fruit to end a meal, with thick clotted cream, yellow and crusty, but runnier than the winter cream (made with scones and hot puddings in mind).

I try to make the best use of those ingredients that are close at hand, both cultivated and wild. Elderflowers, for instance, are very much a traditional English flavouring, but were forgotten for many years until their recent revival. In late May and June elderbushes are suddenly noticeable wherever you look. They have a musky scent, and are a natural partner with gooseberries. Dipped in batter and deep-fried, they make subtle sweet fritters, and their scent can be captured by infusing in vinegar (see page 59). Rose petals, too, give a pretty fragrance and colour to creams, sorbets and jams.

Similarly, peach leaves and blackcurrant leaves have been overlooked. I use both to flavour custards, creams and ice creams. The almondy taste of peach leaf custard or ice cream is sensational with hot baked peaches on brioche – top a buttered slice of brioche with skinned, sliced peaches, moisten with a dash of brandy, dust with vanilla sugar and bake for about 8 minutes in a hot oven, before browning briefly under the grill.

The Dartmouth Regatta takes place in mid to late August. It is the high point of the summer season. During the weeks that follow, trade and tourism begin to slacken off, and it is time to make the Christmas puddings. As well as laying up an ample supply for the restaurant itself, we send off consignments to David Mellor's Kitchen Shop in Covent Garden, and sell them in local outlets. I've experimented with several different recipes but in the end return to Eliza Acton's Christmas Pudding, which for a Victorian recipe is amazingly light. For a month or two there's a wonderful smell of dried fruits and spices wafting through the building.

There's no time to mourn the passing of summer bounty before blackberries, heralding autumn, are ripe for picking. The wild brambles are best, with an intensity of flavour that the fatter perfect-looking cultivars can't touch. They make a delicious fool-based ice cream (see page 279). Next come the new season apples, pears and quinces.

I planted a quince tree in the garden when I first moved into my house some twenty years ago. The first year it produced just two quinces, but now I get baskets full of golden fruit. It is a real blessing, and means that I can make my fill of quince puddings without having to scour the local greengrocers' shops in the hope that one of them will be daring enough to stock them. City dwellers are often rather luckier in this respect – in areas with large Greek or Greek Cypriot communities quinces are a fairly commonplace sight among the apples and pears in the autumn.

Cold winter weather means chocolate and fresh chestnuts, and our English classics – steamed puddings like the Steamed Marmalade Roll and Sticky Toffee. On a lighter note are puddings based round the imported exotic fruit, mango, papayas and cranberries, and the ever increasing collection of citrus fruits, oranges, limes, pink and yellow grapefruits. Seville oranges arrive in January for marmalade making, naturally, and to flavour baked custards and other puddings. And then it is blood oranges, with their stunning ruby-red juice, the last of the citrus fruit bringing us back full circle to spring.

USING ROSE PETALS

Rose petals, from scented, old-fashioned roses, should be used with restraint to perfume puddings. Rose petal recipes are not too common, and those that one does come across usually call for whole rose petals. However, it is easy enough to adapt basic cream-based recipes (for example, custards, bavarois, whipped creams for meringues, ice creams) by replacing the flavouring ingredient with a judicious amount of rose petal purée.

To make the purée, process rose petals with lemon juice and a spoonful or two of stock syrup (see page 290) in a processor or blender. The lemon juice is particularly important to preserve the colour. Without it the purée turns an unprepossessing, bluish colour. The purée can be frozen in small batches to be used within the next one to two months.

USING QUINCES

One of the nicest ways is to bake them whole (without coring) – just place in a pan, with a little water and a few spoonfuls of honey and bake in a preheated oven, 180°C/350°F/gas mark 4, for about 45 minutes, until tender. Their flavour is powerful, however, and this may be too strong for some tastes. If you can only lay your hands on a couple of quinces, you may well feel that this is squandering a fruit that lends its flavour out well.

The answer is to combine a small quantity of quinces with three or four times as many apples or pears. A compote of pears and quinces, sliced and simmered until tender in a vanilla syrup and eaten cold with clotted cream, is a most elegant autumn pudding. The quinces take much longer to cook than the pears – at least 30 minutes – so start them off on their own, adding the pears when the quinces are almost tender.

Quince purée, which can be frozen, can be made by baking the quinces, for the most intense flavour (see page 289), or simmering, which is quicker and so may be more convenient (see Apple and Quince Tart, page 321).

USING GELATINE

I find leaf gelatine much easier to use than the powdered variety. It dissolves more evenly into warm liquids, rarely leaving blobs of pure gelatine lurking in the depths. Although it is not as widely available as the boxed sachets of powdered gelatine, it is by no means rare. I certainly think it is worth buying several packets whenever you come across it in delicatessens and specialist food and kitchen shops.

Of course, in most recipes the two are interchangeable – they are, after all, exactly the same substance, differing only in presentation. One exception is the Chicken in Jelly with Plums on page 169, where the leaves of gelatine are layered with chicken and plum, rather than dissolved into a liquid.

Wherever gelatine is used, the important measurement is the weight required, rather than number of sheets, or sachets, and even this may need to be increased by about one-third if, say, the weather is particularly warm, or the unmoulded jelly or terrine has to survive intact for some length of time in a warm room. Where you are adding the gelatine to a very thick base, such as mayonnaise, you can, conversely, use a smaller amount than usual. If you wish to make a plain fruit jelly, set and served in individual glasses with no need for unmoulding, you can get away with using 11 g/scant ½ oz to set 900 ml/1½ pints of juice.

Whether you use leaf or powdered gelatine, check the instructions on the packet before using. Leaves of gelatine are normally soaked in cold water for 15–20 minutes, until soft. It is important to drain them thoroughly, squeezing gently to get rid of excess water. Then they are ready to be stirred into the hot (but not boiling) liquid used in the recipe, making sure that they have completely dissolved before moving on to the next stage.

GELATINE CONVERSION CHART						
(All conversions are approximate)						
Weight		Gelatine			Will Set	
Grams	Ounces	In sheets	In sachets (powder)	In rounded teaspoons	Litres/millilitres	Pints
25	1	12	2	6	1.2 l	2
20	¾	9	1½	5	900 ml	1½
15	scant ¾	8	1⅓	4	800 ml	1⅓
11	scant ½	6	1	3	600 ml	1
8	⅓	4	⅔	2	400 ml	⅔
6	scant ¼	3	½	1½	300 ml	½
4	⅙	2	⅓	1	200 ml	⅓
2	¹⁄₁₂	1	⅙	½	100 ml	⅙

Powdered gelatine is usually sprinkled over 3–4 tablespoons of water in a small pan, then left to soak for 5 minutes. It is heated slowly without boiling, stirring until it has dissolved. It should be cooled if necessary, so that it is at about the same temperature as the liquid to which it is to be added.

It is worth noting that different brands of leaf gelatine may have different weights. Some sheets are longer or wider or thicker than others. The German brand I use is very thin, and dissolves quickly – there are six sheets to 11 g/scant ½ oz, enough to set 600 ml/1 pint of liquid. Other brands may be heavier, with only three or four sheets needed to set the same amount of liquid. Always check carefully before using.

The small sachets of powdered gelatine each contain 11–13 g/scant ½ oz gelatine (3 rounded teaspoons), again enough to set 600 ml/1 pint of liquid.

TWO ORANGE TERRINE WITH MINT AND A RASPBERRY SAUCE

The brief season for blood oranges comes in early spring. Make the most of it while it lasts. The startling scarlet juice makes a refreshing drink, and set with gelatine and layered with ordinary orange juice, gives a jellied fruit terrine a dramatic twist. If you are only able to obtain the blood orange juice, see the alternative method on page 304.

SERVES 6

FOR THE TERRINE
300 ml/½ pint blood orange juice
50 g/2 oz caster sugar
11 g/scant ½ oz leaf gelatine (6 sheets), soaked, see page 301
3 oranges, peeled and separated into segments
1 tablespoon finely chopped mint
300 ml/½ pint orange juice
5 blood oranges, peeled and separated into segments

FOR THE RASPBERRY SAUCE
225 g/8 oz raspberries
50 g/2 oz caster sugar

To make the terrine, place the blood orange juice in a pan with half the sugar and 3 sheets of the gelatine. Heat gently without boiling, stirring constantly, until both the sugar and gelatine have dissolved. Rinse out a 1.2 litre/2 pint mould with cold water, or line with clingfilm. Pour a thin layer of the blood orange jelly over the base. Leave in the fridge, or even in the freezer (but don't let it freeze), until just set. Set the remaining jelly mixture aside in a warm place and allow to cool but not to set.

While it is setting, skin the plain orange segments carefully and drain on kitchen paper or on a clean tea towel. Arrange on top of the set jelly, and cover with the rest of the blood orange jelly. Sprinkle with half the mint and return to the fridge to set.

Heat the plain orange juice gently in a pan with the remaining sugar and gelatine, stirring constantly, until both the sugar and gelatine have dissolved without boiling. Leave to cool until tepid. Skin the blood orange segments and drain on kitchen paper or on a clean tea towel. Repeat the layering of jelly, then blood orange segments, jelly and mint. Leave overnight in the fridge to set firmly.

To make the raspberry sauce, process the raspberries with the sugar in a processor or blender, and rub through a fine sieve. Just before serving, turn out the terrine and peel off the clingfilm, if used. Slice thickly and serve with the raspberry sauce.

Alternatively, if you are able to obtain only blood orange juice and not the segments, heat the plain orange juice with half the sugar, half the gelatine and the mint. Pour half of this jelly over the base of the mould, stir to distribute the mint, and leave to set. Put the remaining jelly mixture aside as above.

When the jelly has set, place the skinned plain orange segments on top.

Heat the blood orange juice with the remaining sugar and gelatine and leave to cool as above, then pour onto the orange segments and leave to set.

Pour on the remaining plain orange juice and mint mixture, stir to distribute the mint and leave to set. Serve as above.

GOOSEBERRIES IN A HONEY SAFFRON CUSTARD

A few years ago I realized that although I used saffron frequently in savoury dishes, I rarely added it to anything sweet, despite being set in the middle of saffron country with its traditions of saffron cakes and buns. Experiments began, and this pretty, yellowy custard, with flecks of deeper colour traced by the filaments, was one of the most successful outcomes.

The richness of the custard is beautifully set off by the tart layer of gooseberries below. Later on in the year, blue-black damsons take the place of the gooseberries.

SERVES 6

225 g/8 oz gooseberries, topped and tailed
50 g/2 oz caster sugar
6 egg yolks
600 ml/1 pint single cream
75 g/3 oz honey
scant ¼ teaspoon saffron filaments

Put the gooseberries into a pan with the sugar and 2 tablespoons cold water. Cover tightly and stew gently for 5 minutes, until tender. Divide between six ramekins.

Whisk the egg yolks with the cream, honey and saffron, and pour into a bowl set over a pan of simmering water, making sure that the base of the bowl does not touch the water. Cook the custard over a low heat for about 10 minutes, stirring until it is thick enough to coat the back of a spoon.

Strain the custard over the gooseberries. Stand the ramekins in a roasting tin filled with warm water to a depth of 2.5 cm/1 inch. Bake in a preheated oven, 140°C/275°F/gas mark 1, for 45 minutes to 1 hour, until just set. Serve warm or cold.

Variation

DAMSONS IN A HONEY SAFFRON CUSTARD

When damsons are in season, I replace the stewed gooseberries with 225 g/8 oz damsons. Halve and stone the raw damsons, then divide them between the ramekins and sprinkle with 50 g/2 oz caster sugar. Bake in a preheated oven, 140°C/275°F/ gas mark 1, for 30 minutes.

While the damsons are cooking, prepare the saffron custard. Pour on to the hot damsons, and bake (see page 305). Serve warm or cold.

ELDERFLOWER FRITTERS WITH GOOSEBERRY SAUCE

The scent of elderflowers is a strange one – people either love or hate it. The lacy heads of flowers, deep-fried in a case of airy batter, make a dream of a pudding for those who fall into the former camp. For the best fritters, use elderflowers no more than a few hours after they are picked. Choose heads that are relatively insect-free, and growing as far away from a main road as possible.

SERVES 4

8 freshly picked elderflower heads
oil for deep-frying
icing sugar

FOR THE SAUCE
225 g/8 oz gooseberries, topped and tailed
75 g/3 oz caster sugar

FOR THE BATTER
100 g/4 oz flour
1 pinch of salt
2 tablespoons groundnut oil
1 egg white

To make the sauce, wash the gooseberries and put them into a pan with the sugar. Cover tightly, and cook over a gentle heat, shaking occasionally, for about 10 minutes until tender. Rub through a sieve.

To make the batter, sift the flour with the salt into a large bowl. Make a well in the middle and pour in the oil and enough cold water to mix to a thick cream. Set aside until ready to use, then whisk the egg white until it forms stiff peaks and fold in.

Heat the oil to 185°C/360°F. Shake the elderflowers to get

rid of any insects. Dip into the batter, shake off the surplus and deep-fry for about 8 minutes, turning once, until puffed and golden. Drain quickly on kitchen paper. Divide the hot sauce between four plates, arrange the fritters on top and dust with icing sugar.

ROSE PETAL CREAM
WITH STRAWBERRIES

*Greenway House, just a few miles upstream, is set in the midst of
beautiful gardens full of old-fashioned roses. When they bloom in
June and July their glorious scent fills the air. The roses we use to
make this fragrant cream, and other rose petal confections, come from
Greenway, by kind permission of Mrs Hicks.*
*This is the simplest of summery puddings, and one of the most
pleasing, served with* langues-de-chat *or macaroon finger biscuits.*

SERVES 6–8

1 fragrant, dark red rose
150 ml/¼ pint single cream
1 tablespoon caster sugar
lemon juice
150 ml/¼ pint double cream
450 g/1 lb strawberries

Separate the rose petals. Whizz the rose petals with the single
cream, sugar, and a dash of lemon juice in a blender. Mix with
the double cream and whisk lightly. Hull the strawberries and
halve if large. Layer with the rose petal cream in a single bowl
or in individual glasses.

BLACKCURRANT PORT JELLY

*A dark purple-black jelly with the deep, earthy taste of blackcurrants
– just the thing to round off a good meal, cool and soothing, and
glamorously simple. It is even better with a few slices of poached pear
embedded in it.*

SERVES 6

225 g/8 oz blackcurrants
100 g/4 oz granulated sugar
300 ml/½ pint cold water
150 ml/¼ pint port
8 g/⅓ oz leaf gelatine (4 sheets), soaked, see page 301

Simmer the blackcurrants with the sugar, water and port until
tender. Pass through a *mouli légumes* or a sieve to remove seeds.
While the sieved blackcurrants are still warm, add the gelatine
and stir until it has completely dissolved. If necessary, reheat
gently without boiling to finish dissolving the gelatine. Pour
into six glasses, and leave to set in the fridge.

VARIATION

*BLACKCURRANT PORT JELLY
WITH POACHED PEARS*

Peel, core and halve 3 pears. Place in a pan with
100 g/4 oz granulated sugar and 300 ml/½ pint cold water or
red wine and bring to the boil. Simmer gently for 15 minutes,
until tender. Lift out of the cooking liquid and drain on kitchen
paper. Make the blackcurrant jelly as above. Divide about one-
third of it between six bowls and leave to set in the fridge. Set
the remaining jelly aside. Slice each pear and lay the slices on
top of the set jelly. Spoon just enough of the rest of the jelly over

and round the pear slices to anchor them down, but not enough to set them floating. Chill until set, and then divide the remaining jelly between the bowls, covering the pears completely. Chill until set firm.

BLACKCURRANT (OR REDCURRANT) MERINGUE CAKE

This is a super combination of sharp and sweet against the sandy almond shortcrust. What is most appealing is the fresh taste of the fruit. Protected from the fierce blast of heat by the insulating meringue, the currants are warmed until they begin to collapse, but not enough to be cooked. It is just as good made with redcurrants and although I've not yet tried it, I suspect that raspberries might work equally well.

SERVES 8

450 g/1 lb blackcurrants or redcurrants, stripped of stalks
100 g/4 oz caster sugar

FOR THE BASE
150 g/5 oz butter, softened
100 g/4 oz caster sugar
4 egg yolks
75 g/3 oz ground almonds
250 g/9 oz flour, sifted

FOR THE MERINGUE
4 egg whites
100 g/4 oz caster sugar

To make the base, cream the butter with the sugar in a bowl until pale and fluffy. Add the egg yolks and mix well. Fold in the almonds and the flour. Spread the mixture in a buttered 25 cm/10 inch tart tin and bake in a preheated oven, 190°C/375°F/gas mark 5, for 30 minutes, until firm and pale biscuit-brown.

Mix the blackcurrants or redcurrants with the sugar. Spread evenly over the base, leaving a 1.25 cm/½ inch gap round the edge.

To make the meringue, whisk the egg whites until they hold stiff peaks, and add half the sugar. Whisk again until the mixture is shiny and smooth. Fold in the remaining sugar.

Spread over the blackcurrants or redcurrants, roughing up the surface with the tines of a fork. Increase the oven temperature to 220°C/425°F/gas mark 7 and bake the cake for 5–10 minutes, until the peaks are lightly browned and the meringue is just firm. Serve warm or cold.

LEMON CRÉMETS

*We use the traditional French heart-shaped china moulds, which are
pierced to let the whey drain off, for these lemon creams, but less
elegant though they may be, 150 ml/¼ pint yoghurt or cream pots,
pierced with a sharp knife or a hot skewer, do the job just as well.
The crémets are light and creamy, with just enough lemon to prevent
them becoming cloying. Lovely with soft fruit, poached peaches, a
good home-made jam, or on their own with a crisp biscuit.*

SERVES 6

250 ml/8 fl oz single cream
250 ml/8 fl oz double cream
50 g/2 oz caster sugar
juice and finely grated zest of 1 lemon
2 egg whites

Put the creams into a bowl with the sugar, lemon zest and juice.
Whip until it forms soft peaks. Whisk the egg whites until they
hold stiff peaks and fold into the whipped cream.

Line six pierced moulds with muslin and divide the cream
between them. Tap the moulds gently to settle the filling. Fold
the muslin over the surface of the cream. Stand the moulds on a
rack over a tray in a cool place and leave to drain overnight.

Turn out and peel off the muslin.

PEACH LEAF CUSTARD

*Many people who own a peach tree spend so much time nursing
along the fruit, without realizing that the leaves, too, are of culinary
value. They give a bitter almond flavour to this thick custard, which
is delicious on its own, or with the Pistachio and Almond Loaf (see
page 325). Increase the sugar, fold in 300 ml/½ pint whipped
double cream, freeze and you have a rich peach leaf ice cream.*

SERVES 6

8 egg yolks
600 ml/1 pint single cream
1 tablespoon vanilla sugar
6 peach leaves

Whisk the egg yolks with the cream and sugar and pour into a
bowl set over a pan of simmering water, making sure that the
base of the bowl does not touch the water. Add the peach
leaves. Cook the custard over a low heat for about 5 minutes,
stirring until it is thick enough to coat the back of the spoon.

Strain into individual glasses or pots, or a single serving dish,
and leave to set.

LIQUEUR BAVAROIS

I'm particularly partial to the taste of Cointreau or Grand Marnier in this velvety bavarois, but any good liqueur can be used. I've sometimes replaced the alcohol with the same quantity of rose petal purée (see page 299). Peach leaves give a good flavour (see Peach Leaf Custard on page 315 for method), and so too do bitter almonds.

In fact, this is really just a basic bavarois recipe which you can flavour as you wish. For an even posher pudding, layer two or three flavours or set it in a ring mould and fill the centre with a tumble of fresh raspberries or redcurrants.

SERVES 6

4 egg yolks
300 ml/½ pint milk
100 g/4 oz caster sugar
8 g/⅓ oz leaf gelatine (4 sheets), soaked, see page 301
300 ml/½ pint double cream
1 tablespoon liqueur (Cointreau or Grand Marnier, for example)

Whisk the egg yolks with the milk and sugar and pour into a bowl set over a pan of simmering water, making sure that the base of the bowl does not touch the water. Cook the custard over a low heat for about 5 minutes, stirring until it is thick enough to coat the back of the spoon. Strain.

Stir the gelatine into the warm custard until it has dissolved. Cool in the fridge until almost set.

Whip the cream lightly with the liqueur. Fold into the custard. Either divide between six individual glasses, or rinse out one large mould with cold water and fill with the bavarois. Leave to set in the fridge and, if you have used a single, decorative mould, just before serving dip the mould into hot water for a couple of seconds and turn the bavarois out on to a serving dish.

BROWN SUGAR MERINGUES

These brown sugar meringues make a nice change from ordinary meringues. They are not quite so sweet, and have a hint of caramel. Serve them with whipped cream or, even nicer, with thick, yellow clotted cream, and soft fruit, or pipe tiny rosettes to serve with coffee. The slower you cook meringues the better they are. I make the meringue mixture in the evening, give them 15 minutes at 110°C/ 225°F/gas mark ¼ and turn off the heat without opening the door, leaving just the warmth from the pilot light and residual heat of the oven to dry them out overnight. The meringues are dry and crumbly through to the heart.

MAKES AROUND 12 FULL-SIZE MERINGUES

100 g/4 oz caster sugar
100 g/4 oz dark muscovado sugar
4 egg whites

Mix together the two sugars. Whisk the egg whites until they hold stiff peaks and add half the sugar, a tablespoonful at a time, whisking in well before adding the next. Continue to beat until the mixture is smooth and shiny. Fold in the remaining sugar.

Pipe or spoon the meringue on to a baking sheet lined with foil in 5 cm/2 inch rounds or in 10 cm/4 inch nests, building up the sides if you want to fill them with cream or fruit. Bake slowly in a preheated oven, 70°C/150°F/gas mark ¼, for 3 hours, until the meringues are dry and crisp.

GRAPES IN MUSCAT JELLY

*Muscat grapes are grown locally, just down the road in Strete. The
weather here is warm enough for them to develop the full muscat
scent to balance out their intense sweetness. The best of grapes, they
are awaited with keen anticipation as autumn begins. Look out for
imported Italian muscat grapes, plump and at their peak as they
mature from green to a pale honey colour.*

*Here they are set in a Beaumes de Venise jelly, which echoes the
muscat flavour. If you have time, set the grapes in two or three layers
rather than in the single one suggested.*

SERVES 4

150 ml/¼ pint water
150 ml/¼ pint stock syrup, see page 290
8 g/⅓ oz leaf gelatine (4 sheets), soaked, see page 301
300 ml/½ pint Beaumes de Venise or other sweet white wine
juice of ½–1 lemon
48 muscat grapes, peeled and pipped

Heat the water and syrup until hot but not boiling. Add the
gelatine and stir until it has dissolved. Leave to cool until
tepid. Stir in the wine and lemon juice to taste.

Set half the jelly aside, and divide the rest between four
glasses. Leave in the fridge to set. Pile about 12 grapes into each
glass, and pour in the remaining jelly. Return to the fridge to
finish setting.

AUTUMN FRUIT SALAD

This is a delicious autumnal or wintry cooked fruit salad with the contrasting textures and tastes of dried and fresh fruits, bathed in a spiced red wine syrup. Our version is inspired by a recipe from Roger Vergé's Cuisine of the Sun. *We vary the recipe sometimes by adding dried figs, quince slices, walnuts and so on. It tastes good with cream, or a scoop of home-made vanilla ice cream, but best of all with a swirl of Quince Parfait (see page 288).*

SERVES 4

12 prunes
300 ml/½ pint red wine
2 clementines, unpeeled
2 firm Comice pears, peeled, quartered and cored
150 g/5 oz clear honey
8 pecan halves
1 bay leaf
2.5 cm/1 inch piece of cinnamon
½ vanilla pod

Soak the prunes in the wine for 8 hours or overnight. Next day, cut the ends off the clementines and slice each into four rings. Place in a pan or flameproof casserole with the prunes, wine and the remaining ingredients. Bring slowly to the boil, cover and reduce the heat. Simmer very gently for 30 minutes, until the fruit is tender. Remove the spices and bay leaf. Serve lightly chilled.

QUINCE CUSTARDS

The tender slices of quince are a treat waiting to be discovered underneath the depths of honeyed baked custard. This is a very special pudding, rich yet light, with marvellous flavours, delicious hot from the oven, and maybe even better served at room temperature or barely chilled.

SERVES 6

FOR THE POACHED QUINCE
450 g/1 lb quinces
100 g/4 oz caster sugar
1 vanilla pod
150 ml/¼ pint cold water

FOR THE CUSTARD
600 ml/1 pint single cream
6 egg yolks
1 generous pinch of saffron filaments
50 g/2 oz clear honey

Peel, core and slice the quinces. Place in a pan with the remaining poached quince ingredients, cover and cook gently for about 30 minutes, until the quince is tender and the juices are thick and jammy. Remove the vanilla pod. Divide between six ramekins.

Whisk together the custard ingredients and pour into a bowl set over a pan of simmering water, making sure that the base of the bowl does not touch the water. Cook the custard over a low heat for about 5 minutes, stirring until it is thick enough to coat the back of the spoon. Strain and pour over the quinces.

Stand the ramekins in a roasting tin filled with warm water to a depth of 2.5 cm/1 inch. Place in a preheated oven, 140°C/275°F/gas mark 1, and cook for 1 hour, until set. Eat warm or cold.

APPLE AND QUINCE TART

This is a marvellously fragrant, open apple tart, with its hidden layer
of quince purée. Nothing is wasted – all the trimmings from the fruit
are boiled up to extract the last drops of flavour for the final glaze.
I usually make it in a long, narrow flan tin, so that it can be cut into
fingers, but a 23 cm/9 inch circular tart tin can be used instead.

SERVES 8–10

225 g/8 oz sweet flan pastry, see page 349
900 g/2 lb quinces
350 g/12 oz caster sugar
675 g/1½ lb Cox's Orange Pippins

Line a 10 × 23 cm/4 × 9 inch oblong flan tin with the pastry.
Leave to rest in the fridge for 30 minutes. Line the tin with
greaseproof paper, weight with baking beans and bake 'blind'
in a preheated oven, 220°C/425°F/gas mark 7, for 10 minutes.
Remove the beans and paper and return the pastry to the oven
for 5 minutes to dry out. Set the pastry aside.

Peel, quarter and core the quinces. Save the trimmings, and
place the quince quarters in a pan with 75 g/3 oz of the sugar
and 150 ml/¼ pint cold water. Cover and stew gently for about
30 minutes, until the fruit is tender and collapsing. Mash to a
purée and rub through a sieve.

Spread the purée on the pastry. Peel, quarter and core the
apples. Save the trimmings. Slice the apples thinly and arrange
on top of the purée. Sprinkle with 25 g/1 oz of sugar and bake in
a preheated oven, 180°C/350°F/gas mark 4, for 30 minutes.

Place the quince and apple trimmings in a pan with 600 ml/
1 pint cold water. Bring to the boil and simmer gently for 30
minutes. Strain off the liquid – you should have about 300 ml/
½ pint. Stir the remaining sugar into the liquid until it has dissolved. Return to the pan, bring to the boil and boil hard for 5
minutes, or longer if necessary, to make a syrupy glaze. Brush
the glaze over the tart, and leave to cool. Serve warm.

CINNAMON CREAM WITH POACHED PEARS

This cinnamon cream is another variation on the basic French 'crémets', drained moulded cream, lightened with egg white. The warm spiciness of cinnamon makes this an ideal partner for poached pears.
Use either the French heart-shaped, perforated china moulds, or 150 ml/¼ pint yoghurt or cream pots pierced with a sharp knife or a hot skewer so that the whey can drain off.

SERVES 6

FOR THE CREAM
300 ml/½ pint double cream
1 tablespoon caster sugar
1 teaspoon ground cinnamon
1 egg white

FOR THE PEARS
3 firm pears
150 ml/¼ pint red or dry white wine
150 ml/¼ pint stock syrup, see page 290

Whip the cream lightly and fold in the sugar and cinnamon. Whisk the egg white until it holds stiff peaks and fold into the cream. Line six small perforated moulds with muslin, and fill with the cream mixture. Tap the moulds gently to settle the filling. Fold the muslin over the surface of the cream. Stand the moulds on a rack over a tray in a cool place and drain for 8 hours or overnight.

Peel, core and slice the pears. Place in a pan with the wine and syrup and bring to the boil. Simmer gently for 10 minutes, until tender. Remove from the heat and leave to cool in the cooking liquid.

Turn out the creams, peel off the muslin, and serve with the drained, poached pears.

COCONUT CREAM WITH MANGO, LIME AND PINK GRAPEFRUIT

A pudding to set one dreaming of the Caribbean in the depths of our winter, when mangoes, grapefruits and limes are most plentiful. There's a real balancing act going on here – sharp lime, sweet mango with its turpentine scent, fresh pink grapefruit against the creamy coconut mousse. Adapted from a recipe in Jane Grigson's Fruit Book, *it is good too with fresh pineapple.*

SERVES 4

1 mango
1 lime
1 pink grapefruit
extra sugar

FOR THE COCONUT CREAM
150 ml/¼ pint milk
65 ml/2½ fl oz single cream
20 g/¾ oz creamed coconut, grated
20 g/¾ oz granulated sugar
1 vanilla pod
4 g/⅙ oz leaf gelatine (approximately 2 sheets), soaked,
see page 301
lemon juice
150 ml/¼ pint double cream

To make the coconut cream, put the milk, single cream, coconut, sugar and vanilla pod into a pan and warm gently, whisking with a flat whisk to dissolve the coconut. Add the gelatine and mix thoroughly until it has dissolved. Remove the vanilla pod and sharpen with a squeeze of lemon juice. Leave to cool in the fridge until beginning to set.

Whip the double cream lightly and fold into the coconut cream. Line four 150 ml/¼ pint moulds with clingfilm and spoon the cream into them. Leave in the fridge to set.

Peel and slice the mango. Pare the zest off the lime in long strips, being careful to avoid the white pith. Blanch for 1 minute in boiling water then cut into long shreds. Peel the lime and the grapefruit, taking off all the white pith. Separate into segments and carefully pull off the thin skins. Mix together all the fruit and lime shreds and sprinkle with a little sugar.

Turn out the coconut creams, peel off the clingfilm, and serve with the fruit.

PISTACHIO AND ALMOND LOAF
WITH APRICOT SAUCE

*This loaf of ground nuts and citrus zest bound together with the
lightest wine 'soufflé' is marvellously delicate – too delicate, even, to
be sliced straight from the oven, though if you did want to serve it
hot, you could pour it into individual moulds.*
*Hot, warm or cold, surround with a pool of plain apricot sauce, or a
richer Peach Leaf Custard (see page 315) or, better still, both, and
maybe some slices of fresh fruit – peaches or mangoes perhaps. The
recipe comes from Richard Olney's* Simple French Food.

SERVES 6

50 g/2 oz pistachio nuts
100 g/4 oz blanched almonds
finely grated zest of 1 orange
finely grated zest of 1 lemon
75 g/3 oz caster sugar
4 tablespoons dry or medium white wine
3 eggs, separated

FOR THE APRICOT SAUCE
100 g/4 oz dried apricots
juice of ½ lemon
100 g/4 oz vanilla sugar, see page 24

Pour boiling water over the pistachios and leave for 30 seconds.
Drain, skin, and leave to dry. Place the dry nuts in a processor or
blender with the almonds and orange and lemon zests and
whizz to a rough powder. Add the sugar, wine and egg yolks
and whizz again until thick.

Whisk the egg whites until they hold stiff peaks and fold into
the nut mixture. Pour into a clingfilm-lined 900 g/2 lb loaf tin.
Stand the tin in a roasting tin, filled with warm water to a
depth of 2.5 cm/1 inch. Cook in a preheated oven, 160°C/

325°F/gas mark 3, for 45 minutes to 1 hour, until firm. Leave to cool until tepid.

To make the sauce, put the apricots and lemon juice into a pan with 300 ml/½ pint cold water. Cover and cook for about 30 minutes, until tender. Process with the vanilla sugar in a processor or blender, and leave to cool.

Turn the loaf out on to a serving dish, peel off the clingfilm, and serve in thick slices with the sauce.

GRAND MARNIER SOUFFLÉ

A classic, hot, sweet soufflé which provides a tremendous finale to a meal. Enjoy it on its own with just a crisp biscuit, but even more with a fruit compote, or a scoop of ice cream. The contrast of very hot and very cold, and of strong flavours (try a chocolate ice cream, for instance) is excellent.

SERVES 4–6

40 g/1½ oz unsalted butter
2 level tablespoons flour
150 ml/¼ pint milk
75 g/3 oz caster sugar, plus extra for dusting
50 ml/2 fl oz Grand Marnier
4 egg yolks
5 egg whites
icing sugar

Melt the butter in a pan and stir in the flour to form a *roux*. Cook for 1 minute, remove from the heat and gradually stir in the milk. Add the sugar. Return to the heat and bring gently to the boil. Simmer for 10 minutes. Remove from the heat and stir in the Grand Marnier and then the egg yolks. Leave the mixture to cool until tepid.

Butter a 1.4 litre/2½ pint soufflé dish, or six 300 ml/½ pint dishes, and dust with caster sugar. Whisk the egg whites until they hold stiff peaks and fold into the Grand Marnier base. Pour into the prepared dish(es), filling no more than two-thirds full. Stand the dish(es) in a roasting tin, filled with hot water to a depth of 2.5 cm/1 inch. Bake in a preheated oven, 200°C/400°F/gas mark 6, for 25–30 minutes for a single soufflé, 10–15 minutes for individual soufflés, until puffed and browned. Remove from the oven, dust with icing sugar, and serve immediately.

CHOCOLATE POTS

*This is the most wonderfully simple and luxurious chocolate cream,
that takes literally minutes to make, without any worries about
overheating the chocolate. I love it served like this in little ramekins,
with a few crisp finger biscuits, but I occasionally use it as a filling.
One very successful pudding was created by lining a roly-poly mould
with the striped Zebra Cake (see page 336) moistened with brandy,
filling with this chocolate cream, cooled until almost set, and covering
with a last layer of cake. After two hours in the fridge, it sliced
perfectly to give discs of chocolate edged with stripes of dark and light
cake.*

SERVES 6

300 ml/½ pint single cream
200 g/7 oz plain chocolate
1 egg
1 tablespoon brandy

Place the cream in a pan and bring to the boil. Break the chocolate into squares and put into the processor or blender. Add the boiling cream and process until smooth. Add the egg and the brandy and mix well. Pour into six ramekins and leave in the fridge to set.

COFFEE AND PRALINE CHARLOTTE

Both this and the Charlotte Louise which follows are rich, classic puddings that are perfect for a party or special dinner. All the work of lining and filling the mould is done at leisure some 24 hours in advance, so that it merely needs to be turned out just before serving.

SERVES 6–8

50 g/2 oz ground coffee
600 ml/1 pint milk
5 egg yolks
100 g/4 oz caster sugar
11 g/scant ½ oz leaf gelatine (6 sheets), soaked, see page 301
450 ml/¾ pint double cream
24 sponge finger biscuits
2 tablespoons Tia Maria
2 tablespoons stock syrup, see page 290

FOR THE PRALINE
50 g/2 oz hazelnuts
50 g/2 oz caster sugar

To make the praline, spread out the hazelnuts on a baking sheet and toast in a preheated hot oven for 5–10 minutes. When cool enough to handle, rub between the palms of your hands to remove the papery skins. Chop roughly.

Place the sugar in a small pan with 1 tablespoon cold water. Stir over a medium heat, without boiling, until the sugar has dissolved, then increase the heat. Boil until it turns a light brown, watching the pan constantly. Immediately tip in the hazelnuts, bring back to the boil and remove from the heat. Pour on to a lightly oiled baking sheet and leave to cool and harden. Break into pieces, and grind to a powder. Store until needed in an airtight container.

To make the charlotte, put the coffee and milk into a pan, and bring to the boil. Remove from the heat, cover, and leave to infuse for 20 minutes. Strain through muslin, return to the pan and reserve.

Whisk the egg yolks with the sugar until light and fluffy. Bring the coffee-flavoured milk to the boil and pour on to the egg yolks and sugar, whisking constantly. Return to the pan and stir over a low heat for about 5 minutes, without boiling, until the custard is thick enough to coat the back of the spoon. Strain.

Stir the gelatine into the warm custard until thoroughly dissolved. Leave to cool. When almost set, whip the cream lightly and fold in with the praline.

Take a 1.75 litre/3 pint mould – a soufflé dish, or an oblong mould, for instance – line with clingfilm, and cover the base with finger biscuits, curved side down, cut into wedges so that they can be arranged like the petals of a flower. Stand more finger biscuits upright round the sides, again curved sides against the mould, wedged tightly into position. Make sure there are no gaps, and reserve the remaining biscuits for the top. Mix together the Tia Maria and the syrup and sprinkle three-quarters of it over the biscuit-lined mould.

Fill the mould with the praline cream, tapping it against the work surface to expel any air bubbles. Cover the top with the remaining biscuits and any trimmings and sprinkle with the rest of the Tia Maria. Cover with clingfilm and chill for 12 hours or overnight. Turn out before serving and peel off the clingfilm.

CHARLOTTE LOUISE

The recipe for Charlotte Louise was given to us by Sally Jaine. It really is a splendid pudding with its filling of chocolate, orange and cream enclosed in a shell of finger biscuits.

SERVES 6

18 sponge finger biscuits
25 ml/1 fl oz Orange Curaçao
225 g/8 oz plain chocolate
50 g/2 oz butter
juice and finely grated zest of 2 small oranges
300 ml/½ pint double cream

Line a 900 ml/1½ pint mould with clingfilm, then with the sponge finger biscuits, sprinkling with the Curaçao, as for the Coffee and Praline Charlotte (see page 329).

Break the chocolate into squares and place in a bowl with the butter. Set over a pan of simmering water, making sure that the base of the bowl does not touch the water. When the chocolate and butter have melted, remove from the heat and, little by little, stir in the orange zest and juice. Leave to cool.

Whip the cream lightly and fold into the chocolate. Fill the lined mould with this mixture and finish as for the Coffee and Praline Charlotte.

CHOCOLATE AND CHESTNUT CAKE

This flourless cake is one of the first recipes I turn to when fresh chestnuts come into season. It really does have to be freshly cooked and sieved chestnut, not tinned purée, but the delicate cake that emerges from the oven is more than ample reward for all the extra work.
See the recipe for Chestnut and Walnut Pie on page 267 for method of cooking the chestnuts, but rub them through a sieve rather than chop them.

SERVES 8–10

FOR THE CAKE
4 eggs, separated
225 g/8 oz caster sugar
225 g/8 oz cold, sieved, cooked chestnut
75 g/3 oz chocolate, grated

FOR THE FILLING
150 ml/¼ pint double cream
25 g/1 oz caster sugar
50 g/2 oz cold, sieved, cooked chestnut
1 tablespoon brandy

FOR THE ICING
150 g/6 oz plain chocolate
2 tablespoons caster sugar
50 g/2 oz unsalted butter, diced

To make the cake, beat the egg yolks with the sugar thoroughly in a bowl. Fold in the chestnut and the chocolate. Whisk the egg whites until they hold stiff peaks and fold in. Spread the mixture in two buttered 20 cm/8 inch flan rings on foil-lined baking sheets. Bake in a preheated oven, 180°C/350°F/gas mark 4, for 15–20 minutes, until just firm. Allow to cool, then remove the flan rings and peel off the foil.

To make the filling, whip the cream lightly with the sugar. Mix together the chestnut and brandy and fold into the cream. Sandwich the two cakes together with the filling.

For the icing, break the chocolate into squares and place in a bowl with the sugar and 4 tablespoons cold water. Set over a pan of simmering water, making sure that the base of the bowl does not touch the water. Stir occasionally as it melts. Remove from the heat and beat in the butter, bit by bit. Leave to cool until it begins to thicken. Pour over the cake and smooth the surface and sides of the cake with a palette knife. Leave to set. Serve cut into thick slices.

CHOCOLATE MOUSSE ROULADE

Many years ago, I used melted chocolate in the sponge mixture for the chocolate roulade and very good it was too. But I now use cocoa instead, which I think is even better, giving it a bitter-sweet taste which is sensational with the chocolate mousse filling.
In the summer we often replace the chocolate mousse with fresh strawberries, or even use both in the filling.

SERVES 8

FOR THE SPONGE
oil
6 eggs, separated
150 g/5 oz caster sugar
50 g/2 oz cocoa, sifted

FOR THE FILLING
225 g/8 oz plain chocolate
100 g/4 oz butter
50 ml/2 fl oz brandy or rum
4 eggs, separated
600 ml/1 pint double cream

To make the sponge, brush a 45 × 30 cm/18 × 12 inch baking tin with oil, and line with greaseproof paper or baking parchment. Brush the paper lightly with oil.

Beat the egg yolks with the sugar in a bowl until light and fluffy, then stir in the cocoa. Whisk the egg whites until they hold stiff peaks and fold in. Spread the mixture evenly in the tin and bake in a preheated oven, 190°C/375°F/gas mark 5, for 15 minutes, until firm to the touch. Turn out on to a clingfilm-lined tray, cool and peel off the paper.

To make the filling, break the chocolate into squares and place in a bowl with the butter. Set over a pan of simmering water, making sure that the base of the bowl does not touch the water. When the chocolate and butter have melted, beat in the brandy or rum and egg yolks, and leave to cool until tepid. Whisk the egg whites until they hold stiff peaks and fold into the chocolate mixture.

Whip the cream fairly stiffly. Spread the mousse mixture evenly over the cake and then spread the cream on top. Now carefully roll up the cake, using the clingfilm to mould it into shape as you roll. Wrap tightly in foil or clingfilm and chill for 30 minutes before peeling off the covering and cutting into 1.25 cm/½ inch thick slices.

ZEBRA CAKE WITH CHOCOLATE AND LIQUEUR CREAMS

As you might well have guessed from the name, this glamorous, indulgent cake is streaked with dark chocolate and white stripes. It looks impressive, tastes sensational, but is surprisingly easy to put together. Make it a good twenty-four hours in advance so that it has plenty of time to set.

SERVES 10

FOR THE CAKE BASE
6 eggs
190 g/6½ oz caster sugar
165 g/5½ oz flour, sifted
20 g/¾ oz cocoa, sifted
75 ml/3 fl oz stock syrup, see page 290
50 ml/2 fl oz Grand Marnier

FOR THE FILLING
Chocolate Cream
Grand Marnier Cream

Whisk the eggs in a bowl with the sugar until thick and fluffy. Spoon half the mixture into a separate bowl. Fold 75 g/3 oz of the flour into one half and the remaining flour and the cocoa into the other.

Line a 45 × 30 cm/18 × 12 inch Swiss roll tin with non-stick baking parchment and pipe or spoon alternate lines of plain and cocoa cake mixtures, side by side, diagonally across the tin. Bake in a preheated oven, 180°C/350°F/gas mark 4, for 15 minutes, until firm to the touch. Turn out and cool on a cake rack.

Cut two 23 cm/9 inch circles from the cake, and slip one into a 23 cm/9 inch cake tin lined with clingfilm. Use the trimmings to line the sides of the tin, without leaving any gaps. Mix together the syrup and the Grand Marnier, and sprinkle over the cake to moisten. Fill with alternate spoonfuls of Chocolate and Grand Marnier Cream, smoothing down carefully without mixing. Trim sides level with the filling, and cover with the second circle of cake. Cover and chill for 24 hours before turning out and peeling off clingfilm.

CHOCOLATE CREAM

100 g/4 oz plain chocolate
325 ml/11 fl oz milk
3 egg yolks
100 g/4 oz caster sugar
25 g/1 oz flour
4 g/⅙ oz leaf gelatine (2 sheets), soaked, see page 301
325 ml/11 fl oz double cream

Break the chocolate into small pieces and place in a pan with the milk over a gentle heat. Stir without boiling until the chocolate has dissolved. Whisk the egg yolks in a bowl with the sugar until pale and thick, then fold in the flour. Add the chocolate milk, whisking constantly. Return the mixture to the pan, stir over a medium heat and bring gently to the boil. Cook for 2 minutes, stirring constantly. Remove from the heat and add the gelatine. Stir until it has completely dissolved. Leave to cool until tepid. Whip the cream lightly and fold in.

GRAND MARNIER CREAM

4 egg yolks
75 g/3 oz caster sugar
325 ml/11 fl oz milk
6 g/scant ¼ oz leaf gelatine (3 sheets), soaked, see page 301
65 ml/2½ fl oz Grand Marnier
275 ml/9 fl oz double cream

Whisk the egg yolks in a bowl with the sugar until thick and pale. Bring the milk to the boil, remove from heat and pour in a slow, steady stream on to the egg yolks, whisking constantly. Pour the mixture back into the pan and stir over a gentle heat, without boiling, until it is thick enough to coat the back of the spoon. Strain and quickly stir the gelatine into the warm custard until it has completely dissolved. Add the Grand Marnier and leave to cool until tepid. Whip the cream lightly and fold in.

STEAMED MARMALADE ROLL

'I know I shouldn't, but maybe, just this once . . .' A line that echoes round the dining room at Dartmouth whenever we have this Steamed Marmalade Roll, or the Sticky Toffee Pudding that follows, on the menu. And the worse the weather, the more it's heard. On really horrible damp and cold winter Sundays I can guarantee that there will be no steamed puds left by the time the restaurant empties.

SERVES 8

2 eggs
butter ⎫
caster sugar ⎬ for quantities see method
self-raising flour, sifted ⎭
2 tablespoons milk
225 g/8 oz marmalade

FOR THE TOPPING
100 g/4 oz marmalade
2 tablespoons brandy

Weigh the eggs, and then weigh out equal quantities of butter, sugar and flour. Cream the butter with the sugar in a bowl until light and fluffy. Gradually beat in the eggs, then fold in the flour and add enough milk to mix to a soft dropping consistency. Spread the marmalade over the base of a buttered 30 cm/ 12 inch hinged roly-poly mould or a 1.2 litre/2 pint pudding basin, and spread the cake mixture evenly over it. Close the mould or cover the basin with foil and secure tightly with string. Steam for 1½ hours. Check every 20 minutes or so that the pan has not boiled dry and keep topping up with boiling water.

To make the topping, warm the marmalade in a pan with the brandy, mixing thoroughly. Turn out the marmalade roll on to a warmed serving dish and spread the marmalade and brandy over the top. Serve immediately.

STICKY TOFFEE PUDDING

*At the famous Sharrow Bay Hotel in the Lake District they make a
baked Sticky Toffee Pudding studded with dates. It is a pudding I
love, and was the inspiration for The Carved Angel's Sticky Toffee
Pudding. I use apricots where they use dates, increase the sticky toffee
topping, and steam the mixture instead of baking it. The apricots,
chopped so finely that you barely realize what they are (use a
processor for this), give a mild sharpness.*

SERVES 8–10

FOR THE PUDDING
175 g/6 oz dried apricots, very finely chopped
1 teaspoon bicarbonate of soda
300 ml/½ pint boiling water
50 g/2 oz butter
100 g/4 oz caster sugar
50 g/2 oz vanilla sugar
1 egg, beaten
225 g/8 oz flour
1 teaspoon baking powder

FOR THE TOPPING
215 g/7½ oz dark muscovado sugar
115 g/4½ oz butter
6 tablespoons double cream

Place the topping ingredients in a small pan and stir over a
gentle heat until the butter has melted and the sugar dissolved.
Bring to the boil and simmer for 3 minutes. Pour into two
buttered 900 ml/1½ pint pudding basins.

Place the apricots in a bowl with the bicarbonate and pour
the boiling water over them. Leave to cool thoroughly. Cream
the butter in a bowl with the caster and vanilla sugars until

light and fluffy. Beat in the egg. Sift the flour with the baking powder and fold in. Stir the apricot mixture into the batter and divide between the two pudding basins.

Cover each basin with foil and secure tightly with string, leaving long ends. Knot these to make a handle across the basin so that it can easily be lifted out of the steamer.

Place the bowls on trivets in a large pan and surround with enough hot water to come halfway up. Cover and steam for 1½ hours. Check every 20 minutes or so that the pan has not boiled dry and keep topping up with boiling water. Lift out of the water and turn the puddings out on to a warmed serving dish. Serve immediately.

Pastries, Biscuits *& Petits Fours*

It is often the asides, the *amuse-gueules*, breads and pastries, biscuits and petits fours, that make or break a meal. If the first mouthful of food, however basic or small, is delicious, then the right mood of pleasurable anticipation is set straight from the start. And if your very last morsel, the petits fours that you toyed with over coffee, was so good that you couldn't bear to leave the last one alone on the plate, then the memory you carry away with you is rounded off with satisfaction.

I am as pleased by the sight of a bowl of cool, red radishes, with a pat of unsalted butter, or of olives marinated with herbs and garlic, as by the most intricate of canapés. Cheese sablés, cut into fingers, are barely more effort – the dough, like so many pastries, can be frozen in rolls, and a few slices shaved off and baked at a moment's notice.

No matter how good a filling may be, if the pastry case supporting it is lousy, the overall impression is bound to be poor. Never let small amounts of pastry or biscuit dough go to waste. Even a couple of ounces can be frozen, to be rolled out thinly at a later date to make canapé bases or little tartlet cases. For instance, the Sesame and the Oatmeal savoury biscuit doughs on pages 351 and 352 can both be used in this way. These can be topped or filled with any number of things – an excellent means of stretching some expensive treat just that bit further.

You might mix some poached salmon, crab or lobster with

mayonnaise and herbs, or make a salmon tartare with a little raw salmon and drained yoghurt, or make duck liver pâté and spread it on a biscuit base. I've occasionally made miniature pasties, each filled with a teaspoon of the spiced meat filling stolen from the Dartmouth Pie recipe (see page 216). Left-over puff pastry is a good excuse to bake tiny sausage rolls – wonderful things when the sausage meat is of first-class quality.

People often imagine that brioche is horribly tricky to make but it doesn't have to be at all. The recipe I use is no more complicated than any ordinary yeast dough, and the cooked brioche freezes well. There is barely any sugar in it, which means it is a good all-round brioche, to accompany savoury and sweet dishes. It can be varied by adding nuts and candied peel, orange and lemon zest, or spices.

Although it is customary to offer a selection of very sweet petits fours with coffee, personally I prefer a light, crisp biscuit, a macaroon, or orangine, or a tiny 'palmier' made with left-over puff pastry. Another alternative are those small fruits that can be eaten easily with the fingers – clementines or kumquats in the winter, a few cherries or frosted redcurrants (dipped in egg white, coated with caster sugar and dried briefly on a rack) in summer. Having said that, I must admit that a square of fudge is awfully nice with strong black coffee.

BRIOCHE

This is a very easy brioche to make, with a good buttery flavour. It
can be sliced for toast, or used as a base for peaches or other fruit
baked on brioche. At Easter I spice the brioche with cardamom to
serve with the traditional Russian Pashka, a rich pudding of moulded
cream cheese and glacé fruit.
To get perfect rounds of brioche, I will occasionally bake the dough in
a large, clean tomato can, or in smaller evaporated milk cans.
Whatever the contents once were, the can itself should be straight
sided, with both top and bottom removed. Stand the can on a baking
sheet lined with buttered foil, and half-fill with dough. Exact timings
for baking will vary according to the depth. If the crust is browning
too fast, cover with foil.

MAKES 2 LOAVES

7 g/¼ oz fresh yeast or 1 heaped teaspoon dried yeast
2 tablespoons warm milk
275 g/10 oz strong flour
1 teaspoon salt
1 tablespoon granulated sugar
3 eggs, lightly beaten
175 g/6 oz butter, melted and cooled
beaten egg, to glaze

Mix the yeast into the milk and leave in a warm place for 10
minutes, until frothing. Sift the flour and salt into a bowl and
add the sugar. Make a well in the centre and pour in the eggs,
then the yeast mixture and the butter. Work in the flour to give
a soft, slightly sticky dough. Cover with clingfilm or a saucepan
lid and leave to rise in a warm place for 1½ hours until doubled
in size.

Knock the dough down, and mix briefly. Cover and leave in
a cool place for 4–6 hours or overnight in the fridge to rise again
until doubled in size. Mix again briefly. Divide between two
buttered 450 g/1 lb loaf tins. Cover and prove in a warm place
for 1 final hour. Brush with beaten egg and bake in a preheated

oven, 240°C/475°F/gas mark 9, for 15 minutes, until golden brown. Test with a skewer – plunge it into one of the brioches in a discreet but central spot, and if it comes out dry then the brioche is cooked.

SHORTCRUST PASTRY
(PÂTE BRISÉE)

A plain, well-behaved, all-purpose shortcrust pastry. Any unused pastry can be frozen until needed.

ENOUGH FOR 2–3 TART CASES

275 g/10 oz flour
½ teaspoon salt
1 large pinch of sugar
225 g/8 oz butter, chilled, and cut into small pieces
8–9 tablespoons cold water

Put the flour, salt and sugar in a processor or mixer with the cold butter. Process until it resembles fine breadcrumbs. Gradually add the water to form a firm dough. Gather up into a ball, wrap in clingfilm and rest for at least 30 minutes in the fridge before using.

If you don't have a processor, make sure that all the ingredients are well chilled. Rub the fat into the flour, salt and sugar as quickly as possible. Add enough water to form a firm dough.

PUFF PASTRY

Home-made puff pastry has a marvellous butteriness that is lacking in commercial brands. But the process is time-consuming, so it makes sense to prepare a big batch and freeze what you are not going to use straight away.

ENOUGH FOR 8 PIE CRUSTS

900 g/2 lb flour
2 teaspoons salt
900 g/2 lb butter, chilled
juice of ½ lemon

Sift the flour with the salt into a bowl or a mixer with a dough hook. Rub in 100 g/4 oz of the butter. Make a well in the centre and pour in the lemon juice and enough cold water to form a dough – you'll need around 600 ml/1 pint. Leave to rest, covered, in the fridge for 30 minutes.

Follow the diagram on page 380. Divide the remaining butter in half. Put each half of the butter between two sheets of greaseproof paper and flatten each with a rolling pin into a slab about 20 cm/8 inches square. Peel off the paper, sprinkle the butter with a little flour, wrap in fresh paper and chill until the butter is firm.

Roll out the rested dough on a lightly floured surface into a rectangle roughly 60 × 20 cm/24 × 8 inches. Lay the two slabs of butter side by side over two-thirds of the pastry. Flip over the uncovered third on to the butter. Then fold the buttered pastry on top of the first flap. Give the pastry a quarter turn, so that the folded edges are facing you, and roll out again to a 60 × 20 cm/ 24 × 8 inch rectangle. Rolling puff pastry requires some practice; give the dough short, sharp rolls – avoid pushing the rolling pin along the dough as this tends to push out the butter. Fold in three and leave to rest for 30 minutes in the fridge.

Repeat the turning, rolling and folding twice more. The butter should no longer be visible – if the dough appears streaky, give it another roll and turn. Divide into eight slabs, wrap well and freeze until needed.

ROGER VERGÉ'S SWEET FLAN PASTRY

This unusual sweet pastry recipe with its nip of rum comes from Roger Vergé's Cuisine of the Sun. *It is perfect for fresh fruit tarts – baked blind and filled with summer fruits, and in fact good enough to eat neat as biscuits – cut into fingers or circles, glazed with beaten egg and baked.*

ENOUGH FOR ABOUT 6 FULL-SIZE TART CASES

500 g/1 lb 2 oz flour, sifted
165 g/5½ oz caster sugar
1 pinch of salt
90 g/3½ oz ground almonds
grated zest of 1 lemon
3 tablespoons rum
1 whole egg
2 egg yolks
390 g/13½ oz butter, softened and diced

Mix together the first five ingredients in a bowl. Make a well in the centre and add the rum, egg and egg yolks, and the softened butter. Work into the flour as briefly as possible, to give a soft dough. Chill thoroughly before using.

CHEESE SABLÉS

Use a mature, well-flavoured Cheddar, or a mixture of Cheddar and Parmesan, for these flaky cheese biscuits. Watch them carefully as they cook, since they turn very quickly from golden- to burned-brown!

MAKES ABOUT 60

150 g/5 oz butter
150 g/5 oz flour
150 g/5 oz Cheddar cheese, grated
1 pinch of cayenne pepper
½ teaspoon salt
2 tablespoons cold water
1 egg, beaten
celery or whole cumin seeds

Rub the butter into the flour in a bowl until it resembles fine breadcrumbs. Add the grated cheese and seasonings. Add the cold water to form a soft dough. Chill for 30 minutes. Roll out on a lightly floured surface to 6 mm/¼ inch in thickness. Cut into fingers or diamonds. Lay them on a baking tray, brush with beaten egg, and sprinkle with celery or cumin seeds. Bake in a preheated oven, 190°C/375°F/gas mark 5, for 8–10 minutes, until nicely browned. Cool on a wire rack.

SESAME BISCUITS

A savoury biscuit dough with a multitude of uses. The short, dry texture and nutty taste go beautifully with cheese. The baked biscuit is substantial enough to use for canapé bases or tartlet cases.

MAKES ABOUT 30–40

2 eggs
25 g/1 oz caster sugar
175 g/6 oz wholemeal flour
175 g/6 oz sesame seeds
finely grated zest of 1 lemon

Whisk the eggs with the sugar until thick and fluffy. Mix in the remaining ingredients and knead to a firm dough. Chill for 30 minutes.

Roll out on a lightly floured surface to 6 mm/¼ inch in thickness, stamp out 7.5 cm/3 inch circles and bake on a greased tray in a preheated oven, 180°C/350°F/gas mark 4, for 10–15 minutes, until lightly browned. Cool on a wire rack.

OATMEAL BISCUITS

These biscuits are similar to digestive biscuits, with a delicious short texture. Like the sesame biscuit dough, I sometimes use this one for canapé bases or tartlet cases. For vegetarians, I've filled oatmeal tartlets with a vegetable and tomato ragoût, then topped it with a cheese soufflé mixture, which puffs up quickly in a hot oven.

MAKES ABOUT 30–40

150 g/5 oz brown flour
150 g/5 oz medium oatmeal, plus extra for sprinkling
½ teaspoon salt
1 large pinch of caster sugar
225 g/8 oz butter, chilled
100 ml/4 fl oz egg white (approximately 3 large egg whites)

Mix together the dry ingredients in a bowl and rub in the butter until the mixture resembles fine breadcrumbs. Add enough egg white to form a firm dough. Chill, then roll out on a surface sprinkled with oatmeal to 6 mm/¼ inch in thickness. Stamp out 7.5 cm/3 inch circles. Lay them on a baking sheet and bake in a preheated oven, 180°C/350°F/gas mark 4, for 10 minutes, until the biscuits are lightly browned. Cool on a wire rack.

ORANGINES

These thin biscuits, discovered in The Constance Spry Cookery
Book, *are rather like Florentines, with the almonds and candied
peel, and very little flour. Watch over them as they cook, since the
sugar catches easily. Brittle and orange-scented, they are marvellous
with hot dark coffee. The icing is optional.*

MAKES 40–50

50 g/2 oz blanched almonds
50 g/2 oz candied peel
finely grated zest of ½ orange
40 g/1½ oz flour
50 g/2 oz butter
50 g/2 oz caster sugar
1 tablespoon milk

FOR THE ICING
50 g/2 oz icing sugar
orange juice

Put the almonds and peel in a processor and whizz to chop
finely. Add the remaining ingredients and process until well
mixed, to form a smooth dough. Wrap in clingfilm or
greaseproof paper and roll into logs 2.5 cm/1 inch in diameter.
Chill for at least 30 minutes.

Slice the logs very thinly and lay the slices on a lightly
greased baking sheet. Bake in a preheated oven, 160°C/325°F/
gas mark 3, for 10–15 minutes, until lightly browned. Cool on a
wire rack.

To make the icing, mix the sugar with enough orange juice
to make a thick paste. Spread the cool biscuits with the icing
and leave to dry.

MACAROONS

These are proper old-fashioned macaroons, crisp on the outside and still a little chewy at the centre. Make them finger shaped to serve with puddings, round swirls for tea-time, and tiny little swirls for petits fours. Fold crushed macaroon crumbs into a chocolate mousse mixture and you have a Saint Émilion au Chocolat.

Makes about 70

175 g/6 oz ground almonds
150 g/5 oz vanilla sugar, see page 24
150 g/5 oz caster sugar
20 g/¾ oz flour or arrowroot
3 egg whites
3 drops vanilla essence
rice paper
split or flaked almonds

Mix together the almonds, sugars and flour or arrowroot in a bowl. Add the egg whites and vanilla essence and beat well. Line a baking sheet with rice paper. Pipe the mixture on to the paper in swirls or fingers. Press a split almond in the centre of rounds or scatter a few flaked almonds over fingers. Bake in a preheated oven, 160°C/325°F/gas mark 3, for 20 minutes. Cool on a wire rack.

For petits fours, pipe very small swirls 2.5 cm/1 inch in diameter. Bake for 10 minutes only.

WALNUT BISCUITS

You can vary these biscuits by using toasted, skinned hazelnuts or ground almonds instead of the walnuts. Serve them with ices, poached fruit, baked custards, or for tea, or sandwich them in pairs with clotted or whipped cream and fresh fruit. One marvellous mixture is walnut biscuits sandwiched with clotted cream and bananas tossed in lemon juice, served with Apricot Sauce (see page 325).

MAKES ABOUT 80

75 g/3 oz walnuts, finely chopped
225 g/8 oz self-raising flour
200 g/7 oz butter
150 g/5 oz caster sugar
1 egg

Place the walnuts, flour, butter and sugar in the processor and whizz until the mixture resembles fine breadcrumbs. Add the egg and mix again.

Wrap in clingfilm or greaseproof paper and mould into a log 2.5 cm/1 inch in diameter. Chill. Slice as thinly as possible, turning the roll as you cut, and lay the slices on a baking sheet. Bake in a preheated oven, 180°C/350°F/gas mark 4, for 10 minutes, until lightly browned. Cool on a wire rack.

Alternatively, pipe the mixture while soft into small swirls, 2.5 cm/1 inch in diameter, on to a baking sheet. Bake for 8–10 minutes.

MADELEINES (HONEY BUNS)

I make very small madeleines, little honeyed mouthfuls, to serve with coffee. The honey keeps them moist. They can, of course, be baked in tartlet tins though the temperature of the oven should be lowered to 190°C/375°F/gas mark 5, and the cooking time increased to 10 minutes.

MAKES ABOUT 60–70

2 eggs
65 g/2½ oz caster sugar
1 tablespoon dark muscovado sugar
1 small pinch of salt
75 g/3 oz flour
1 teaspoon baking powder
75 g/3 oz butter, melted and cooled
1 tablespoon honey

Whisk the eggs lightly with the sugars and salt in a bowl. Sift the flour with the baking powder and fold into the egg mixture. Add the butter and honey and mix well. Leave the mixture to rest for 30 minutes. Pour into petits fours paper cases, filling only half full, and place on a baking sheet. Bake in a preheated oven, 220°C/425°F/gas mark 7, for 5 minutes, until golden brown. Cool on a wire rack.

ORANGE CHOCOLATES

The lemon and orange zests give a real boost to white chocolate, making a fondant-like filling for dark chocolate colettes cases or truffles. Serious white chocolate enthusiasts can line cases or coat truffles with white chocolate, though I find this white on white just a little too cloying.

MAKES 30

FOR THE COATING
100 g/4 oz plain chocolate

FOR THE FILLING
juice and finely grated zest of ½ lemon
juice and finely grated zest of ½ orange
25 g/1 oz granulated sugar
50 ml/2 fl oz double cream
225 g/8 oz white chocolate, broken into pieces
25 g/1 oz unsalted butter, diced

To make Orange Chocolate Colettes, break the 'coating' chocolate into squares and melt in a bowl set over a pan of simmering water, making sure that the base of the bowl does not touch the water. As soon as it has melted remove from the heat. Brush the chocolate as evenly as possible over the insides of 30 small petits fours cases, using about half the chocolate. Cool until firm and then give the cases a second layer of chocolate.

For the filling, place the lemon and orange juices in a small pan with the sugar. Stir over a medium heat until the sugar has dissolved then increase the heat and simmer for 5 minutes.

In a separate pan, bring the cream to the boil and pour on to the chocolate pieces. Stir until the chocolate has melted, then whisk in the citrus syrup and lemon and orange zests. Beat in the butter bit by bit. Cool until the mixture just holds its shape. Pipe into the petits fours cases and chill until firm.

To make Orange Chocolate Truffles, make the filling (see page 357) but freeze until the mixture holds its shape. Roll into small balls and chill again in the freezer. Break the 'coating' chocolate into squares and melt in a bowl set over a pan of simmering water, making sure that the base of the bowl does not touch the water. As soon as the chocolate has melted, remove from the heat. Drop each ball into the chocolate, coating completely. Lift out with a fork, tipping to remove any surplus. Leave to set on a baking sheet lined with greaseproof paper, in the fridge.

FUDGE

We use a very ordinary fudge recipe, but it always generates high praise. I'm partial to plain fudge, but it is fun to vary it occasionally by adding a dash of Drambuie or a flavoured sugar. Sometimes I add a handful of raisins or nuts as well.

MAKES 1.25 KG/2½ LB

900 g/2 lb granulated sugar
1 × 415 g/14½ oz can evaporated milk
100 g/4 oz butter

Place all the ingredients in a large pan and add 150 ml/¼ pint cold water. Stir over a medium heat until the sugar has dissolved, the butter has melted and the mixture is evenly mixed.

Bring to the boil and simmer, stirring occasionally, until it reaches soft ball stage. Test by dripping a little of the mixture into a glass of iced water. It should form soft sticky balls. While it bubbles, oil an oblong flan frame, 34 × 10 cm/13½ × 4 inches, set on a foil-lined baking sheet, or a Swiss roll tin, 25 × 15 cm/10 × 6 inches.

Remove from the heat and beat vigorously until the mixture starts to thicken and crystallize. Pour into the prepared mould and cool until just set. Remove the flan frame, cut the fudge into squares, and store in an airtight container.

VARIATIONS

VANILLA FUDGE

Substitute vanilla sugar for granulated, or add 2 vanilla pods – remove before you beat the fudge.

DRAMBUIE OR TIA MARIA FUDGE

Beat in 50 ml/2 fl oz Drambuie or Tia Maria when the fudge has just come off the heat.

BROWN SUGAR FUDGE

Substitute half dark or light muscovado sugar and half white sugar for granulated.

Preserves

As customers enter the dining room of The Carved Angel, they pass the open wooden shelves laden with jams, jellies, preserves and pickles. It is a welcoming sight, a promise of good food to come, of a kitchen that anticipates and delights in the abundance of seasonal produce. Whether he buys a small jar of marmalade, or a large glass urn filled to brimming with olives or goats' cheeses marinated with herbs in olive oil, it is a way for the satisfied customer to take home a reminder of a happy meal.

The contents of these shelves and the larders at the back of the kitchen change constantly. Each season brings its own specialities: Seville oranges and lemons in winter, wild samphire in the late spring, soft fruits and warm weather vegetables in summer, plums and apples in autumn. As the quantities increase and the prices drop, the preserving pans are kept busily bubbling on the stoves.

The whole process of laying up stores of preserves and pickles gives me immense satisfaction. It brings out the squirrel instinct – stashing the filled jars away, ignoring them for a month or more, until the time comes to pick one out, open it up and savour the taste and memory of an earlier season.

PREPARING JARS AND CONTAINERS

Always prepare plenty of containers (jam jars with lids if possible, or proper preserving jars with tight seals) before you get going on the final stages of the preserving process. Wash jars in warm soapy water and rinse well. Dry upside down on a rack in the oven, set to 130°C/250°F/gas mark 1. Leave them there for at least 30 minutes to sterilize, or until preserve is ready to be potted. Fill hot jars with hot preserve. If filling with a cold pickle, let the jars cool in the oven until needed. When making pickles and chutneys with a high degree of acidity, be sure to cover with non-metallic or plastic-lined lids to avoid corrosion.

Cover jars straight away with either an airtight lid, or with discs of waxed paper, and cellophane covers. As the air trapped between the surface of the preserve and the lid cools and contracts it forms a partial vacuum, which helps to preserve the contents of the jar. Clean, label and, when cold, store in a cool, dry, dark cupboard or larder until needed.

PICKLED CABBAGE
WITH ORANGE

This recipe comes from the Marks & Spencer Book of Home
Preserves *and is one of the nicest and most interesting versions I've
come across. The addition of orange and raisins is a real
improvement, giving the cabbage a softer flavour than the sharp
shop-bought pickle. It is delicious with bread and cheese, or any cold
meats, and I love it with a good Irish Stew or Lamb Hot Pot.*

MAKES 1.75 KG/4 LB

1 red cabbage, weighing about 900 g/2 lb
2 tablespoons salt
600 ml/1 pint Spiced Vinegar, see page 367
juice and finely grated zest of 2 large oranges
1 large onion, thinly sliced
50 g/2 oz raisins
1 tablespoon brown sugar

Quarter the cabbage, remove the core and shred. Put into a large
bowl with the salt and mix well. Leave overnight to extract
moisture. Rinse and drain the cabbage thoroughly.

Put the vinegar into a pan with the remaining ingredients.
Stir over a medium heat until the sugar has completely dissolved, then bring to the boil. Pour over the cabbage and mix
well. Pack into clean jars, cover and seal while still hot. Store
for at least a month in a cool, dark place.

CUCUMBER PICKLE

A classic, the best of all bread and cheese pickles, with its clean fresh taste. It goes well with sausages and fatty meats such as Grilled Pigs' Trotters (see page 235). Towards the end of the summer is the time to make cucumber pickle, when the growers are clearing out their greenhouses, selling off the twisted and misshapen cucumbers at bargain prices.

MAKES 3 KG/6½ LB

1.6 kg/3½ lb cucumbers
450 g/1 lb onions, finely sliced
1 green pepper, seeded and sliced
40 g/1½ oz salt
275 g/10 oz brown sugar
40 g/1½ oz mustard seeds
1 teaspoon celery seeds
1 teaspoon ground turmeric
1 teaspoon ground mace
600 ml/1 pint white wine vinegar

Peel and slice the cucumbers thinly – you should end up with about 1.4 kg/3 lb of prepared cucumber. Mix with the onions, green pepper and salt. Set aside for 2–3 hours, then drain, rinse under the cold tap and drain again, pressing down gently to extract as much moisture as possible without damaging the slices.

Put the sugar, spices and vinegar into a pan large enough to take the vegetables as well. Stir over a medium heat until the sugar has dissolved, then bring to the boil. Simmer for 2 minutes and add the vegetables. Bring back to the boil, stir well and remove from the heat. Pack into clean jars, cover and seal while hot. Store for at least a month in a cool, dark place.

PICKLED SAMPHIRE

*I collect wild rock samphire from the walls bounding the gardens of a row of small cottages beside the lower ferry across the River Dart. No one else seems to be particularly interested in it – the elderly ladies who live in the cottages are happy to let me pick as much as I need.
The first tender shoots are ready to be culled in April, and it eventually flowers in August. While still young, samphire, lightly blanched, makes a wonderful addition to salads. Fresh fish steamed with a little samphire is one of early summer's most pleasing dishes. Towards the end of the season (but before it has flowered) we crop it by the carrier-bag full so that we can pickle enough to take us through the winter. The strange iodine flavour of the sea in the rock samphire produces a pickle that is ideal with oily fish like salmon, or deep-fried goujons of sole, or against the creaminess of the Brain Fritters on page 243.
Both rock and marsh samphire, which tastes more of salt than iodine, are occasionally sold by enterprising inland fishmongers. Marsh samphire can be used in the same way as rock samphire.*

samphire
black peppercorns
fresh horseradish, if available
salt
dry cider
white wine or cider vinegar

Pick over the samphire, throwing out the tougher thick stalks and damaged leaves. Wash and dry. Pack into preserving jars, adding 10 peppercorns, 1 slice of horseradish, if using, and 1 teaspoon salt per 1 litre/1¾ pint jar.

Bring equal quantities of cider and wine or vinegar to the boil and pour over the samphire, covering well. Cover loosely and place in a preheated oven, 140°C/275°F/gas mark 1, to infuse for 1 hour. Seal tightly and cool. Store in a cool, dark place for at least a month before using.

PICKLED GREEN TOMATOES

*If you grow your own tomatoes, make a point of culling enough hard
unripened fruit to make this unusual pickle. I keep it hidden away
from temptation until the late autumn, when it is brought out to set
off the earthy flavours of game terrines and pies.*

MAKES 2.25 KG/5 LB

1.4 kg/3 lb small green tomatoes
100 g/4 oz salt
900 g/2 lb granulated sugar
300 ml/½ pint white wine vinegar
1 vanilla pod or 1 cinnamon stick

Wash the tomatoes and put in a pan. Add the salt to 2.25 litres/4
pints cold water in a separate pan and stir until it has dissolved
completely, then bring to the boil. Pour enough over the tomatoes to cover. Simmer for 10 minutes then drain and peel the
tomatoes.

Place the sugar, vinegar, vanilla pod or cinnamon stick and
150 ml/¼ pint cold water in a pan large enough to take the
tomatoes as well. Stir over a medium heat until the sugar has
dissolved, then bring to the boil. Add the tomatoes and simmer
very gently for 5 minutes. Remove from the heat and leave to
cool in the syrup for 8 hours or overnight.

Strain off the syrup into a separate pan and bring it to the boil
again. Boil for 10 minutes, and add the tomatoes. Simmer for a
further 5 minutes, then remove from the heat. Pack into clean
jars and seal while still hot. Store in a cool, dark place for at
least a month before using.

SPICED VINEGAR

I always prepare a copious quantity of spiced vinegar at the beginning of the autumn ready to be used in pickles and preserves whenever the occasion arises.

MAKES 1.2 LITRES/2 PINTS

1.2 litres/2 pints white or red wine vinegar
5 cm/2 inch piece of cinnamon stick
1 tablespoon whole allspice berries
2 bay leaves
1 tablespoon whole cloves
1 tablespoon roughly crushed mace
1 tablespoon black peppercorns

If you have the time, put all the ingredients into a bottle, seal tightly and leave in a cool, dark place for one to two months, shaking occasionally.

Otherwise, put them all into a large pan and bring to the boil. Remove from the heat and set aside until cool. Strain and bottle. Can be used immediately.

SPICED ORANGES

Delicious with the Sweetbread Terrine on page 115, cold cooked meats, grilled chicken and guinea fowl, or game.

MAKES 3.25 KG/7 LB

18 small oranges
1.25 kg/2½ lb granulated sugar
600 ml/1 pint white wine vinegar
1½ cinnamon sticks
1 teaspoon whole cloves
6 blades of mace

Cut the oranges into 7 mm/¼ inch thick slices, discarding the ends and removing pips. Place in a wide, flameproof casserole and cover with cold water. Bring to the boil and simmer gently for about 40 minutes, until the peel is soft, being careful not to overcook to a mush. Gently tip the pan to drain off the juices and set the pan aside.

Place the remaining ingredients in a large pan and stir over a medium heat until the sugar has completely dissolved. Bring to the boil and boil for 4 minutes. Pour carefully over the orange slices. Cover the casserole and cook in a preheated oven, 140°C/275°F/gas mark 1, for another hour until the peel is translucent. Set aside for 24 hours.

Pack the slices carefully into jars – this is best done with your hands, even if it is sticky work. Pour over the syrup to cover. Seal and leave in a cool, dark place for at least six weeks before using.

LEMON OR LIME CHUTNEY

This is a pungent pickle, to serve with spicy dishes and curries. Though the chutney is ready to be dipped into after one month, it tastes even better if it can be left to mature for a whole year!

MAKES 4.5 KG/10 LB

1.75 kg/4 lb lemons or limes
900 g/2 lb onions, sliced
50 g/2 oz salt
25 g/1 oz whole allspice berries
15 g/½ oz whole cardamom pods
15 g/½ oz coriander seeds
1.2 litres/2 pints white wine vinegar
50 g/2 oz green chilli peppers, chopped
100 g/4 oz fresh root ginger, grated
1.4 kg/3 lb caster sugar

Slice the lemons or limes and remove the pips. Place in a bowl with the onions and salt. Tie all the spices together in a square of muslin and add to the bowl with the vinegar. Leave for 8 hours or overnight.

Pour into a large heavy-based pan, and add the chillis and the ginger. Bring to the boil and simmer gently for 1½ hours. Remove from the heat and add the sugar. Stir until it has dissolved, then return to the heat. Boil fast for 20 minutes, stirring frequently to prevent catching. Remove the spice bag. Ladle the chutney into clean jars, cover and seal while hot. Keep for at least one month in a cool, dark place before opening.

MEDITERRANEAN CHUTNEY

This is really a pickled ratatouille and, like ratatouille, you can adjust the balance of ingredients according to resources. As long as you keep the total weight of vegetables (excluding the tomatoes) the same, you could reduce the quantity of aubergine or peppers and increase the number of courgettes, say, depending on what is cheap and plentiful or what you like best.
Serve this chutney with bread and cheese, or with thin slices of cold lamb.

MAKES 3.5 KG/8 LB

1.75 kg/4 lb tomatoes, skinned and chopped
900 g/2 lb onions, chopped
900 g/2 lb courgettes, diced
450 g/1 lb green peppers, diced
450 g/1 lb red peppers, diced
450 g/1 lb aubergines, diced
6 cloves of garlic, crushed
2 tablespoons salt
2 tablespoons cayenne pepper
2 tablespoons sweet paprika
2 tablespoons whole coriander seeds, crushed
600 ml/1 pint red wine vinegar
675 g/1½ lb caster sugar

Put all the vegetables, including the garlic, in a pan with the salt and spices. Cover and cook over a very gentle heat, stirring occasionally, until the juices run out. Uncover and bring to the boil. Simmer for 1 hour, until all the vegetables have softened and almost all the liquid has evaporated.

Add the vinegar and sugar and stir until the sugar has dissolved. Simmer for 1 more hour, until very thick and with no trace of wateriness. Ladle into clean jars, cover and seal while hot. Leave for at least one month in a cool, dark place.

SPICED PLUMS OR DAMSONS

This spiced plum pickle with its hint of ginger goes particularly well with a plate of charcuterie, or Christmas cooked ham, sliced thick from the bone.

MAKES 4 KG/9 LB

2.25 kg/5 lb small plums or damsons
1.4 kg/3 lb caster sugar
900 ml/1½ pints red wine vinegar
½ cinnamon stick
1 teaspoon whole cloves
1 teaspoon ground allspice
1 teaspoon whole coriander seeds
25 g/1 oz grated fresh root ginger

Prick the plums or damsons with a needle and arrange in a roasting tin or flameproof casserole in layers no more than two or three deep, so that the weight of the fruit above does not squash the lowest layer.

Place the sugar in a pan with the vinegar and all the spices, including the ginger. Stir over a medium heat until the sugar has dissolved, then bring to the boil. Simmer for 5 minutes and pour over the fruit. Place over a direct heat and bring back to the boil. Leave to cool for 8 hours or overnight.

Strain off the syrup into a pan and pack the fruit into clean jars. Bring the syrup to the boil and boil hard until reduced by a third. Strain and pour over the fruit. Cover and seal while still hot. Keep for at least a month in a cool, dark place before using.

SPICED APPLE JELLY

I prefer this jelly when it is made with rather less sugar than I've suggested in the recipe below – 350 g/12 oz to 600 ml/1 pint apple juice – but reducing the sugar also reduces its longevity. So if you wish to keep the jelly for longer than a couple of months, or intend to give it to friends as presents, it is best to stick with the full quantity. Use it as an accompaniment to roast meats such as rabbit, lamb or kid.
By cutting out the vinegar and spices, and adding sloes, angelica or rose petals you can make delicious scented jams to spread on hot toast, or eat with cream cheese.

MAKES 1.4 KG/3 LB

2 kg/4½ lb cooking or crab apples
2 lemons, unpeeled, sliced and pipped
25 g/1 oz fresh root ginger, unpeeled
1 cinnamon stick
½ teaspoon whole cloves
200 ml/7 fl oz white wine vinegar
granulated sugar

Chop the apples roughly, without peeling or coring them, and place in a heavy-based pan with the lemons. Slice the ginger. Add to the pan with the cinnamon, cloves, vinegar and 1.75 litres/3 pints cold water. Bring to the boil, reduce the heat, cover and simmer gently for 45 minutes to 1 hour, until the apple is very soft. Mash well.

Line a large colander with a double layer of muslin and set over a large bowl. Ladle the apple mixture into the colander and leave to drain for 1 hour. Gather up the edges of the muslin and knot, then hang up to drain over the bowl for 8 hours or overnight.

Measure the liquid in the bowl and weigh out 450 g/1 lb sugar for every 600 ml/1 pint. Put the liquid and sugar in a large, heavy-based pan, stir over a medium heat to dissolve the sugar, then bring to the boil, stirring constantly. Boil hard until it reaches setting point – test after 5 minutes by spooning a few drops on to a cold saucer. Turn the heat off. Cool the saucer rapidly for a few seconds in the freezer then nudge the drops with your finger. If a skin has formed and wrinkles up, then the jelly is ready. If it does not, switch the heat on and boil for a further 5 minutes, before testing again.

Remove the jelly from the heat and skim off any scum. Ladle into clean, warm jars, cover and seal while hot. Store in a cool, dark place for a month before using.

VARIATIONS

APPLE AND SLOE JELLY

Omit the spices, replace the vinegar with the same amount of water and use only 1.6 kg/3½ lb apples, with 450 g/1 lb sloes.

APPLE AND ANGELICA OR ROSE PETAL JELLY

Omit the spices, replace the vinegar with the same amount of water and add 2 stalks of fresh angelica, chopped, or the petals of 8 fragrant red roses.

APPLE AND MEDLAR JELLY

Omit the spices, replace the vinegar with the same amount of water and use only 1 kg/2¼ lb apples, with 1 kg/2¼ lb medlars.

PUMPKIN JAM

In the run-up to Bonfire Night pumpkins are cheap and abundant, and it is a shame to let them go to waste. This jam, with its glorious orange colour, is a superior version of the more commonplace marrow and ginger jam, lovely for breakfast, even better with fresh cream cheese, or fromage frais for pudding. The quantity made will obviously depend on the size of your pumpkin.

1 pumpkin
For each 450 g/1 lb of prepared pumpkin (see below):
25 g/1 oz fresh root ginger, grated
450 g/1 lb granulated sugar
juice of ½ lemon

Slice the pumpkin, then peel and remove seeds and stringy fibres. Cut into 2.5 cm/1 inch dice, and weigh. Calculate the required quantities of ginger, sugar and lemon juice.

Steam the pumpkin for 20 minutes, until tender. Place in a bowl with the ginger, sugar and lemon juice. Cover and leave for 24 hours. Place in a large, heavy-based pan and stir over a medium heat until the sugar has dissolved. Bring to the boil and cook until the jam is thick and translucent.

Ladle the jam into clean, warm jars, cover and seal while hot. Store in a cool, dark place for at least a month before using.

RHUBARB AND ANGELICA OR ROSE PETAL JAM

This is a fragrant summer jam, another one that I often serve with a home-made cream cheese. Rhubarb and fresh angelica is a lovely combination, and one that I use in other ways as well. The rhubarb and angelica leaf upside-down pudding was a memorable success.

MAKES 1.4 KG/3 LB

900 g/2 lb rhubarb
900 g/2 lb granulated sugar
juice of 1 lemon
5 angelica leaves, finely shredded, or 1 handful of fragrant,
dark red rose petals

Wipe the rhubarb, trim the ends and slice. Put in a bowl with the sugar and mix well. Cover and leave for 8 hours or overnight. Place the fruit and sugar in a pan with the lemon juice and angelica leaves or rose petals. Stir over a medium heat until the sugar has completely dissolved then increase the heat and boil until the rhubarb is thick, stirring occasionally to prevent catching. Ladle into clean, warm jars, cover and seal while hot. Store in a cool, dark place for at least a month before using.

APRICOT AND
HAZELNUT CONSERVE

*This luxurious winter jam, dotted with hazelnuts and laced with
brandy, is an old favourite. It makes a welcome present – if you can
bear to part with it.*

MAKES 3.25 KG/7 LB

900 g/2 lb dried apricots
450 g/1 lb lemons
1.75 kg/4 lb granulated sugar
100 g/4 oz hazelnuts, toasted and skinned
150 ml/¼ pint brandy

Soak the apricots in 2.25 litres/4 pints cold water for 8 hours or
overnight. Drain the water into a large pan and add the finely
grated zest of the lemons, their juice and the sugar. Place over a
medium heat and stir until the sugar has dissolved. Bring to the
boil and simmer for 15 minutes.

Add the apricots and simmer gently for about 45 minutes
until the apricots are just tender, but still whole. Stir in the
hazelnuts and brandy and continue to cook for 15 minutes,
until thick and jammy. Ladle into clean, warm jars, cover and
seal while hot. Store in a cool, dark place for at least a month
before using.

Glossary of Cooking Terms

al dente
Italian term most often applied to pasta or vegetables, meaning cooked until just done but still with a little firmness.

amuse-gueules
Hot or cold, bite-sized appetizers often served with aperitifs.

à point
Term for meat, e.g. steak, or fish, cooked to medium.

ballotine
Boned and rolled meat, poultry or game, served hot or cold.

bard
To cover meat, poultry or game with thin slices of pork fat or bacon before roasting. This protects and bastes the food during cooking.

bavarois
Light, gelatine-set mould enriched with cream. Various flavours can be added.

blanquette
A white stew of chicken, lamb, veal or fish simmered in stock then finished with egg yolks and cream.

chine (to)
Remove the backbone from ribs on a loin or rib roast before cooking.

colettes
Small chocolate cases filled with liqueur chocolate mixture.

confit
Preserved meat, especially goose, pork or duck, cooked and packed in its own fat.

crémets
Drained, moulded cream eaten as a dessert with fruit, etc.

dariole mould
A small, cylindrical mould with sloping sides used for making individual sweet or savoury dishes, especially bavarois, custards or steamed puddings.

duxelles
Finely chopped mushrooms and shallots (or onions) sautéed in butter. Used in sauces, as flavouring or in stuffings.

emulsion
Tiny globules of fat held in suspension in a smooth liquid, as in mayonnaise or creamed mixture of butter, sugar and eggs.

essence
Concentrated meat or poultry juices or stock.

farce
Stuffing or forcemeat.

galantine
Boned and stuffed meat or poultry simmered in stock, cooled, pressed and glazed in aspic (with or without additional coating sauce). Always served cold.

infuse
Extract flavour from e.g. herbs, fruit peels, by steeping them in a (usually hot) liquid.

julienne
Food cut into thin matchstick-sized strips.

langues-de-chat
Crisp, dry, sweet biscuits which are long and thin – said to resemble cats' tongues.

mandoline
Flat slicing machine.

mouli légumes
A circular sieve operated by a handle which strains out pips, skins and small bones.

mousseline
Mixtures lightened and enriched by the addition of whipped cream. Also, small mousses used as stuffings or served with a sauce.

panada
A thick white mixture comprised of flour or breadcrumbs, fat, milk or stock. Basis of choux pastry, for example; also used as binding agent.

quenelle
Mixture of finely minced fish, poultry or meat combined with egg whites, seasoning and cream, then moulded into small, oval shapes and poached gently in stock or water. Served with a sauce.

roux
A cooked mixture of fat and flour which forms the base of a sauce or is used as a thickening agent.

sweat
To cook vegetables gently in a little fat in a covered pan until they release their juices.

velouté
A creamy, white coating sauce made from a roux, white stock, egg yolks and cream.

zest
The outer coloured skin of citrus fruits which contains strongly flavoured oil.

Techniques

MAKING FILO PASTRY TRIANGLES

1 Cut a sheet of filo pastry into 8 strips crossways, and brush each strip with melted butter.
2 Place a small teaspoon of filling in the corner of one end of each strip.
3 Fold the top corner down to the bottom edge to enclose the filling.
4 Fold the bottom corner of the triangle over to the right to form the second triangle.
5 Fold the bottom corner up to the top edge, and repeat the sequence until all the strip has been used and a neat triangle formed.

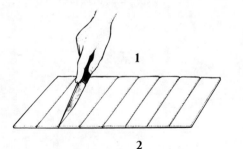

1

4

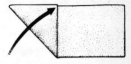

2

5

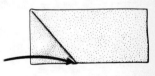

3

MAKING PUFF PASTRY

1 Knead the dough into a ball. Place it in a bowl, cover and leave in the fridge for 30 minutes.
2 Roll out the dough to a 60 × 20 cm/24 × 8 inch rectangle.
3 Place one 20 cm/8 inch slab of butter on the top third of the pastry. Place the second slab of butter about 1.25 cm/½ inch below it on the second third of the pastry.
4 Fold the uncovered bottom third of the pastry up over the second slab of butter, then fold the top buttered third down to cover it.

   Repeat the turning, rolling and folding as in the recipe on page 347.

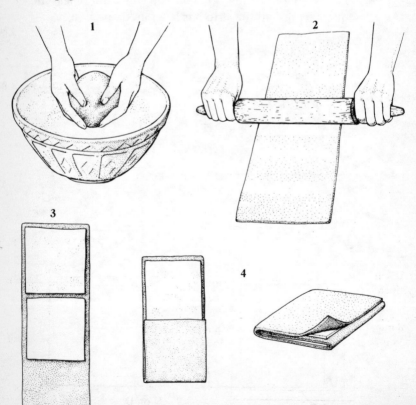

MAKING PUFF PASTRY TWISTS

1 Roll out puff pastry to a 20 cm/8 inch square, 4 mm/
⅛ inch thick. Cut into four 10 cm/4 inch squares.
2 Using the point of a small, sharp knife, mark a line
8 mm/⅓ inch in from the edge of the pastry but stop 1.25
cm/½ inch short at corners E and F. Cut through the
pastry along the line, stopping short at corners E and F,
thus keeping these two diagonally opposite corners intact.
Brush lightly with egg wash 8 mm/
⅓ inch in from cut line.
3 Lift corner A gently and fold over neatly onto B.
4 Lift corner C gently and fold over neatly onto D. Gently
press the edges onto the base, making sure they are all
aligned. Chill until needed.

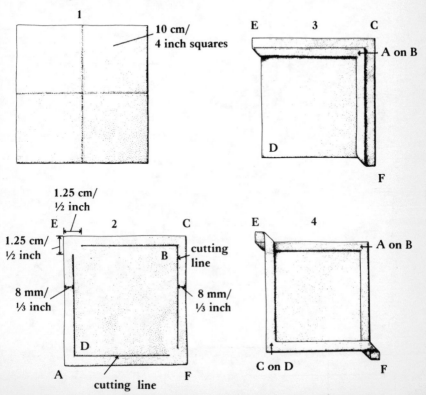

BONING A DUCK FOR BALLOTINE OF DUCK

1 Lay the duck breast-side down on a board and, using a small, sharp knife, cut along the backbone from neck to tail. Keeping the knife blade against the ribcage, cut the flesh away from the bones on one side of the ribcage and peel back. Cut through the leg and wing joints to sever the limbs from the carcass. Repeat on the other side.
2 Grasp the ribcage in one hand and, keeping the blade of the knife against the bone, cut the ribcage away from the breast along the breast bone and lift it off. Set the carcass aside. The duck should now be lying, skin-side down, flat on the board.

1

3 Cut off the bony ends of the legs and wing tips. Slice
  through the flesh to the bone down the length of the legs
  and wings, cut the flesh away and remove the bones and
  sinews.
4 Remove half the leg and breast meat from the skin, and
  follow the recipe on page 107.
5 Spread the duck, skin-side down, on a board and spread
  half the *farce* over the flesh to within 2.5 cm/1 inch of
  the edges. Cover this with a layer of the strips of
  marinated ingredients and the nuts, then spread the
  remaining *farce* over. Roll up the ballotine and sew the
  edges together using button thread.

3

5

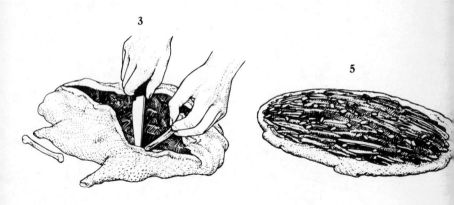

4

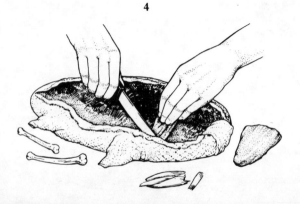

JOINTING A HARE/RABBIT

1 Place the hare on its side on a board with its head facing left. Chop off the head and set aside.* Holding the shoulder in your left hand, cut in a curve around the shoulder to release it from the carcass, cutting through the ball and socket joint. Turn the hare over and remove the other shoulder in the same way. Remove the hind legs in the same way.

2 You will be left with a complete back. Remove the heart, liver and blood from the chest cavity, tipping it all into a bowl.* Trim off the belly flaps and set aside.*

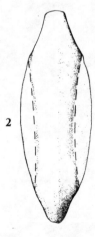

3 The back is covered with two layers of skin – the first loose and easily removed, the second fine and silvery and more difficult. Detach the top loose skin and discard. Using a very sharp knife, remove the second skin, taking off thin strips at a time. This step is essential as, if left on, the skin will contract and toughen when the meat is cooked.

   The skinned back can be roasted whole, or the top ribs can be chopped off and cooked with the legs, leaving a more compact saddle for roasting.

* The head, heart and belly flaps can be used to make stock or soup. The blood can be strained off and used to thicken a civet of hare. The liver, trimmed of gall, can go into a pâté.

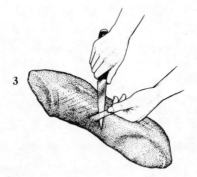

FILLING AND KNOTTING SAUSAGE CASINGS

A Using a piping bag – for fresh sausages and boudins

1 Place the filling in a large piping bag fitted with a large plain tube. Working with lengths of sausage casing about 1 metre/3 feet long, feed the washed casing onto the piping nozzle, getting as much on as possible and holding it in place with your left hand (1). Do not tie a knot in the end of the casing as this will trap air as the casing is filled.

   Twist the piping bag above the filling and, holding the bag in your right hand, gently squeeze the filling into the casing, gradually releasing the casing as it fills up. Pack the casing well, leaving no air bubbles. Leave a short length of casing unfilled at each end.

2 When the casing is filled, remove from the nozzle and, using button thread or very fine string, knot the far end tightly. Knot with thread or string at 10 cm/4 inch intervals to make the individual sausages (2).

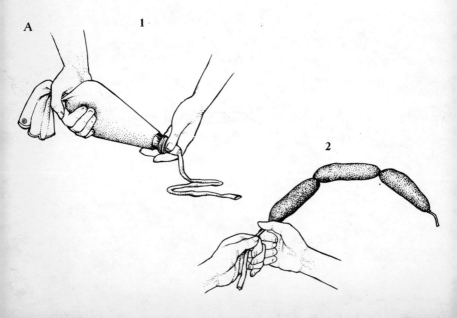

B Using a funnel – for salami-style sausages

1 Hold a wide-mouthed funnel in your left hand and feed the washed casing onto the narrow end of the funnel, leaving a length of casing about 7.5 cm/3 inches. Hold the casing in place with your left hand.

2 Place the filling in the funnel and, using a plunger or wooden spoon, press it through into the casing; pack it tightly and leave no air bubbles.

3 When the casing is filled, remove from the funnel and, using button thread or very fine string, knot the far end tightly. At 30 cm/12 inch intervals along the sausage, make two tight knots and then cut between the knots to give individual salamis, etc.

Bibliography

Here is a short list of the books mentioned in the text and also of ones I have particularly enjoyed and would recommend reading.

Acton, Eliza *Modern Cookery for Private Families*. 1845

Blanc, Georges *Ma Cuisine des Saisons*. Macmillan, 1987

Blanc, Raymond *Recipes from Le Manoir Aux Quat'Saisons*. Macdonald Orbis, 1988

Boxer, Arabella *Mediterranean Cookbook*. J. M. Dent & Sons, 1981; Penguin Books, 1983

Brown, Linda *Fresh Thoughts on Food*. Chatto & Windus, 1986

Burrow, Jackie *Home Preserves*. St Michael Cookery Library, Marks & Spencer, 1979

Cassell's Dictionary of Cookery. Published *c*. 1890–1900

Costa, Margaret *Four Seasons Cookery Book*. Nelson, 1970; Papermac, 1981

David, Elizabeth *French Country Cooking*. John Lehmann, 1951; Penguin Books, 1959
French Provincial Cooking. Michael Joseph, 1960; Penguin Books, 1964
Italian Food. Macdonald, 1954; Penguin Books, 1963
An Omelette and a Glass of Wine. Robert Hale, 1984; Penguin Books, 1986

Davidson, Alan *Mediterranean Seafood*. Penguin Books, 1972
North Atlantic Seafood. Revised edition, Penguin Books, 1986

Girardet, Fredy *Cuisine Spontanée*. Macmillan, 1985

Gray, Patience *Honey from a Weed*. Prospect Books, 1986; Papermac, 1987

Grigson, Jane *Charcuterie and French Pork Cookery*. Michael Joseph, 1967; Penguin Books, 1970
Fruit Book. Michael Joseph, 1982; Penguin Books, 1983

Hartley, Dorothy *Food in England*. Macdonald, 1954; Futura, 1985

Holt, Geraldine *French Country Kitchen*. Penguin Books, 1987

Hom, Ken *East Meets West*. Macmillan, 1987

Jaffrey, Madhur *Indian Cookery*. BBC Publications, 1982

Larkcom, Joy *Salads the Year Round*. Hamlyn Paperback. First published 1980
The Salad Garden. Frances Lincoln/Windward, 1984

Olney, Richard *Simple French Food*. First published 1974. Revised edition Jill Norman, 1981; Penguin Books, 1983

Phillips, Roger *Wild Food*. Pan Books, 1983

Roden, Claudia *A New Book of Middle Eastern Food*. Viking, 1985; Penguin Books, 1986

Roux, Albert and Michel *New Classic Cuisine*. Macdonald, 1983
Pâtisserie. Macdonald, 1986

Spry, Constance *The Constance Spry Cookery Book*. Dent, 1956
Come into the Garden, Cook. First published Dent, 1942

Stobart, Tom *The Cook's Encyclopaedia*. Batsford, 1980 (also in paperback)

Time-Life *Good Cook series: Soups*. Time-Life Books, 1979

Vergé, Roger *Cuisine of the Sun*. Macmillan, 1979

Index